Computing Before Computers

Computing Before Computers

Edited by William Aspray

Contributors
- W. ASPRAY
- A. G. BROMLEY
- M. CAMPBELL-KELLY
- P. E. CERUZZI
- M. R. WILLIAMS

IOWA STATE UNIVERSITY PRESS / AMES

Typesetting by Michael R. Williams, University of Calgary. Iowa State University Press is grateful to Prof. Williams for his contribution to the composition of *Computing Before Computers*.

Manufactured in the United States of America

First edition, 1990

Library of Congress Cataloging-in-Publication Data

Computing before computers / edited by William Aspray.
     p.   cm.
  ISBN 0-8138-0047-1
    1. Calculators — History. 2. Computers — History. I. Aspray, William.
QA76.C5834 1990   89–26745
681′.14 — dc20

Table of Contents

Contributing authors

William Aspray, author of the Introduction, Chapter 3, and the Epilogue, is Director, IEEE Center for the History of Electrical Engineering, 345 E. 47 St., New York, NY 10017.

Allan G. Bromley, author of Chapters 2 and 5, is Senior Lecturer, Basser Department of Computer Science, University of Sydney, Sydney, N.S.W., AUSTRALIA.

Martin Campbell-Kelly, author of Chapter 4, is Lecturer, Computer Science Department, University of Warwick, Coventry, ENGLAND CV4 7AL.

Paul E. Ceruzzi, author of Chapters 6 and 7, is Curator, Space History, National Air and Space Museum, Smithsonian Institution, Washington, DC 20560.

Michael R. Williams, author of Chapter 1, is Professor, Computer Science Department, University of Calgary, Calgary, Alberta, CANADA T2N 1N4.

Introduction

Wherever we turn we hear about the "Computer Revolution" and our "Information Age." This is testimony to the public awareness of the invention and rapid development of the computer since the Second World War and the fundamental changes it has driven in the way we conduct business, perform scientific research, and spend our leisure time. With all of this attention to the computer we tend to forget that computing has a rich history that extends back beyond 1945. Since antiquity societies have had a need to process information and make computations, and they have met this need through technology.

We offer here a concise survey of computing technology prior to the development of the modern computer. We show the continuity of the history of computing by tracing several distinct older traditions that over the last forty years have converged in today's technology. Our study ends essentially in 1945, at the time when the plans for the first electronic, stored-program computer were being made. However, we do follow the exit of these earlier technologies, none of which survived long after the commercialization of computers in the 1950s.

All of the contributors to this volume are historians or computer scientists who have specialized in the study of computer history for at least a decade. We have tried here to wear our scholarship lightly. All efforts have been directed toward providing a balanced and accurate account of our subject, while writing at a level accessible to the general reader. We have attempted to relate technical innovations to their intellectual, social, and institutional contexts: to consider not only the machines and devices that were built and the innovations they incorporate but also the purposes for which they were to be used, the financial and organizational constraints and opportunities that shaped their developments, and the impact they had on individuals and institutions. We recognize, however, that computing has only recently come under historical scrutiny and that our remarks, especially on the context of technological development, are of only a preliminary nature.

This book includes seven chapters, an introduction, and an epilog. The first chapter covers two millennia of effort to develop arithmetic and the means to facilitate its computation. The story takes a modern turn in the late–nineteenth century when the desk calculator, invented 200 years earlier, became economically viable for American and European businesses. The essay traces the steady improvement in desk calculators in the twentieth century, their incorporation into the business world, and their diminished role after the invention of the computer.

The second chapter, on difference and analytical engines, examines nineteenth-century attempts to build machines to compute mathematical tables. The prominent figure here is the British mathematician Charles Babbage, who in the plans for his analytical engine originated the fundamental idea of program-controlled computing. The need for machines to calculate mathematical tables continued in the twentieth century, and this line is traced through the work in the 1940s of Howard Aiken and George Stibitz.

Computers are able to process symbols and control logical operations as well as calculate numerical problems. The first serious efforts to mechanize logical processes, in nineteenth-century Britain, are the starting point of the next essay. It continues with the development of logic machines in the twentieth century and, more significantly, the increasing knowledge of the relationship between logic and computing that forms a basis for computer science theory today.

Punched-card sorting and tabulating equipment was first built to process information from the 1890 United States Census. By the 1930s punched-card machinery became commonplace in medium-sized and large businesses in Europe and the United States. At the same time astronomers and other scientists began to adapt it to their own uses. These business and scientific users provided the original customer base for the electronic stored–program computer, while their punched-card equipment was adopted as peripheral equipment for the first electronic computing systems.

By the 1930s a rich array of calculating technology existed in the form of desk calculators, punched-card equipment, and analog computers (in which numerical values are measured rather than counted). The next chapter examines a range of analog devices used especially during the 1930s and the Second World War for scientific and engineering calculation. These include differential analyzers, wind tunnels, network analyzers, and gunnery computers. Analog and hybrid digital-analog computers were built until the 1960s, but they were eventually overtaken for almost every scientific and engineering application by the speed, precision, and programming flexibility of digital computers.

A major reason for the success of the modern computer is its processing speed. Until the 1930s most calculating equipment was slow by comparison, due to the slow rate of operation of mechanical switches. In the 1930s, in independent projects in the United States and Germany, computing devices were developed that used electromechanical relays for switching. These provided marked increase in speed over mechanical calculators. The next chapter examines the electromechanical calculators built at Harvard University and Bell Laboratories in the United States and by Konrad Zuse in Germany.

Even electromechanical relays were too slow to solve cryptanalytic and ballistic table-making problems confronting the Allied countries during the Second World War. These problems were met by the first serious attempts to develop electronic calculating equipment, notably the American calculator ENIAC and the British Colossus. The seventh chapter traces the move to computing with electricity, a critical step in the advance to the modern computer.

The convergence of these prewar calculating technologies in the modern computer is the topic of the epilog. It shows how calculator users and applications were already well established by the 1930s; how various pieces of the new technology (e.g., the program-control concept, electronic switching, and punched-card peripherals) were already in place; and how many of the precomputer projects grew into projects to build the first generation of computers.

Note

We appreciate the assistance given by the Charles Babbage Institute of the University of Minnesota in the editing of this volume.

Further Reading

Annals of the History of Computing. Published quarterly by Springer-Verlag, New York. A leading international journal devoted to the history of computing.

Cortada, James W., ed. *An Annotated Bibliography on the History of Data Processing.* Westport, Conn.: Greenwood Press, 1983. A useful guide to the available literature.

Goldstine, Herman H. *The Computer From Pascal to Von Neumann.* Princeton: Princeton University Press, 1972. A generally reliable and readable account by one of computing's pioneers.

Metropolis, N., J. Howlett, and Gian-Carlo Rota, eds. *A History of Computing in the Twentieth Century.* New York: Academic Press, 1980. A collection of essays, mainly by participants, of the first two decades of electronic computing.

Randell, Brian, ed. *The Origins of Digital Computers.* New York: Springer-Verlag, 3d ed., 1982. A collection of excerpts of important papers on computing, with historical introductions and a useful bibliography by the editor.

Computing Before Computers

Chapter 1

Early Calculation

Introduction

This chapter covers many different aspects of the history of calculation, describing the first steps in numeration and continuing through some of the nineteenth- and twentieth-century developments of mechanical calculating machinery. It is quite impossible to make this story completely chronological because of many different overlapping developments; however, an effort has been made to show the broad flow of historical events in the approximate order in which they occurred. Some topics, for example the contributions of the nineteenth-century British mathematician Charles Babbage, are left to be described in other chapters because they logically belong to a different line of development than that described here.

The main emphasis in this chapter is on the historical development of mechanical aids to calculation. By the early 1600s the progress of calculation takes two different routes: the first is based on the mathematical development of logarithms and leads into a discussion of John Napier, Napier's bones, logarithms, and slide rules; the second is more of a mechanical than an intellectual achievement and leads into the early development of calculating machinery, finally culminating with the very sophisticated desk-top machines of the early twentieth century.

Numeration

Counting

We will never know when or how humans first developed the ability to count. The process does not leave any physical evidence behind for archaeologists to find. What we do know is that the process is extremely ancient. Any of the so-called primitive peoples that have been studied have all had a highly developed sense of number and, to at least some degree, an ability to represent numbers in both words and symbols.

Of course the very earliest civilizations would not have had the same need for a sophisticated number system, or the arithmetic that goes with it, as we do today. In fact, the general level of numerical knowledge that we now take for granted is a fairly recent development for the common individual. Some evidence of this can be found in that, prior to the eleventh century, British law stated in order for a man to be considered as a creditable witness in court, he had to be able to count up to nine. To apply such a criterion today would be ridiculous.

Once humans had developed the ability to count, it must have become necessary to have a method of recording numbers. Elementary situations do not require any sophisticated numeral system, just an ability to reconstruct the final figure at some later date. A typical instance would be the shepherd who puts one pebble in a bag for every sheep he lets out of the pen in the morning and removes one for every sheep herded back at night. If pebbles are left over after all the sheep are back in the pen, he knows that he has to go back and look for the strays.

Written Number Systems and Arithmetic

Humanity's first attempt at numerical notation was likely a simple pictorial system in which five cows would be drawn to represent five cattle or, with a slight generalization, seven tents might represent seven family groups. This pictorial stage is of very little interest from the point of view of the development of any arithmetic abilities, which did not usually arise until various civilizations had developed reasonably sophisticated systems of numerical notation.

The physical evidence we have, at the moment, seems to indicate that several different groups in different parts of the world had reached this stage by about 3000 B.C.

Once a culture had reached the point at which semipermanent recording of numerical information was necessary, the actual system that they developed appears to have been dependent on such factors as the type of writing materials available, the base of the number system being used, and cultural factors within the group. These cultural factors eventually dictated which of the two major notational systems, the additive or the positional, was adopted.

The additive notational system uses one distinct symbol to represent each different unit in the number base, this symbol being repeated as often as necessary to indicate the magnitude of the number being written. The classic example of an additive system is the one developed by the ancient Egyptians; however, for purposes of illustration, the Old Roman Numeral system will be much more familiar.

The Modern Roman Numeral system, which uses the subtractive forms of IV for 4 and IX for 9, is a development out of the Old Roman Numeral system, which, although it was seen as early as A.D. 130, did not become popular until about A.D. 1600. In the Old Roman system it was possible to express any number less than 5,000 by a sequence of symbols in which no individual sign needed to be repeated more than four times. For example, the number 3,745 would be represented as MMMDCCXXXXV. It was the custom to write down the symbols in decreasing order of their magnitude (M = 1000, D = 500, C = 100, X = 10, V = 5, I = 1), but this was not necessary. The same number could have been represented as CXXCXXMMVMD, but it never was because of the obvious ease of reading the number when the symbols are written in the order of descending value.

The pure additive system of notation is quite easy to use for simple calculations, even though it does not appear so at first glance. Addition involves the two step process of simply writing down the individual symbols from each number, then collecting together the sequences of smaller valued symbols to make larger valued ones so that the number regains its canonical form. For example:

| 2319 | = | MM CCC X V IIII |
+ 821	=	DCCC XX I
3140	=	MMDCCCCCCXXXVIIIII

The second step now takes over and, because IIII = V, VV = X, CCCCC = D, and DD = M, the final result is written as MMMCXXXX.

Multiplication, although slow, is not really difficult and only involves remembering multiples of 5 and 10. For example:

$$
\begin{array}{rcl}
28 & = & \text{XXVIII} \\
\times\ 12 & = & \text{XII} \\
\hline
336 & &
\end{array}
$$

$$
\begin{array}{rcl}
\text{XXVIII} \times \text{I} & = & \text{XXVIII} \\
\text{XXVIII} \times \text{I} & = & \text{XXVIII} \\
\text{XXVIII} \times \text{X} & = & \text{CCLXXX} \\
\hline
& & \text{CCLXXXXXXXVVIIIIII}
\end{array}
$$

which would be written as CCCXXVI.

The operations of division and subtraction are a little more cumbersome; however, they were aided by standard doubling and halving operations (as was multiplication) which are no longer in use today. These techniques of "duplation" and "mediation" were actually developed from similar methods used by the Egyptians.

Although more cumbersome than systems of positional notation, the additive systems are not without their merits, and computation is not difficult once the rules are mastered. The modification of such a number system to include subtractive elements, such as the IV = 4 or IX = 9 of the Modern Roman system, tend to make matters very much more difficult as far as arithmetic is concerned, but this device is not to be found at all in most examples of additive notation.

In positional number systems, like the one most of us use today, the values being represented are denoted entirely by the position of the symbol in the string of characters representing the number. Each position corresponds to a certain power of the 'base' being used. The base in most common use today is, of course, ten; the positions representing units, tens, hundreds, thousands, etc. This means that it is necessary to have a zero symbol to indicate an empty position. The Chinese actually had a mechanism of using a positional number system without a zero symbol, but this is very much the exception in this type of notation.

The rules of calculation in a positional system are more complex than those used with additive systems, and they usually require that the user memorize some form of multiplication table. Because of the fact that everyone is familiar with the working of our own positional number system, no attempt will be made to describe it in detail.

The Abacus

Introduction

The abacus is usually considered as being an object in the same class as a child's toy. This is quite the wrong impression, for in the hands of a trained operator it is a powerful and sophisticated aid to computation. Some appreciation of the power of the abacus can be gained by noting the fact that in 1947 Kiyoshi Matsuzake of the Japanese Ministry of Communications used a soroban (the Japanese version of the abacus) to best Private Tom Wood of the United States Army of Occupation, who used the most modern electrically driven mechanical calculating machine, in a contest of speed and accuracy in calculation. The contest consisted of simple addition and subtraction problems, adding up long columns of many-digit numbers, and multiplication of integers. Matsuzake clearly won in four out of the five contests held, being only just beaten out by the electrically driven calculator when doing the multiplication problems. Although both men were highly skilled at their jobs, it should be pointed out that it took Matsuzake several years of special training in order to develop such a high order of skill at using the soroban and it is unlikely that the average abacus user would ever develop such speed and accuracy of operation. However, it does illustrate that, at least in the hands of even a moderately skilled operator, the abacus is far from being only an interesting toy.

The origin of the abacus is, literally, lost in the dusts of time. It likely started out as pebbles being moved over lines drawn in the dirt. Many cultures have used an abacus or counting board at some stage in their development, but as in most European countries, once paper and pencil methods were available the use of an abacus died out so completely that it is hard to find any cultural memory of the abacus being an important part of the arithmetic process. Today we tend to think of the abacus as a Far Eastern device, only because that is one of the few places where its use is still noticeable. In fact the abacus, in its present form, was only introduced into China in historical times (about A.D. 1200) and was taken from there to Korea (about A.D. 1400) and then to Japan (about A.D. 1600).

Although we know that the abacus was in general use in Europe until only about 250 years ago, we have remarkably little physical evidence of its presence, particularly from the earliest Greek and Roman times. What evidence we do have is usually in the form of quotations from the ancient writers. For example, Demosthenes (circa 384 B.C.– circa 322 B.C.) wrote of the need to use pebbles for calculations that were too difficult to do in your head. The use of the abacus was not confined to the Old World. We know very little about the various forms of abacus used by the Indians of North and South America, but we do know that some of these groups used the device. In 1590 a Jesuit, Joseph de Acosta, recorded some facts about the Inca culture that would indicate the common use of an abacus:

> In order to effect a very difficult computation for which an able calculator would require pen and ink . . . these Indians make use of their kernels of grain. They place one here, three somewhere else and eight I know not where. They move one kernel here and three there and the fact is that they are able to complete their computation without making the smallest mistake. As a matter of fact, they are better at calculating what each one is due to pay or give than we should be with pen and ink.[1]

It would seem likely that a number of North American Indian cultures were advanced enough to require some form of calculating device to be in use but almost no records remain of anything even as primitive as de Acosta's description. It is possible that the abacus was being used by some groups but that very few Europeans were concerned with recording anything except their own conquest of these Indian cultures.

The European Abacus

One of the few interesting bits of physical evidence for the early use of the table abacus comes from Greece. It is an actual abacus table, found on the island of Salamis (see Figure 1.1) just a few miles off the Greek coast near Piraeus. The Salamis abacus is now broken into two pieces, but was once a large marble slab about 5 feet long and 2 feet 6 inches wide. There is no indication of when it might have been made. From its size, it must have been used in some large public institution, perhaps as a bank or money changer's table. We know very little about how it may have been used except that it seems to be designed for counters to be placed on or between the various lines and the inscriptions appear to refer to numerical values and to certain types of coins, such as drachmae, talents, and obols. It has been speculated by many different people that the spaces between the five separate lines at one end of the abacus are intended for calculations involving fractions of the drachma.

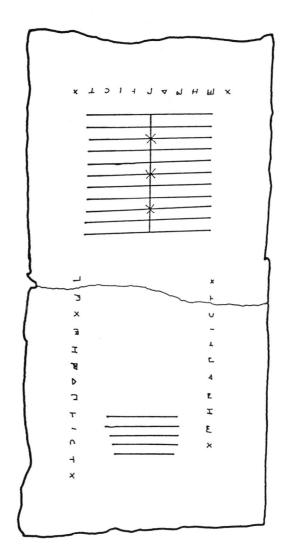

Figure 1.1. A drawing of the Salamas Abacus.

The word *abacus* itself can be of some help in determining the origins of the European version. The manipulation of pebbles in the dust, or the use of a finger or stylus in fine dust or sand spread upon a table, is known to have been used as an aid to calculation from very early times. The Semitic word *abaq* (dust) is thought by many to be the root of our modern word *abacus*. From the Semitic, the word seems to have been adopted by the Greeks who used *abax* to denote a flat surface or table upon which to draw their calculating lines. The term then appears to have spread to the Romans who called their table an *abacus*.

The term *abacus* has meant many different things during its history. It has been applied to the simple dust table, or wax tablet, which was generally used only as a substitute for pen and ink, as well as to the various forms of table abacus and different wire and bead arrangements used in the Far East. Because most early arithmetic was done on the abacus, the term became synonymous with 'arithmetic' and we find such oddities as Leonardo of Pisa (Fibonacci) publishing a book in 1202 called *Liber Abaci* (*The Book of the Abacus*), which did not deal with the abacus at all but was designed to show how the new Hindu-Arabic numerals could be used for calculation. In Northern Europe, the phrase *Rechnung auf der linien* (calculating on the lines) was in common use as a term meaning "to do arithmetic" even long after the use of the abacus had been abandoned.

Several of our modern mathematical and commercial terms can be traced to the early use of the table abacus. For example, the Romans used small limestone pebbles, called *calculi*, for their abacus counters; from this we take our modern words *calculate* and *calculus*. A more modern example comes from the fact that in England the table abacus was generally referred to as a *counting board* or simply as a *counter;* of course every merchant would have a counter in his shop upon which to place the goods being purchased and upon which the *account* could be calculated.

By the thirteenth century the European table abacus had been standardized into some variant of the form shown in the diagram below. It consisted of a simple table, sometimes covered by a cloth, upon which a number of lines were drawn in chalk or ink. The lines indicated the place value of the counters: the bottom line representing units and each line upwards representing ten times the value of the line below. Each space between the lines counted for five times that of the line below it. No more than four counters could be placed on a line and no more than one in any space. As soon as five counters appeared on a line, they were removed and one placed in the next higher space; if two appeared in a space, they were removed and one placed on the next higher line. When performing a computation on the table abacus, any counters in a space were considered to be grouped together with those on the line below: the use of the space simply being a device to keep the eye from being confused by having a large number of counters on one line. A cross or star was usually placed next to the fourth (thousands) line to guide the eye, much as we use a comma today to mark off groups of three digits. An example of such an abacus is shown in Figure 1.2.

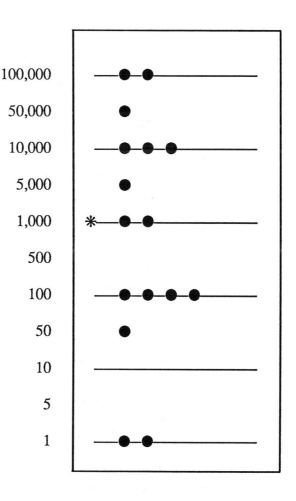

Figure 1.2. Table abacus set out to represent 287,452.

Very few of these *reckoning tables* still exist. We know that they once existed in great numbers for they are often mentioned in wills and in household inventories, but, being a common object, nobody thought to preserve them and only a handful are known still to exist in various museums.

By the thirteeth century the counters had changed from the simple pebbles used in earlier days into specially minted coinlike objects. They first appeared about 1200 in Italy, but because it was there that the use of Hindu-Arabic numerals first replaced the abacus, the majority of the counters now known come from north of the Alps. These coinlike counters were cast, thrown, or pushed on the abacus table, thus they were generally known by some name associated with this action. In France they were called *jetons* from the French verb *jeter* (to throw), while in the Netherlands they were known as *werpgeld* (thrown money). The older English usage of *to cast up an account* or *to cast a horoscope* also illustrates the mode of operation of a good abacist.

The counters, now commonly called *jetons*, are still to be found in quite large numbers. This is not surprising when you realize that the average numerate man would possess at least one set of copper jetons while a merchant would likely have several. Individuals possessing larger wealth or authority in the community would often have their jetons struck in silver with their coat of arms or portraits as the decoration.

The table abacus was used extensively in Britain even after it had been abandoned by the majority of people on the Continent. Illustrated in Figure 1.3 is one page from the first widely used printed book on arithmetic in the English language. This book, by Robert Recorde, was in print from 1542 right up to the start of the 1700s. It clearly shows (besides two errors in the illustration which are left as a puzzle for the reader) that abacus arithmetic was being taught to school children throughout this period.

The illustration for Recorde's book clearly shows the usual method of working a table abacus. For addition the two numbers were simply set down side by side and the two groups of jetons were simply moved together to accomplish the addition. Subtraction was slightly more difficult but was easily accomplished especially when one was able to literally "borrow" a jeton from a higher valued row in order to accomplish the process. The methods for multiplication and division were slightly different in various parts of Europe, but they

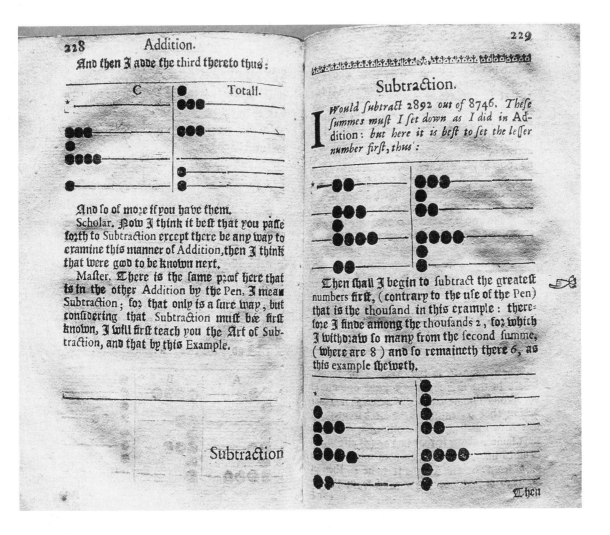

Figure 1.3. A page from Robert Recorde's book on arithmetic.

largely retained the doubling and halving processes that were started by the Egyptians.

When the Hindu-Arabic numerals became firmly established in Europe, the use of the table abacus died out completely. Its use was forgotten to the extent that, when Napoleon invaded Russia in 1812, his soldiers brought back examples of the Russian abacus as being a curiosity of the area; this was at a time when their own great-grandfathers had been daily users of the device in France.

The Abacus in the Orient

The oriental wire and bead abacus appears to have its origin in the Middle East some time during the early Middle Ages. A type of abacus was developed that had several wires, each of which was strung with ten beads. The Turks called this a *coulba*, the Armenians a *choreb*, and the Russians, where it can still be seen in use today, referred to it as a *stchoty*. This device almost certainly entered the Far East through the standard trade routes of the day, the merchant class being the first to adopt its use and then it slowly spread to the upper levels of society. Its introduction may well have been helped by international traders, such as Marco Polo, who had to travel through several different countries on their way to China and thus had ample opportunity to pick up different techniques along the way.

By the time it was firmly entrenched in Chinese society, about the year A.D. 1300, the abacus consisted of an oblong frame of wood with a bar running down its length, dividing the frame into two compartments. Through this bar, at right angles to it, are usually placed seventeen (but sometimes more) small dowels with seven beads strung on each one, two on the upper side (heaven) of the bar and five on the lower side (earth). Each bead in the lower section is worth one unit, while those in the upper section are worth five. Thus, it is possible to represent any number from 1 to 15 on the individual dowels, although anything greater than 9 would naturally occur only as an intermediate result in the process of a calculation. The Chinese called this device a *swan pan* (counting board). The term *swan* was derived from an older term meaning to "reckon with the rods"—a reference to an earlier oriental technique of using short bamboo rods to represent numbers on a flat calculating board (Figure 1.4).

From China the concept of a wire and bead abacus spread to Japan. Again it was likely the merchant class who actually spread the idea, for there was a great deal of trade going on between the two countries during the period A.D. 1400-1600. It is entirely possible that the soroban was being used in Japan for at least one hundred years before it was officially noticed by the ruling classes some time about 1600. At that time, the rulers of Japan were known to despise the lower classes; any knowledge of business affairs, or even of the value of the different coins, on the part of the nobility was considered a sign of inferior breeding. The soroban generally resembles the swan pan, except that there is only one bead in heaven and four in earth, and the beads themselves have been changed in shape to provide a sharper edge so that the operators fingers made better contact for flipping them up and down the dowels (Figure 1.5). These changes meant that the Japanese operator had to be a little more aware of how to work quickly with additions or subtractions, which may require a carry, or borrow, to or from the next column. It is, perhaps, with the soroban that the abacus reached its ultimate development. As was pointed out earlier, a well-trained soroban operator can compete with an electrically driven, four-function, mechanical calculator as far as speed and accuracy are concerned.

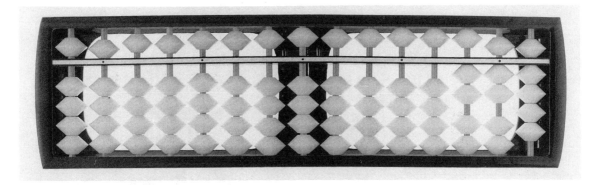

Figure 1.5. A Japanese soroban.

Figure 1.4. A Chinese swan pan.

Calculating Aids

Napier and His Bones

The Scottish Reformation was just starting as John Napier (Figure 1.6) was born in 1550 and the upheavals that it caused added to the misery of both the nobles and the common folk alike. In the middle of the sixteenth century, Scotland was torn apart by both political and religious strife, with war between the different groups being a constant occurrence. The cultural level of the time is said to have seldom risen above that of barbarous hospitality. Before Napier's time, Scotland had produced several men of note in the field of literature but only one in science, the thirteenth-century mathematician Michael Scott. With the study of academic subjects being held in low regard, it is very surprising that some of the most fundamental advances in mathematics and computation should have come out of this environment.

Figure 1.6. John Napier (1550–1617).

Napier was born near Edinburgh, but that is almost all we know of his early life. His father was one of the first people to take up the cause of the Protestant movement in Scotland and, presumably, he influenced John from his earliest days to believe that the pope was the sole bar to the salvation of all humanity. Certainly John held this belief right up to the time he died in 1617.

Napier is best known for his invention of logarithms, but he spent a large part of his life devising various other schemes for easing the labor involved in doing arithmetic. One of the best known of these devices is his *Rabdologia*, or as they are more commonly known *Napier's Bones*. The name *bones* arose from the fact that the better quality sets were constructed from horn, bone, or ivory. Various authors have preferred to call them "numbering rods," "multiplying rulers," or even "speaking rods," but the name *bones* just refused to to die out. Today they are usually considered a mere curiosity.

Napier did not at first consider this invention worthy of publication; however, several friends pressed him to write it up, if only to avoid others claiming it as their own. His descriptions appeared in 1617, the year of his death and three years after the publication of his description of logarithms, in a small book entitled *Rabdologia*.

The idea for the bones undoubtedly came from the Gelosia method of doing multiplication. This method is known to be very old; it likely developed in India and there are records of its use in Arabic, Persian, and Chinese societies from the late Middle Ages. The method was introduced into Italy sometime in the fourteenth century, where it obtained its name from its similarity to a common form of Italian window grating. The method consists of writing down a matrixlike grid, placing one digit of the multiplicand at the head of each column and one digit of the multiplier beside each row, the product of each row and column digit is then entered in the appropriate box of the matrix—the tens digit above the diagonal and the units digit below. The final product is obtained by starting in the lower right-hand corner and adding up the digits in each diagonal with any carry digits being considered as part of the next diagonal. Figure 1.7 illustrates the Gelosia method, showing 456 multiplied by 128 with the product (058368) being read off starting from the upper left-hand corner.

Napier's bones are simply a collection of strips of all possible columns of this Gelosia table as is shown in Figure 1.8. To perform the multiplication of 456 by 128 one would select the strips headed 4, 5, and 6, place them side by side, read off the partial products of

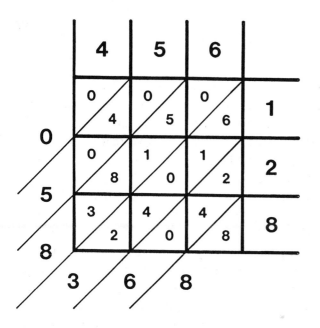

Figure 1.7. The Gelosia method of multiplication.

456 times 1, 456 times 2 and 456 times 8 (by adding up the digits in each parallelogram to obtain each digit of the partial product), and then add together the partial products. Division was aided by the bones in that multiples of the divisor could be easily determined, saving time that would normally be spent in trial multiplication.

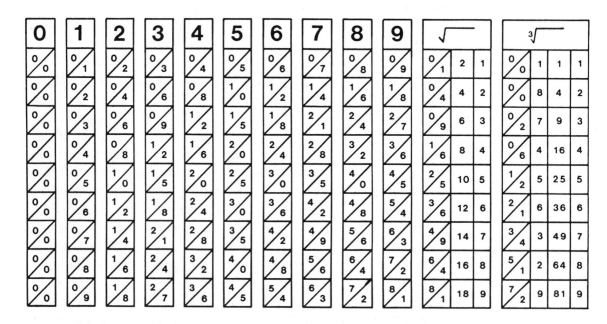

Figure 1.8. A modern set of Napier's bones.

The use of Napier's bones spread rapidly, and, within a few years, examples could be found in use from Europe to China. It is likely that the two Jesuits, Gaspard Schott and Athanasius Kircher, were partially responsible for their spread, particularly to China, where two other Jesuits held office in the Peking Astronomical Board. Both Schott and Kircher were German mathematicians during the time when the Jesuit order was sending its technically trained members around the world as missionaries for both the Christian faith and the wonders of European technology.

Schott was aware of the physical problems involved in using a standard set of arithmetic bones: such things as locating the correct bones, having some convenient device to ensure they line up correctly, etc. Several others had suggested incorporating Napier's bones into some form of mechanical assembly but none of them had published any of their ideas, so Schott was left on his own to invent a similar device. The result was a series of cylinders with a complete set of Napier's bones inscribed on each, the individual bones running the length of the cylinder. Several of these cylinders were then mounted in a box so they could be turned and any individual bone could be examined through slits cut in the top of the box. Figure 1.9 shows a photograph of Schott's device, the top of the box containing an addition table to aid the operator.

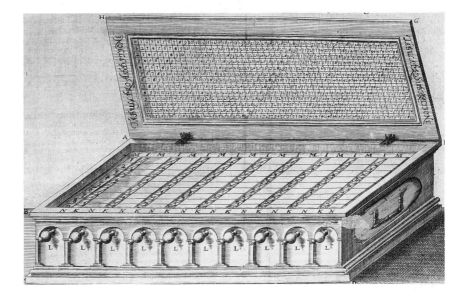

Figure 1.9. Gaspard Schott's version of Napier's bones.

Although it was an interesting attempt at making the bones easier to use, the system proved to be a failure. The parallelograms containing the digits to be added together span two adjacent bones and the space required to mount the cylinders meant that these digits were widely separated. This led to a greater tendency to make mistakes and the device was soon abandoned. Schemes, similar to Schott's, were tried by different people in different countries (most notably by Pierre Petit, the French mathematician and friend of Pascal) but they all failed for the same reason.

The final chapter in the development of Napier's bones as a computational instrument took place in 1885 when, at the French Association for the Advancement of Science meetings, Edouard Lucas presented a problem on arithmetic that caught the attention of Henri Genaille, a French civil engineer working for the railway. Genaille, who was already quite well-known for his invention of several different arithmetic aids, solved Lucas's problem and, in the process, devised a different form of Napier's bones. These "rulers" eliminated the need to carry digits from one column to the next when reading off partial products (Figure 1.10). He demonstrated these rulers to the association in 1891. Lucas gave these rulers enough publicity that they became quite popular for a number of years. Unfortunately he never lived to see their popularity grow, for he died, aged 49, shortly after Genaille's demonstration.

The rulers, a set of which are shown in Figure 1.10, are similar in their use to a standard set of Napier's bones. There is one ruler for each digit from 0 to 9. Each ruler is divided into nine sections with several digits inscribed in each section, and one or two arrows point to the left towards a particular digit in the next ruler. In order to find the product of 3271 by 4, the rulers for 03271 (note the need for always having a leading zero ruler) are placed side by side. Starting with the fourth section of the right-most ruler, you select the digit at the top of this section (4 in this case) and then simply follow the arrows towards the left, reading off the digits as you come to them (the product being 13084 in the case shown in Figure 1.11).

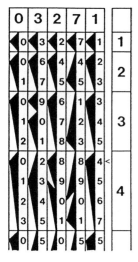

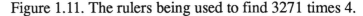

Figure 1.11. The rulers being used to find 3271 times 4.

21

Figure 1.10. A set of the Genaille-Lucas rulers.

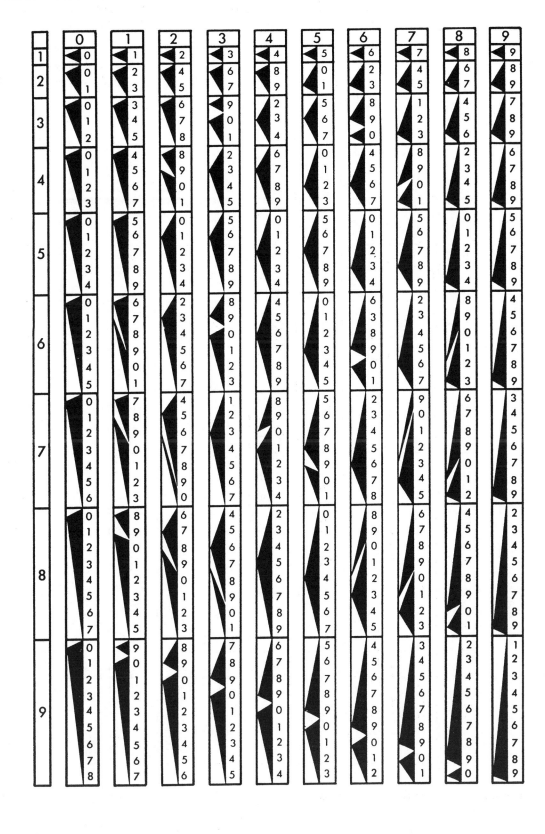

Once the problem of eliminating the carry digits had been solved by Genaille, the creation of a specific set of rulers for division was quickly accomplished. The division rulers are similar to the multiplication ones except that the large arrows are replaced by a multitude of smaller ones. Figures 1.12 and 1.13 show a complete set of division rulers together with an example of how they could be used to divide the number 6957 by 6.

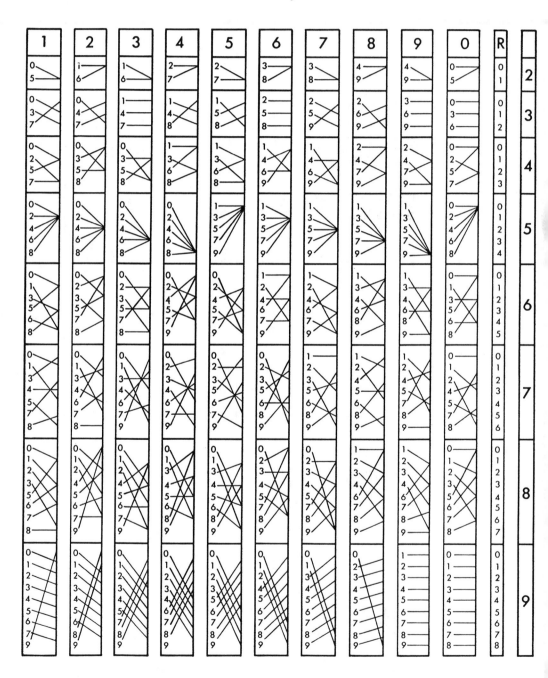

Figure 1.12. A set of the Genaille-Lucas division rulers.

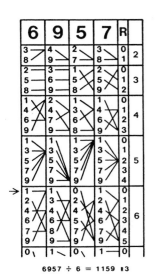

6957 ÷ 6 = 1159 r3

Figure 1.13. Genaille-Lucas division rulers used to divide 6957 by 6.

Note that a special ruler (marked R) must be placed on the right-hand side of the set in order to determine the remainder, if any, of the division operation. The division rulers are used in the opposite direction from the multiplication ones. In order to divide the number by 6, you start at the left hand side of the sixth section with the topmost digit (1 in the case shown here) and proceed to the right, following the arrows and reading off the digits as they are encountered (1159 with a remainder of 3).

In the era before the mechanical desk-top calculating machine industry had been developed, these simple instruments were one of the two main forms of computational assistance for anyone engaged in scientific or business calculations more complex than elementary addition and subtraction. The other main computational aid, like these various forms of Napier's bones, also began with some pioneering work of John Napier and is discussed below.

Logarithms

Many writers have suggested that the invention of logarithms came like a bolt from the blue, with nothing leading up to them. This is not exactly the case because, like almost every other invention, examples can be found of parallel development by other people. John Napier is always given the credit for logarithms because these other developments were either left unpublished or, in some cases, not recognized for what they were at the time.

The major computational problems of Napier's time tended to involve astronomy, navigation, and the casting of horoscopes, all of which are interrelated. These problems led to a number of sixteenth-century scientists devoting their time to the development of trigonometry. About twenty-five years before Napier published his description of logarithms, the problem of easing the workload when multiplying two sines together was solved by the *method of prosthaphaeresis*, which corresponds to the formula:

$$\sin a \times \sin b = [\cos(a - b) - \cos(a + b)]/2$$

Once it had been shown that a rather nasty multiplication could be replaced by a few simple additions, subtractions, and an elementary division by 2, it is entirely likely that this formula spurred scientifically oriented individuals, including Napier, to search for other methods to simplify the harder arithmetical operations. In fact several other such formulae were developed during Napier's time, but only the method of prosthaphaeresis was of any real use, except in special circumstances. We know that Napier knew of, and used, the method of prosthaphaeresis, and it may well have influenced his thinking because the first logarithms were not of numbers but were logarithms of sines.

Another factor in the development of logarithms at this time was that the properties of arithmetic and geometric series had been studied extensively in the previous century. We now know that any numbers in an arithmetic series are the logarithms of other numbers in a geometric series, in some suitable base. For example, the following series of numbers is geometric, with each number being two times the previous one:

natural numbers 1 2 4 8 16 32 64 128 256 512 1024.

And the series below is an arithmetic one whose values are the corresponding base 2 logarithms:

logarithms   0 1 2 3 4 5 6   7   8   9   10.

It had long been known that if you take any two numbers in the arithmetic progression, say 3 and 4, their sum, 7, would indicate the position of the term in the geometric series that is the product of the terms in the corresponding positions of the geometric series, e.g., $3 + 4 = 7$ and $8 \times 16 = 128$ (the third times the fourth = the seventh). This is starting to look very much like our own conception of logarithms as being the powers to which some base number is raised, a concept that was not understood in Napier's time. Often the use of a good form of notation will suggest some basic mathematical principle. Our use of indices to indicate the power to which a number is being raised seems to have an obvious connection with logarithms, but without this form of notation, the connection is vague at best.

John Napier came at the idea of logarithms not by algebra and indices but by way of geometry. When first thinking about this subject, he used the term *artificial number* but later created the term *logarithm* from a Greek phrase meaning "ratio number." He decided on this term because his logarithms were based on the concept of points moving down lines in which the velocity of one point was based on the ratio of the lengths of the line on either side of it.

We know almost nothing about how long Napier worked before he felt that the idea of logarithms was sufficiently refined to be worthy of publication, but in July of 1614 he published a small volume of fifty-six pages of text and ninety pages of tables entitled *Mirifici Logarithmorum Canonis Descriptio*. At best, it is translated as *Description of the Admirable Cannon (Table) of Logarithms*. It was common in those days to dedicate a book to a nobleman, often in the hope that some patronage would result. Unfortunately Napier had the bad luck to dedicate the *Descriptio* to the then Prince of Wales, who, when he later became King Charles I, was beheaded by Cromwell.

The *Descriptio* was just that, a description of the cannon or table of logarithms of sines, with the rules to be followed when using them to perform multiplication, division, or the computation of roots and powers. It contained a statement that, if these tables were accorded the reception that Napier hoped, he would describe in some future publication exactly how they were discovered and the methods used to calculate them.

Our story now shifts to London, where one of the most famous English mathematicians of the day, Henry Briggs (1561-1631), was Professor of Geometry at Gresham College. By the early years of the 1600s his reputation had spread far enough that people like Johann Kepler were consulting him on the properties of the ellipse. In the later months of 1614 he obtained a copy of Napier's *Descriptio* and, by March of the following year wrote that

> Napier, lord of Markinston, hath set my head and hands at work with his new and admirable logarithms. I hope to see him this summer, if it please God; for I never saw a book which pleased me better, and made me more wonder.[2]

Briggs immediately began to popularize the concept of logarithms in his lectures and even began to work on a modified version of the tables. Several years later, in 1628, Briggs's newly calculated logarithms were published and he stated in the Latin preface

> That these logarithms differ from those which that illustrious man, the Baron of Merchiston published in his Cannon Mirificus must not

surprise you. For I myself, when expounding their doctrine publicly in London to my auditors in Gresham College, remarked that it would be much more convenient that 0 should be kept for the logarithm of the whole sine . . . . And concerning that matter I wrote immediately to the author himself; and as soon as the season of the year and the vacation of my public duties of instruction permitted I journeyed to Edinburgh, where, being most hospitably received by him, I lingered for a whole month.[3]

What Briggs was suggesting was that the base of the logarithms should be changed in order to make them easier to use. Napier had evidently already seen the same thing, for as Briggs states:

But as we held discourse concerning this change in the system of Logarithms, he said, that for a long time he had been sensible of the same thing, and had been anxious to accomplish it, but that he had published those he had already prepared, until he could construct tables more convenient, if other weighty matters and his frail health would suffer him so to do. But he conceived that the change ought to be effected in this manner, that 0 should become the logarithm of unity, and 10,000,000,000 that of the whole sine; which I could but admit was by far the most convenient of all. So, rejecting those which I had already prepared, I commenced, under his encouraging counsel, to ponder seriously about the calculation of these tables; and in the following summer I again took journey to Edinburgh, where I submitted to him the principal part of those tables which are here published, and I was about to do the same even the third summer, had it pleased God to spare him so long.[4]

The result of these changes was to create the common (base 10) logarithms that we know today.

Henry Briggs never did finish his complete recalculation of Napier's logarithms. His tables, first published in 1624, contained the logs of the numbers from 1 to 20,000 and from 90,000 to 100,000 all calculated to 14 decimal places. There are 1161 errors in these original tables, or just under 0.04 percent of the entries. Almost all of them are simple errors of plus or minus 1 in the last decimal place; however, several more are printing or copying errors such as the printing of 3730 instead of 4730, but these are easily seen by users of the tables because they stand out as being quite different from the surrounding entries.

The concept of logarithms spread rapidly. In the same year as Briggs's tables appeared, Kepler published his first set of logarithms and, a year later, Edmund Wingate published a set in Paris called *Arithmetique Logarithmique*, which not only contained logarithms for the numbers from 1 to 1000, but also contained Edmund Gunter's newly calculated log sines and log tangents. The first complete set of logarithms for the numbers from 1 to 101,000 was published by a Dutch printer, Adrian Vlacq (circa 1600-1667), who was noted for his ability at printing scientific works. He filled in the sections missing from Briggs's work, and published the whole table in 1628. Vlacq's tables were copied by many others in later years. Although the publishers seldom acknowledged the source of the logarithms, it was obvious where they came from because Vlacq's original errors were copied along with the correct logarithms. It was not until the first quarter of the nineteenth century, when Charles Babbage published his famous log tables, that correct sets of tables were readily available.

Within twenty years of the time that Briggs's tables first appeared, the use of logarithms had spread worldwide. From being a limited tool of great scientists like Kepler, they had become commonplace in the schoolrooms of the civilized nations. Logarithms were used extensively in all trades and professions that required calculations to be done. It is hard to imagine an invention that has helped the process of computation more dramatically than has logarithms, the one exception being the modern digital computer. During a conference held in 1914 to celebrate the three hundredth anniversary of the publication of the *Descriptio*, it was estimated that, of all the calculation done in the previous three hundred years, the vast majority had been done with the aid of logarithms.

The Slide Rule

Although logarithms were usable in the form in which Napier invented them, it was the work of Henry Briggs that actually made them easier to use. Briggs's work naturally came to the notice of Edmund Gunter, another professor at Gresham College, who was a very practically minded teacher of astronomy and mathematics. Gunter was primarily interested in the problems of astronomy, navigation, and the construction of sun dials (the only reasonable method of telling time in his day), all of which required large amounts of calculation involving trigonometric elements. Because of the trigonometric content of these problems, the logarithm tables being produced by Briggs were only of marginal help, so Gunter sat down and completed the calculations for tables of the logarithms of sines and the logarithms of tangents for each minute of the quadrant. These eight figure tables were published in 1620 and did much to relieve the burden of calculation for finding one's position at sea.

Gunter had some earlier experience in the development of calculating instruments, having been one of the major figures in the perfection of an instrument known as a *sector*. This device used a pair of dividers to measure off different values inscribed along several different linear scales. This experience soon led him to realize that the process of adding together a pair of logarithms could be partially automated by engraving a scale of logarithms on a piece of wood and then using a pair of dividers to add together two values in much the same way as he would have done when using a sector. Not only did this method eliminate the mental work of addition, but it also removed the necessity for the time-consuming process of looking up the logarithms in a table. Gunter's piece of wood soon became known as Gunter's Line of Numbers. Its use spread rapidly through England and was quickly popularized on the Continent.

Gunter's Line of Numbers consisted of a simple piece of wood, about two feet long, (often the shaft of a cross-staff, a simple navigational sighting instrument of the time) marked off with a logarithmic scale, much the same way as one axis of a piece of logarithmic graph paper is marked today. If he wished to multiply A times B, he would open up a pair of dividers to the distance from 1 to A on his line of numbers, putting one point of the compass on the point B, he would read off the number at which the other point sat. The accuracy was limited to two or three digits, depending on the care with which the instrument was used, but he had produced the first logarithmic analog device able to multiply two numbers together. Gunter would likely have added further refinements to his Line of Numbers, for he was a master at the design and use of instruments, but he died, aged 45, in 1626, before he was able to get enough time from his other duties to return to the subject of logarithmic calculating instruments. The next developments were left to a highly individualistic clergyman named William Oughtred.

William Oughtred (circa 1574-1660) was one of the leading mathematicians of his day. In 1604, after having taken a degree at Cambridge, he was appointed as the rector of a small parish in Surrey and, a few years later, was moved to the parish of Albury where he lived for the rest of his life. He was the bane of his bishop, being the subject of several complaints that he was a pitiful preacher because he never studied anything other than mathematics (which tends to make for dull sermons). In the days before regular scientific journals, information was published by sending it to several people who were known to be in regular contact with other scientific men—Athanasius Kircher, mentioned in connection with Napier's bones, and Fr. Martin Mersenne of Paris being the noted "postboxes" on the Continent, while William Oughtred was one of the main distribution points for England.

Oughtred was what we would now classify as a "pure" mathematician. Although he had a contempt for the computational side of mathematics and considered the people who used calculational instruments simply as "the doers of tricks," he was quite familiar with the mathematical instruments then available. There are records of his visiting Henry Briggs in 1610 and, while there, meeting Edmund Gunter, and discussing mathematical instruments with him at great length.

Oughtred noted that Gunter's Line of Numbers required a pair of dividers in order to measure off the lengths of logarithmic values along the scale and quickly came up with the idea that, if he had two such scales marked along the edges of the pieces of wood, he could slide them relative to each other and thus do away with the need for a pair of dividers. He also saw that if there were two disks, one slightly smaller than the other, with a Line of Numbers engraved around the edge of each, that they could be pinioned together at their centers and rotated relative to one another to give the same effect as having Gunter's scale engraved on two bits of wood.

Because of his general disdain for mathematical instruments he did not consider it worth his trouble, time, or effort to publish a description of how he had improved Gunter's Line of Numbers into a practical slide rule. He did, however, describe the system to one of his pupils, Richard Delamain, who was a teacher of mathematics living and working in London. Delamain used Oughtred's ideas quite openly and based his teaching on various methods of instrumental calculation.

In 1630 another of Oughtred's pupils, William Forster, happened to mention that in order to gain more accuracy when using Gunter's Line of Numbers he had resorted to using a scale six feet long and a beam compass to measure off the lengths. Oughtred then showed him how he could dispense with the beam compass by simply having two of Gunter's scales sliding over one another and also showed him a circular disk with Gunter's Line of Numbers marked off along the edge with two indices, like a pair of dividers, extending from the center. The latter device, which Oughtred called his "Circles of Proportion" (shown in Figure 1.14), he claimed to have invented sometime in 1622. Forster was so impressed that he demanded Oughtred publish a description of these inventions. Oughtred, still under the impression that these "playthings" were not suitable objects for the true mathematician, initially decided against it but, when Delamain's book appeared claiming them as his own invention, Oughtred agreed to publish and even let Forster translate his Latin into English so that the subject matter would be more widely distributed than if it had remained in academic Latin.

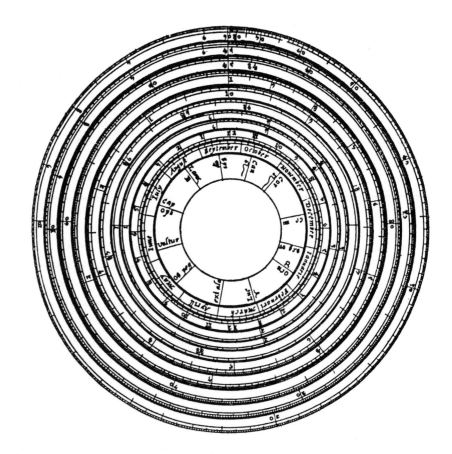

Figure 1.14. Oughtred's circles of proportion.

The slide rule may have been developed and publicized in the 1630s and obtained its current form as a movable slide between two other fixed blocks of wood about the middle 1650s, but very little use was actually made of the device for almost two hundred years. However several special slide rules were developed and became quite popular; for example, a special slide rule was created for the use of timber merchants, but the average educated man still clung to the older sector as his main calculating instrument.

James Watt, better known for his work on the steam engine, was responsible, at least in part, for one of the first really well-made slide rules in the very late 1700s. He had spent the early part of his life as an instrument maker at Glasgow University and so was familiar with the techniques of engraving accurate scales upon instruments. After he had set up a workshop for his steam engine business in Soho, Birmingham, he discovered that he needed a device to let him perform quick calculations concerning the volumes and power levels of various engines. He devised a simple slide rule consisting of one sliding piece between two fixed stocks (a design that had been in use for a considerable period of time), carefully engraved the face with four basic scales, and put tables of various constants on the back. His rule was accurate enough that others soon requested copies for themselves and Watt manufactured this so-called Soho Slide Rule for several years. Even with the example of the Soho Slide Rule, the general public seemed to ignore the power of the instrument. The great English mathematician Augustus De Morgan, when writing an article about the slide rule for the popular press in 1850, had to explain that

> for a few shillings most persons might put into their pockets some hundred times as much power of calculation as they have in their heads.[5]

The big breakthrough for the slide rule came in 1850, when a nineteen-year-old French artillery officer, Amedee Mannheim (1831-1906), designed a very simple slide rule much like that manufactured by Watt, but added the movable double-sided cursor, which we think of as such an integral part of the slide rule today. This was not the first time that a movable cursor had been combined with the simple sliding logarithmic scales, indeed the first time had been almost two hundred years earlier on a slide rule designed for British naval use, but it had been largely ignored until Mannheim reinvented it. The cursor enabled fairly complex operations to be easily carried out on a simple, yet well-made, slide rule (Figure 1.15). Mannheim's design was adopted as the standard for the French artillery and, after a few years, examples of it began to appear in other countries. Mannheim survived his army service and was eventually appointed Professor of Mathematics at the celebrated École Polytechnique in Paris, a post that did nothing to harm the evergrowing reputation of his slide rule.

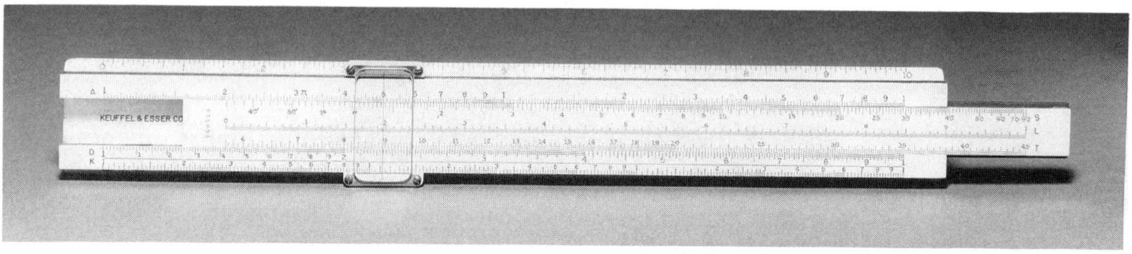

Figure 1.15. A modern version of the Mannheim slide rule.
Courtesy Smithsonian Institution.

Despite the fact that the Europeans began to adopt the "slip stick" for many forms of quick calculation, it remained unpopular in North America until 1888, when several examples of the Mannheim design were imported. The North American market grew until, in 1895, there was enough of a demand that the Mannheim rules were manufactured in the United States. Even with a local source of manufacture, the slide rule was still not totally accepted in North America until the twentieth century. A survey in the journal *Engineering News* reported that, as late as 1901, only one-half of the engineering schools in the United States gave any attention at all to the use of the slide rule.

Once established, the progress of the slide rule was extremely rapid. Many different forms were produced by several different major manufacturers. The number of scales to be found on each instrument increased to the point that eighteen or twenty different scales were regularly engraved on the better quality instruments. Both sides of the rule were used and the center, sliding portion could often be turned over or completely replaced to provide even more combinations of scales. Special slide rules incorporating such things as a scale of atomic and molecular weights were created for chemists, and almost any branch of science or engineering could boast that at least one manufacturer produced a slide rule designed for their particular use. The accuracy of the slide rule was improved by several people who modified the basic form so that the logarithmic scales were wrapped around cylinders or into spirals. One device, known as Fuller's Slide Rule (Figure 1.16), was equivalent to a standard slide rule over eighty-four feet long, yet could be easily held in the hand. It was possible to work correctly to four figures, and sometimes even five, with this particular unit.

Figure 1.16. Fuller's slide rule.

The slide rule became a symbol that was often used to represent the advancing technology of the twentieth century. It was a status symbol for engineering students in the 1950s and 1960s and could almost always be found clipped to their belt as a statement of their chosen profession. It was, however, to be a transient symbol. The development of the hand-held electronic calculator offered many times the accuracy and convenience and the slide rule quickly sank into obscurity. The demise was so rapid that it is possible to find many examples of people who differ in age by only four or five years, one of whom relied entirely on the slide rule for all calculations required during university education, and the other, who took the same course of studies, would not know how to use it to multiply two numbers together. In a matter of a few years the major manufacturers of slide rules had to either transfer their expertise to other products or face bankruptcy.

Mechanical Calculating Machines

Introduction

Though the various analog instruments were capable of performing a great deal of useful arithmetic, the story of devices that ultimately led to fully automatic computation really starts with the invention and development of mechanical devices to perform the four standard arithmetic functions. By devising a system in which mechanical levers, gears, and wheels could replace the facilities of human intellect, the early pioneers in these devices showed the way towards the complete automation of the process of calculation. Needless to say the early efforts were very crude not because the inventors lacked the intelligence to construct better devices but because the technical abilities of the workmen and the materials with which they had to work were often not up to the demands put upon them by these new machines. There was also the problem that whole new techniques had to be invented in order to get mechanical devices to produce some of the motions required of them when doing simple arithmetic.

Some of the mechanical techniques became available about the start of the seventeenth century, when, in response to a demand for mechanical automata to amuse the rich, methods of producing various motions in mechanical systems were developed. The construction techniques were further advanced by the developing trade of the clock maker—several early computing machines were built by people trained in horological arts.

Most of the very early attempts at constructing a simple adding machine relied on the human operator to adjust the mechanism whenever a carry occurred from one digit to the next, much the same way as was done when using a table abacus. There is no point in detailing the development of this type of mechanism as they were all of the most elementary kind and, in general, only constructed from crude materials. The real development of mechanical computing machinery only began when people attempted to incorporate mechanisms to automatically deal with the problem of adding a carry from one digit to the next.

It used to be thought that Blaise Pascal invented the first adding machine to contain a carry mechanism; however, investigative work in the 1950s and 1960s showed that that honor belongs to Wilhelm

Schickard, who produced a machine about the year 1620, some twenty years before Pascal's attempt. It is quite possible that further investigation will reveal yet an earlier device, but nothing now suggests that any work of importance was done before Schickard. There are many stories of people creating adding machines before Schickard, some even as early as the year 1000. For example, the monk Gerbert (later Pope Sylvester II) is reputed to have developed some form of early calculating device, but it is almost certain that these legends refer to things like Gerbert's abacus rather than an actual mechanical device. Even if people like Gerbert did produce some form of mechanical mechanism, it is most unlikely that the technology have allowed anything to be produced matching the sophistication of the Schickard or Pascal machines.

The Machines of Wilhelm Schickard (1592-1635)

Wilhelm Schickard was Professor of Hebrew, Oriental languages, mathematics, astronomy, geography, and, in his spare time, a protestant minister in the German town of Tübingen during the early 1600s. He has been compared to Leonardo da Vinci in that they both had far-ranging interests and enquiring minds. Besides being an excellent mathematician, with some of his mathematical methods being in use until the later part of the nineteenth century, he was a good painter, a good enough mechanic to construct his own astronomical instruments, and a skilled enough engraver to provide some of the copper plates used to illustrate Kepler's great work *Harmonices Mundi*.

Figure 1.17. Wilhelm Schickard (1592-1635).

It is known that Schickard and Kepler not only knew each other but that they also worked together several times during their lives. It was one of these joint efforts that resulted in Schickard producing the first workable mechanical adding machine. Kepler and Schickard are known to have discussed John Napier's invention of logarithms and Napier's bones as early as 1617. During one of Kepler's visits to Tübingen he showed Schickard some of his new results and examples of Napier's bones and logarithms, which he had used in their calculation. This seems to have inspired Schickard to consider the design of a machine that would incorporate both a set of Napier's bones and a mechanism to add up the partial products they produced in order to completely automate the process of finding the product of two numbers.

On September 20, 1623, Schickard wrote to Kepler saying that

> what you have done in a logistical way (i.e., by calculation), I have just tried to do by mechanics. I have constructed a machine consisting of eleven complete and six incomplete (actually "mutilated") sprocket wheels which can calculate. You would burst out laughing if you were present to see how it carries by itself from one column of tens to the next or borrows from them during subtraction.[6]

Kepler must have written back asking for a copy of the machine for himself because, on February 25, 1624, Schickard again wrote to Kepler giving a careful description of the use of the machine together with several drawings showing its construction. He also told Kepler that a second machine, which was being made for his use, had been accidentally destroyed when a fire leveled the house of a workman Schickard had hired to do the final construction.

Their two letters, both of which were found in Kepler's papers, give evidence that Schickard actually constructed such a machine. Unfortunately, the drawings of the machine had been lost and no one had the slightest idea of what the machine looked like or how it performed its arithmetic. Fortunately, some scholars, attempting to put together a complete collection of Kepler's works, were investigating the library of the Pulkovo Observatory near Leningrad. While searching through a copy of Kepler's Rudolphine Tables they found a slip of paper that had seemingly been used as a book mark. It was this slip of paper that contained Schickard's original drawings of the machine. One of these sketches is shown in Figure 1.18. Little detail can be seen, but with the hints given in the letters it became possible to reconstruct the machine.

Figure 1.18. Schickard's drawing of his machine.

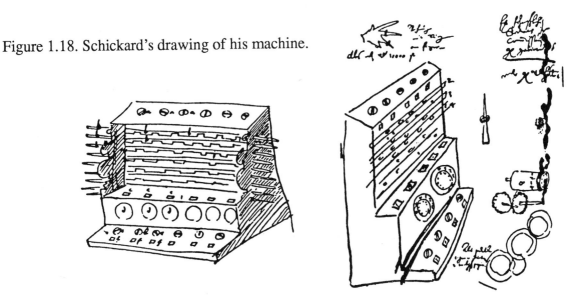

In the stamp illustration, the upper part of the machine is set to show the number 100722 being multiplied by 4. The result of this multiplication is added to the accumulator using the lower portion of the machine. The upper part is simply a set of Napier's bones (multiplication tables) drawn on cylinders in such a way that any particular "bone" may be selected by turning the small dials (marked *a* in Schickard's drawing). Moving the horizontal slides exposes

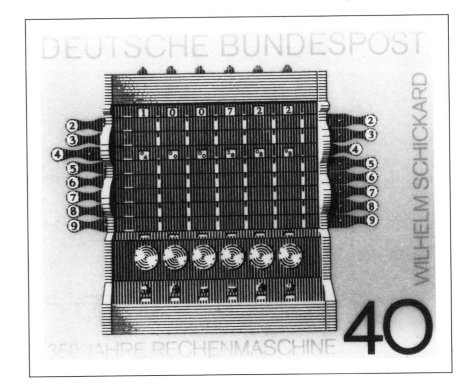

Figure 1.19. A stamp produced to honor the 350th anniversary of the invention of Schickard's machine.

different sections of the "bones" to show any single digit multiple of the selected number, the fourth multiple is shown exposed in Figure 1.19. This result can then be added to the accumulator by turning the large knobs (marked d) and the results appear in the small windows just above (marked c). The very bottom of the machine contains a simple *aide-memoire*. By turning the small knobs (e) it was possible to make any number appear through the little windows (f); this avoided the necessity of having pen, ink, and paper handy to note down any intermediate results for use at some later time in the computation.

The mechanism used to effect a carry from one digit to the next was very simple and reliable in operation. As shown in the drawing (Figure 1.20), every time an accumulator wheel rotated through a complete turn, a single tooth would catch in an intermediate wheel and cause the next highest digit in the accumulator to be increased by one. This simple-looking device presents problems to anyone attempting to construct an adding machine based on this principle. The major problem is created by the fact that the single tooth must enter into the teeth of the intermediate wheel, rotate it 36 degrees

Figure 1.20. The Schickard carry mechanism.

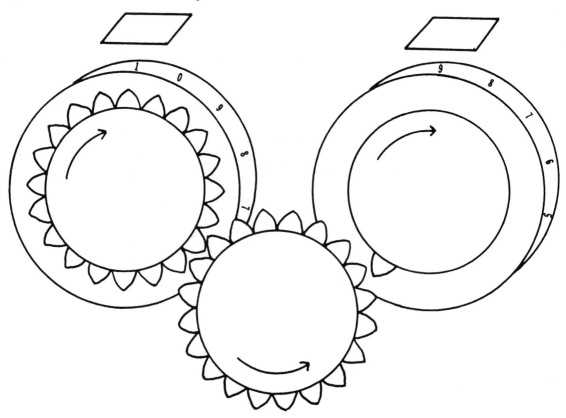

(one-tenth of a revolution), and exit from the teeth, all while only rotating 36 degrees itself. The most elementary solution to this problem consists of the intermediate wheel being, in effect, two different gears, one with long and one with short teeth, together with a spring loaded detente (much like the pointer used on the big wheel of the gambling game generally known as the "crown and anchor"), which would allow the gears to stop only in specific locations. It is not known if Schickard used this exact mechanism, but it certainly works well in the modern reproduction of his machine.

The major drawback of this type of carry mechanism is the fact that the force used to effect the carry must come from the single tooth meshing with the teeth of the intermediate wheel. If the user ever wished to do the addition $999,999 + 1$, it would result in a carry being propagated right through each digit of the accumulator. This would require enough force that it might well do damage to the gears on the units digit. It appears that Schickard was aware of the limitations of the strengths of his materials because he constructed machines with only six digit accumulators even though he knew that Kepler would likely need more figures in his astronomical work. If the numbers became larger than six digits, he provided a set of brass rings that could be slipped over the fingers of the operators hand in order to remember how many times a carry had been propagated off the end of the accumulator. A small bell was rung each time such an "overflow" occurred, just to remind the operator to slip another ring on his finger.

Although we know that the machine being made for Kepler was destroyed in a fire, there is some mystery as to what happened to Schickard's own copy of the device. No trace of it can be found and it is unlikely to ever be found now that complete studies of Schickard's papers and artifacts have been done.

The Machines of Blaise Pascal (1623-1662)

The great French mathematician and philosopher Blaise Pascal made the next major attempt to design and construct a calculating machine. The fact that he was not the first to construct such a device in no way reduces the magnitude of his achievement because his machine was entirely different from Schickard's and it is almost certain that Pascal would not have known of Schickard's machine, much less have seen it in operation.

Figure 1.21. Blaise Pascal (1623 - 1662).

Pascal came from the area of Clermont in southern France west of Lyon. The Pascal family was one of the noble houses of the area. When he was only nineteen years old he managed to design the first of his many calculating machines. He hired a group of local workmen and, showing them his carefully done drawings, asked them if they could make the instrument. What they produced was quite unworkable because they were more used to constructing houses and farm machinery than they were delicate instruments. This led Blaise to train himself as a mechanic, even spending time at a blacksmith shop to learn the basics of constructing metal parts. He experimented with gears made out of ivory, wood, copper, and other materials in an attempt to find something that could stand the strain of being used in a machine of his design.

Although he produced about fifty different machines during his lifetime, they were all based on the idea incorporated in his first machine of 1642. The device was contained in a box that was small enough to fit easily on top of a desk or small table. The upper surface of the box, as can be seen in Figure 1.22, consisted of a number of toothed wheels above, which were a series of small windows to show the results. In order to add a number, say 3, to the result register, it was only necessary to insert a small stylus into the toothed wheel at the position marked *3* and rotate the wheel clockwise until the stylus encountered the fixed stop, much the same way that you would dial a telephone today. The windows through which the results were read actually consisted of two separate sections, with a brass slide to cover the section not in use at the moment. The upper window was used for normal addition and the lower window, which displayed the nines complement (5 is the nines complement of 4 because 9 - 4 = 5) of the number held in the result register, was used for subtraction. This arrangement was necessary in that, due to the internal construction of the machine, it was not possible to turn the dials backwards in order to do a subtraction; instead one added the nines complement of the number one wished to subtract.

Figure 1.22. The top of Pascal's machine.

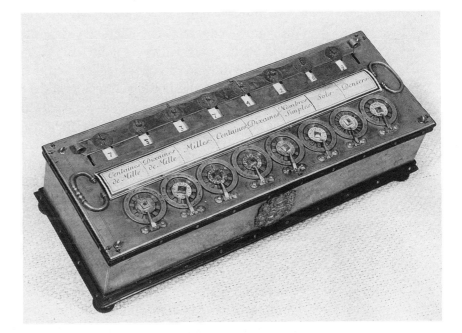

Pascal seems to have realized early on that the single tooth gear, like that used by Schickard, would not do for a general carry mechanism. The single tooth gear works fine if the carry is only going to be propagated a few places but, if the carry has to be propagated several places along the accumulator, the force needed to operate the machine would often be of such a magnitude that it would do damage to the delicate gear works. Pascal managed to devise a completely new mechanism that took its motive force from falling weights rather than from a long chain of gears.

The entire mechanism is quite complex, but the essentials can be seen in Figure 1.23. If the wheel marked *A* was connected to the units digit of the accumulator and the one marked *B* was connected to the tens digit, then any carry would be propagated from one to the other by the device marked *W* between the two shafts. Device *W* is a weight that is lifted up by the two pins attached to the wheel *A* as it rotates. When the wheel rotates from 9 to 0, the pins slip out of the weight allowing it to fall and, in the process, the little spring-loaded foot, shown in black, will kick at the pins sticking out of wheel *B*, driving it around one place. This gravity assisted carry mechanism was placed between each pair of digits in the accumulator and, when a carry was generated through several digits, could be heard to go "clunk," "clunk," "clunk" for each successive carry.

This carry mechanism, which would have been the pride of many mechanical engineers one hundred years after Pascal, eliminated any strain on the gears. However it did have the drawback that the wheels could only turn in the one direction and this meant that it was only possible to add and not to subtract with the machine. As mentioned earlier, the subtraction problem was solved by simply adding the nines complement of the required number, a process that limited the use of the machine to those with a better than average education.

Pascal attempted to put the machine into production for his own profit. This was not a successful venture, but it did result in a large number of units surviving to the present day. They are all slightly different in that they have different numbers of digits in the accumulator or have slight differences in the internal mechanisms. None of the surviving models functions very well, and it is doubtful if they functioned perfectly even in Pascal's day. The mechanism, although ingenious, is rather delicate and prone to giving erroneous results when not treated with the utmost care. Some of them will, for example, generate extra carrys in certain digits of the accumulator when they are bumped or knocked even slightly.

The Machines of Gottfried Wilhelm Leibniz (1646-1716)

Gottfried Wilhelm Leibniz was born in Leipzig on July 1, 1646. His father, a professor of moral philosophy, only lived until Leibniz was six years old, but he and his library were a great influence on the young Leibniz's early education. After he obtained a doctor of laws degree, the University of Altdorf offered him a professorship.

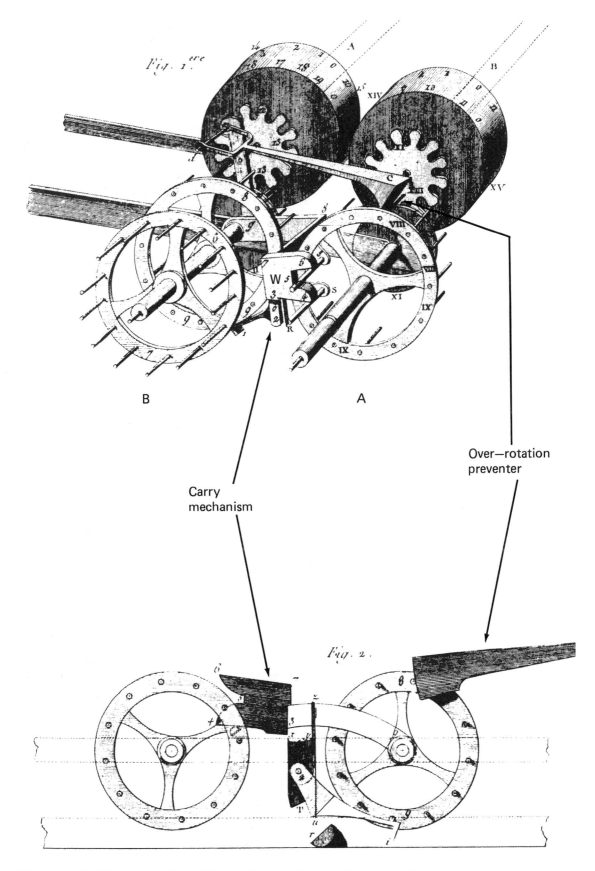

Figure 1.23. The internal workings of Pascal's machine, including the carry mechanism.

Figure 1.24. Gottfried Wilhelm Leibniz (1646-1716).

Wanting a more active job, he refused the offer and accepted a job as an advisor to the Elector of Mainz, one of the most famous statesmen of his day.

While he was in service to the Elector of Mainz he traveled a great deal to other European countries, acting as the elector's personal representative. During these travels he managed to meet most of the famous men of his day. This resulted in his being made a member of the British Royal Society and, later, a member of the French Academy.

Exactly when Leibniz became interested in the problem of mechanical calculation is not certain. It is known that when he heard that Pascal had invented a mechanical adding machine he wrote to a friend in Paris asking for details of its construction. We do not know if Leibniz ever actually saw one of Pascal's machines, but we do know that, at least in his early years, he did not completely understand its workings. In Leibniz's notes is a series of suggestions and drawings for an attachment to be placed on top of Pascal's device in order to enable it to perform multiplication. Although it was an interesting idea, the device could not have worked because no more than one wheel of Pascal's machine could rotate at any given instant. Presumably Leibniz either found this out or the pressure of other work caused him to put the idea aside until it no longer had any relevance, for he never seems to have continued along this line of thought.

The machine for which Leibniz is most famous, his mechanical multiplier, was actually lost to us for about two hundred years. Many records exist to prove that he had actually constructed a machine, but the actual device was not known. It appears that sometime in the late 1670s the machine was given to A. G. Kastner at Göttingen for overhauling and that somehow it was stored in the attic of one of the buildings of Göttingen University, where it remained for the next two hundred years. In 1879 a work crew attempting to repair a leaking roof discovered it lying in a corner. The workings of the machine are based upon one of Leibniz's inventions, the stepped drum, as illustrated in Figure 1.25.

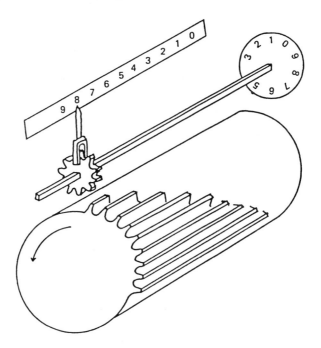

Figure 1.25. The Leibniz stepped drum mechanism.

A result wheel, shown at the end of the square shaft, could be rotated to any of ten different positions to register the digits 0 to 9. In order to add a quantity, say 8, to the result indicated on the wheel, it was only necessary to cause the square shaft to rotate 8 steps. This was done by having the small gear on the shaft mesh with 8 teeth on the large drum below the shaft. The small gear could slide up and down the square shaft so that, depending on its position, it would interact with a different number of teeth on the major drum. Leibniz's machine had eight of these mechanisms so that, when a number was registered on the machine by setting the small pointers (which controlled the position of the gears on the square shafts), a turn of a crank would cause all eight stepped drums to rotate and add the digits to the appropriate counters. To multiply a number by 5, one simply turned the crank five times. The actual machine was constructed in two layers so that, when one needed to multiply a number by 35 the following steps were performed:

1. the number to be multiplied was set up by moving the gears along the square shafts so that the pointers indicated the desired number;

2. the crank was turned five times;

3. the top layer of the machine was shifted one decimal place to the left; and

4. the crank turned another three times.

One of the biggest problems when attempting to design this type of machine is how to deal with the possibility of a "carry" being generated from one digit to the next when the first digit rotates from the 9 position through to the 0 position. Leibniz only partially solved this problem. Although it appears complex, the diagram of the full mechanism is really quite simple when explained. Figure 1.26 shows two digit positions of the machine, the stepped drums being denoted by the digit 6. The gears in front (labeled 1, 2, and 3) are really just part of the drive mechanism and can be ignored. The more complicated mechanics, consisting of the levers, star wheels, cogs, and pentagonal disks (12, 11, 10 and 14) are all part of the carry mechanism.

When a carry was needed, the small lever 7 would interact with the star wheel 8 and partially turn the shaft so that one of the points of the star 11 would assume a horizontal position (compare the two star wheels marked 11 to note the two different positions they could assume). This would put it into a position in which the lever 12 (which turns once for each turn of the addition crank) could give it a little extra push to cause the result wheel to flip over to the next digit (i.e., add the carry to the next digit).

Note that this does not complete all the requirements of the carry

Figure 1.26. The full mechanism of the Leibniz machine.

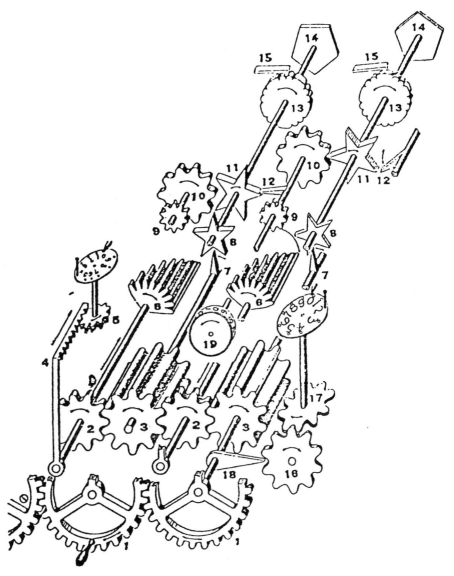

mechanism, for this carry could, in turn, cause another carry in the next higher digit. There is no way that this simple mechanism can be used to ripple a carry across several digits. Note the two different positions of the pentagonal disk *14*: it can have a flat surface uppermost (which would be flush with the top cover of the machine and, thus, not noticeable to the operator) or it could have one of its points projecting above the top surface. This disk is so arranged that whenever a carry is pending, the point is up and when the carry has actually been added into the next digit, the point is down. After turning the crank to add a number into the register, if a ripple carry was generated, one or more of these points would project from the top of the machine, indicating that the need for a carry was detected but that it had not yet been added to the appropriate digit. The operator could reach over and give the pentagonal disk a push to cause the carry to be registered on the next digit and the point to slide back down into the mechanism. If that carry, in turn, caused another carry, further pentagonal disks would push their points through the slots in the top of the machine to warn the operator that he had to give the machine a further assist.

We know that Leibniz started to think about the problems involved in designing such a machine sometime about 1671. In January of 1672 he happened to be in London and was able to demonstrate a wooden model (which did not work properly) to the members of the Royal Society. Leibniz promised to make some technical changes and bring his machine back when it was properly functional. The secretary of the Royal Society did not invite Leibniz to the next meeting but suggested that when a proper working model was available they would like to have it demonstrated. Several letters remain in existence between the secretary and Leibniz concerning the progress of the machine over the next two years.

But Leibniz was plagued by the same types of problems that were faced by Pascal and others—poor workmen and poor materials with which to work. The final machine was only put together because Leibniz had found, during his stay in Paris, a French clockmaker named Olivier, who was both honest and a fine craftsman. No one knows for sure, but it is assumed that Leibniz simply explained the problems to M. Olivier and then let the clockmaker get on with the real construction work. The final version of the machine, which is now housed in the Landesbibliothek in Hannover, was put together in the summer of 1674.

As previously mentioned, the machine consists of two basic sections, the upper one contains the setup mechanism and the result register; the lower part, the basic Leibniz stepped gear mechanism. When the multiplicand digits have been entered into the setup slides, the handle on the front is turned once for every time that the multiplicand should be added to the answer dials. The large dial on the top right of the machine has a pin to set into it at the position

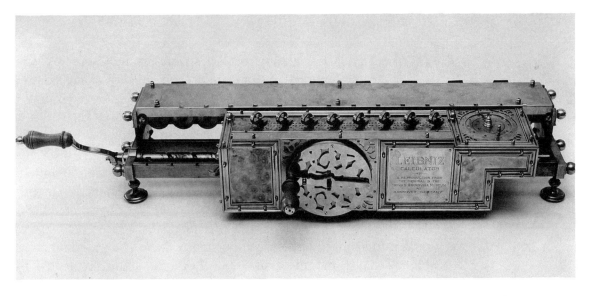

Figure 1.27. The Leibniz calculator.

indicated by the multiplier digit (e.g., 5) and, after five turns of the front handle, it brings this pin up against the stop to be seen at the top of the dial, preventing the operator from adding the multiplicand to the result too many times. After a single digit of the multiplier is processed, the crank at the far left of the machine is turned once to shift the top section of the machine over by one digit place so that the next digit of the multiplier can be considered. Thus, this machine was simply the mechanical version of the common shift-and-add procedure used for multiplication on many digital computers.

Leibniz is more widely known for his work in mathematics and philosophy than for his invention of a calculating machine. It is interesting to note, however, that the principle of the stepped drum gear was the only practical solution to the problems involved in constructing calculating machines until late in the nineteenth century.

Leibniz died on November 14, 1716, enfeebled by disease, harassed by controversy (not the least with Newton over the invention of calculus), and embittered by neglect. Men like him are often very difficult to get along with and there was an almost audible sigh of relief from his contemporaries when he finally died. An eyewitness tells us that

> he was buried more like a robber than what he really was, the ornament of his country.[7]

Nineteenth- and Twentieth-Century Developments

Mechanical calculating machines were essentially useless toys during the first two centuries of their development. The level of technology of the day guaranteed that any attempt to produce a reliable, easy to use instrument was doomed to failure. The real spur to the production of sound machines came with the increase in commercial transactions in the early nineteenth century. It became quite obvious that many hours were being spent in adding up long columns of figures, and many different people attempted to modify the older designs and create new ones in order to bring some relief to the drudgery of the accounting house practices.

The first machine that can be said to have been a commercial success was a modification of the Leibniz calculator created by Charles Xavier Thomas de Colmar, a French insurance executive, in 1820. Although Thomas was not aware of the early work of Leibniz, the internal workings of the machine rely on the same stepped drum principle. Thomas was able to produce an efficient carry mechanism and, in general, the machine was very well-engineered for its day (Figure 1.28). The Thomas firm developed many different models of the basic system and it remained in production until the start of the twentieth century. Although it had been available to the general public

Figure 1.28. An early example of the Thomas de Colmar Arithmometer. Rick Vargas photograph; courtesy Smithsonian Institution.

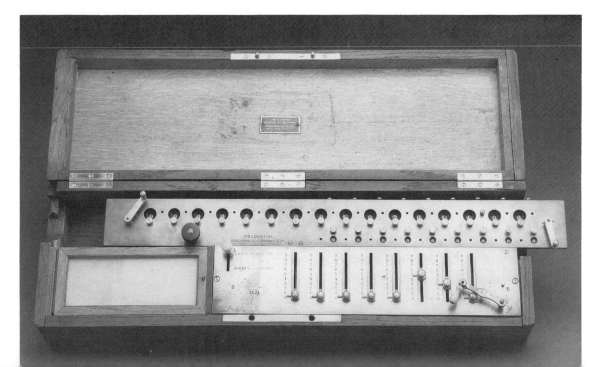

from the early 1820s, the early versions were not all that popular. The expense of the machine, combined with a lack of advertising, resulted in few sales until the machine was exhibited in the Paris Exposition of 1867. It was so far superior to the one other calculator exhibited that it won praise from the judges and finally became quite popular for both business and scientific calculations.

Like any good idea, the Thomas Arithmometer resulted in the production of many rival machines. Several different arrangements of the Leibniz stepped drums were tried, both to avoid simply having a carbon copy of the Arithmometer and in an attempt to reduce the size and weight of the resulting device. One of the most successful of these was the Edmonds Circular Scientific Calculator, which arranged the drums and associated gearing in a circle, the drive mechanism being a crank protruding from the top of the box.

Any real attempt at creating a smaller mechanical calculating machine had to wait until some mechanism was developed that could replace the Leibniz drum with a smaller and lighter device. The purpose of the drum was to provide a mechanism for engaging a gear with a variable number of teeth and, until late in the 1800s, no one had managed to find a workable system to produce gears that could quickly change the number of teeth projecting from their surface.

The true variable-toothed gear appeared in both Europe and America at about the same time. In America Frank S. Baldwin managed in 1873 to construct a model of a calculating machine, based on his invention of a variable-toothed gear. He immediately applied for a patent on the idea that, when granted in 1875, resulted in the device becoming known as "Baldwin's 1875 machine" (Figure 1.29).

Figure 1.29. The Baldwin 1875 machine. Courtesy Smithsonian Institution.

It was only three years later when Willgodt T. Odhner, a Swede working in Russia, produced almost the exact system in Europe. This coincidence resulted in this type of machine being referred to as a Baldwin machine in America and an Odhner machine in Europe. Odhner never claimed to have invented this style of machine and, in his first American patent, he makes it quite clear that he limits his claims to simply making several improvements in the design.

The concept of the variable-toothed gear is quite simple, as can be seen in Figure 1.30. A cam mechanism can be rotated by means of a lever so that as the cam contacts the different spring loaded rods they are forced to protrude from the surface of the disk in which they are mounted. Thus, it is possible to set the lever to the fifth position, resulting in a gear having five teeth. When this gear is rotated, the five teeth cause a result wheel to be turned to indicate that the number 5 has been added to whatever digit had been stored on the wheel.

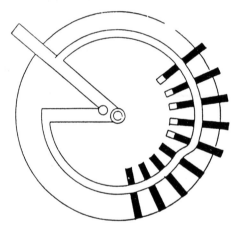

Figure 1.30. The variable-toothed gear mechanism.

The disk form of the variable-toothed gear allows a number of them to be mounted side by side on one axle to provide the arithmetic facilities of a multidigit register in a very compact package. Many different firms immediately started to produce machines based on this design, one of the most famous being the German firm of Brunsviga (Figure 1.31). The popularity of the calculator can be judged from the records of the Brunsviga firm, which indicate that they started production in 1892 and were able to ship their twenty thousandth machine in 1912.

Figure 1.31. A Brunsviga calculating machine (Dupla model). The levers for setting the variable-toothed gears are in the central portion of the device.

All of these machines were better suited to scientific calculations requiring many operations on a few numbers than they were to the problem of adding up long lists of numbers often found in business applications. The labor of setting up a number on the machine, by moving a slide on the Arithmometer type of machine or setting a lever on the Brunsviga type, was slow enough that it made the devices impractical for many commercial firms. Although various models existed that used some form of depressible keys as the input mechanism, these were generally not reliable enough for high-speed operation.

It had long been realized that the action of pushing a key contained enough energy not only to set the number on some form of input device but also to cause the gears to rotate and effect the addition to the result wheels. Unfortunately, no one had been able to invent a mechanism that incorporated both actions in one device. Any of the early attempts usually had the result wheels being turned either too far or not far enough, depending on the force used by the operator in hitting the key. A young American machinist, Dorr E. Felt, found a workable solution in the middle 1880s.

All the early attempts at producing key-driven adding machines relied on the action of depressing a key being communicated to the result wheel by means of a ratchet mechanism that rotated the result wheel by an amount dependent on which key had been pushed. Not only was it found impossible to stop the fast moving result wheel in the proper location but any mechanism designed to carry a digit to the next higher result wheel was always so slow in its action as to limit drastically the speed of operation. A highly trained operator could push keys at a rate that would only allow 1/165 of a second for any carry to be transmitted to the next digit. This meant that any attempt at producing a mechanism based on something as simple as the odometer system found in modern automobiles was doomed to failure.

Dorr E. Felt managed to invent several different mechanical arrangements that he thought might solve most of the problems inherent in a key-driven adding machine. Unable to afford to have his ideas properly constructed from metal, he built his first prototype from rubber bands, meat skewers, staples, bits of wire, and an old macaroni box for the casing (Figure 1.32).

Felt set up a partnership with a man named Robert Tarrant in 1887 and the pair of them started producing commercial quantities of "Comptometers." The success of their key-driven model (Figure 1.33) was so spectacular that no other key-driven adding machine was able to compete with it until after 1912.

One of the next major advances in the production of calculating machines was the incorporation of special devices to automate the operations of multiplication and division. These developments actually took place simultaneously with the Baldwin and Odhner inventions, but they were generally incorporated into machines based on the older Thomas de Colmar design. In all earlier machines it was necessary to perform multiplication by a series of repeated addition operations. This usually required the operator to turn the machine's crank as many times as was represented by the sum of the digits of the multiplier. Single-digit, or even two-digit, multipliers presented little problem when working with the Thomas type of machine, but multipliers of many digits resulted in both the expenditure of considerable physical effort and the passing of long periods of time before the answer could be obtained.

The usual mode of operation in a machine with automatic

Figure 1.32. Felt's macaroni box model.

Figure 1.33. A production model of the comptometer.

multiplication features required that the handle be turned only once for each digit in the multiplier. Typical, and perhaps most popular, of these automatically multiplying machines was the "Millionaire" (Figure 1.34) invented by Otto Steiger of Munich in the early 1890s. Steiger started manufacturing the Millionaire in Zurich and, because of its speed and reliability, it was soon being sold to scientific establishments throughout Europe and America. Its popularity lasted until 1914, when the First World War interrupted the organization of sales and support.

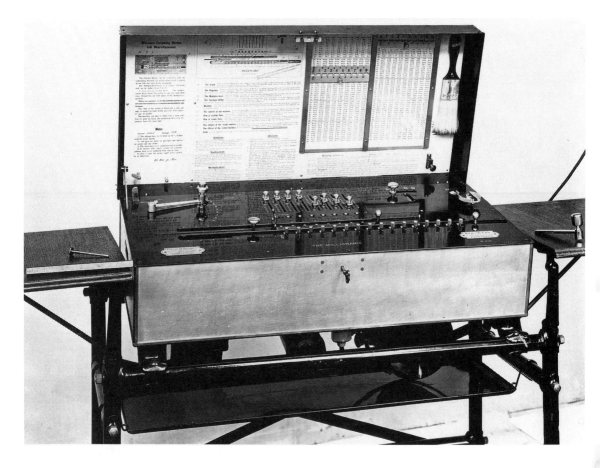

Figure 1.34. A Millionaire. Courtesy Science Museum.

The late nineteenth and early twentieth centuries saw many other firms start to produce calculating machines of different types. By the start of the First World War it was possible to obtain easily machines that incorporated automatic mechanical multiplication devices (much like a mechanical version of Napier's Bones), machines that could print their results on paper or ledger cards, machines that were driven by both electric or spring-driven motors, and even machines having a combination of these features. Several specialty firms even produced machines that consisted of many calculators ganged together in different ways in order to simplify certain special types of calculations. Once the basic technology had been developed, only the limit of human imagination (and the laws of physics) constrained the different forms taken by mechanical calculators. They ranged from desk-sized objects full of features to small examples that were based on Swiss watch technology and capable of being held in one hand yet able to perform all the basic arithmetical functions.

Notes

1. H. Wassen as quoted by James R. Newman, in *The World of Mathematics* (New York: Simon and Schuster, 1956), 463-464.

2. In D. E. Smith, *History of Mathematics, Vol. II* (New York: Dover Publications, 1958), 516.

3. In C. G. Knott, ed., *Napier Tercentenary Memorial Volume* (London: Longmans, Green for the Royal Society of Edinburgh, 1915), 126.

4. Mark Napier, *Memoirs of John Napier* (Edinburgh: William Blackwood, 1834), 410.

5. In R. T. Gunter, *Historic Instruments for the Advancement of Science* (Oxford: Oxford University Press, 1925), 25.

6. As quoted in a lecture at Los Alamos by Dr. Baron von Freytag Loringhoff, 1975.

7. *Encyclopaedia Britannica*, 11th ed., s.v. "Leibniz."

Further Reading

Dantzig, T. *Number, the Language of Science*. New York: Macmillan Co., 1930. Contains a good discussion of the early development of number systems.

Gillings, R. J. *Mathematics in the Time of the Pharaohs*. Cambridge, Mass.: MIT Press, 1972. A fine description of most aspects of Egyptian numbers and mathematical systems.

Heath, T. *A History of Greek Mathematics*. Oxford: Oxford University Press, 1921. The standard reference work on Greek mathematics.

Horsburgh, E. M. *Handbook of the Napier Tercentenary Celebration*. 1914. Reprint. Los Angeles: Tomash Publishers, 1982. This volume contains some fine descriptions of mechanical calculating machines prior to 1914; it also has a substantial description of logarithms and slide rules.

Menninger, K. *Number Words and Number Symbols*. Cambridge, Mass.: MIT Press, 1969. Good descriptions of early numeration systems.

Smith, D. E. *History of Mathematics*. Boston: Ginn and Co., 1926. Reprint. Dover Publications, 1958. This volume contains information on almost every topic in Chapter 1.

Turck, J. A. V. *Origin of Modern Calculating Machines*. Chicago: Western Society of Engineers, 1921. Reprint. Arno Press, 1972. A good description of the development of the Comptometer and related business machines.

Williams, Michael R. *A History of Computing Technology*. Englewood Cliffs, N.J.: Prentice-Hall Inc., 1985. This volume contains further information on many of the topics covered in this section.

Chapter 2

Difference and Analytical Engines

Introduction

The development of a successful computing machine requires the provision of mechanism for at least two basic functions—the storage and arithmetic manipulation of numbers, and some control mechanism whereby a series of arithmetic operations may be combined to produce the result of a desired calculation. The previous chapter described the development of such mechanisms—the commercially successful machines of Thomas de Colmar in the 1820s being the first to combine a practical design with an effective method of manufacture. In these machies the control function was provided by the human operator.

Developments were slow, however, and it was not until the 1880s and 1890s that "scientific" machines (capable of multiplication and division) following the designs of de Colmar or Odhner and "commercial" machines (capable of addition, or addition and subtraction only) by Felt and Tarrant, Burroughs, and others began to appear in quantity. The need for these was spurred by the demands of the larger businesses bred by the Industrial Revolution. In turn the Industrial Revolution made possible the economic mass production of the calculators themselves.

Devices for the automatic control of mechanisms have a much longer history, leading back to the ancient Greek civilizations.

Automatic mechanisms were extensively developed in the great astronomical clocks of the Renaissance and the automata of the eighteenth century. Two devices of particular importance to our story, the pin barrel music box and the punched card Jacquard loom, were well established by the early nineteenth century. Of considerable importance, but in a more abstract intellectual sense, was the development by Stephenson of the ball governor for the steam engine and the idea of feedback that it embodies.

By the early nineteenth century, therefore, the basic mechanisms and ideas existed from which an automatic calculating machine could be developed. This was done by the English mathematician Charles Babbage, who developed, single-handedly, most of the basic ideas inherent in the logical design of modern digital computers—an intellectual tour de force seldom equalled in the history of science and technology. Babbage's ideas were embodied in the design of two calculating machines, the Difference Engine and the Analytical Engine, which form the main topics of this chapter.

Charles Babbage

Charles Babbage was born in south London on December 26, 1791, the son of Benjamin Babbage, a London banker. Charles was a somewhat sickly youth whose education was irregular and mainly conducted at the hands of private tutors. As a youth he was his own instructor in algebra, of which he was passionately fond, and was well-read in the continental mathematics of his day, particularly the calculus of Leibniz.

Upon entering Trinity College, Cambridge, in 1811, Babbage found himself in mathematics far in advance of his tutors who, along with most English mathematicians, were stultified by an overstrict adherence to the unfortunate notations of the calculus of Newton and to geometrical forms of argument in general. As an undergraduate, with John Herschel, Peacock, and others, Babbage founded the Analytical Society for promoting continental mathematics—the "D'ism of Leibniz in opposition to the Dot'age of the University." In time this campaign was successful and played an important role in the revitalization of English mathematics in the mid-nineteenth century.

In his twenties Babbage worked as a mathematician. He was

elected a Fellow of the Royal Society in 1816 and played a prominent part in the formation of the Astronomical Society of London (later the Royal Astronomical Society) in 1820. It was about this time that Babbage first acquired the interest in calculating machinery that became his consuming passion for the remainder of his life. From this time he did no more serious mathematical work.

Throughout his life Babbage worked in many intellectual fields and made contributions that would have assured his fame irrespective of the Difference and Analytical Engines. His interests are well-represented by his published works. He wrote *A Comparative View of the Various Institutions for the Assurance of Lives* (1826) concerning the actuarial principles underlying life insurance. His *Table of Logarithms of the Natural Numbers from 1 to 108,000* (1827) was a paradigm of accuracy and was extensively used into the twentieth century. *Reflections on the Decline of Science in England* (1830) is the best known of Babbage's many polemics against the scientific institutions of his day and fueled much debate at the time and after. Babbage's interest in this area is also seen in his important role in the establishment of the Association for the Advancement of Science (a direct outgrowth of the publication of *Decline of Science*) and the Statistical Society (later the Royal Statistical Society), and in his extensive contacts with continental scientific institutions. *On the Economy of Machinery and Manufactures* (1832), the best known of Babbage's books, is a masterly study of the manufacturing techniques of his day and their economic base. It is seen by some as laying the foundations of the study of operations research. The *Ninth Bridgewater Treatise* (1837) is the most curious of Babbage's works. It was written as Babbage's unsolicited addendum to the *Bridgewater Treatises*, which aimed to prove the existence of God through the richness of natural phenomena. By analogy with his machine, Babbage postulated the existence of a hierarchy of natural laws (an idea that rose to prominence in the twentieth century with the development of relativistic and quantum mechanics) and used this idea to provide a rational explanation of natural miracles. The autobiographical *Passages from the Life of a Philosopher* (1864) is a charming though idiosyncratic view of nineteenth-century life. It contains the most extensive accounts in Babbage's hand of the principles and capabilities of his machines though, unfortunately, written at a very elementary level.

Despite his many achievements, the failure to construct his calculating machines and, in particular, the failure of the government to support his work (as we shall describe later), left Babbage in his declining years a disappointed and embittered man. His bitter, but well-warranted, campaign against street musicians became an easy cliché of the last years of his life and the basis of the "irascible genius" myth that so poorly represents the strengths of his personality and his stupendous achievements. Babbage died at his home on Dorset Street, London, on October 18, 1871.

The Genesis of the Difference Engine

The idea of an automatic calculating machine first came to Babbage about 1820. In one account, written many years later, he describes how he was engaged with his friend, the astronomer John Herschel, in proofreading a set of tables prepared for astronomical calculations. In a moment of exasperation with the errors they found, Babbage remarked, "I wish to God these calculations had been executed by steam." Herschel's reply, "It is quite possible," set Babbage thinking and in a short time, a few days, he had formulated the general idea of the machine that later became known as the Difference Engine.

The idea of the method of differences, which underlies Babbage's first automatic calculating machine, was much in vogue at that time. Consider the formula

$$T = x^2 + x + 41$$

of the variable x. It generates a sequence of values for T—many of which happen to be prime numbers, as seen in the table in Figure 2.1. If we take the differences between successive values of T, the column labeled Δ in the table, these so-called first differences follow quite a simple rule. If we take the differences between the differences, known as the second differences, the result is even more striking—the second difference, Δ^2, is a constant. With this knowledge, the table can be built up in a very simple way, as shown by the box in the table. Take the second difference, 2, and add it to the first difference to form a new first difference

$$4 + 2 = 6.$$

Take this new first difference and add it to the tabular value to form a new tabular value

$$47 + 6 = 53.$$

By simply repeating this process the table of the function T may be extended indefinitely using no other mathematical operation than simple addition (Figure 2.1).

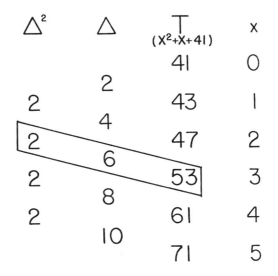

Figure 2.1. Tabulation of a quadratic using the method of differences. The box shows the successive updating of the differences required to form one new tabular value.

The process can be generalized. In our example the second difference is constant because the function T is a quadratic, i.e., a polynomial of degree 2. If the function T were a cubic, such as

$$T = x^3,$$

the second difference would vary, but the third difference, the difference between successive second differences, would be constant. In general a polynomial of degree n will have a constant nth difference and each successive new value of the function can be obtained by n simple additions.

The usefulness of difference techniques is greatly increased by the fact that any section of a well-behaved continuous function can be approximated by a polynomial. The shorter the section and the higher the degree of the polynomial the closer the approximation. So if we wished to tabulate a function, such as a sine or the time of sunset, it is only necessary to divide the function into short enough intervals and find a suitable approximating polynomial for each interval. (Mathematical techniques for doing this were much improved later in the nineteenth century.) The method of differences can then be used to tabulate the function throughout the interval. This process is known as *sub-tabulation*.

Babbage realized that a machine could carry out this sub-tabulation process. First, he needed a mechanism for storing, separately, the numbers corresponding to the values of the tabular value, T, the first difference, Δ, the second difference, Δ^2, etc. and a mechanism to add each difference to the value of the preceding difference. A quadratic, for example, could be tabulated by the machine shown schematically in Figure 2.2.

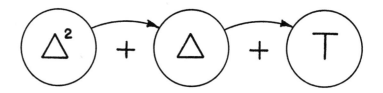

Figure 2.2. Schematic arrangement of the operations required to tabulate a quadratic using the method of differences. The mechanism of Babbage's Difference Engine corresponds exactly to this schematic.

By early 1822 Babbage had constructed just such a machine as this and applied it to the tabulation of

$$T = x^2 + x + 41$$

among other functions—the first thirty values being tabulated in two and a half minutes. Unfortunately, Babbage's first Difference Engine has not survived and his notes and drawings are lost. The only details we have of it are contained in several short letters he wrote in 1822. It was probably similar in general arrangement and design to the later design of 1830. It is important to note that this model was a working machine, though undoubtedly very limited in its numerical capacity. Ideas for a more general range of calculating machines, for extracting roots of equations, multiplying, and computing primes, had occurred to Babbage at this time and had been partially worked out, but no details remain.

A complete Difference Engine requires, in addition to the mechanisms shown in Figure 2.1, a means for controlling the actions of the various parts so that they are performed in the correct sequence. It seems that Babbage's original model acted automatically in this way, but we have no idea of the mechanisms employed.

From the beginning, Babbage was concerned with producing accurate mathematical, astronomical, and other tables. Performing the necessary calculations is only half of the problem. The other half is to transfer the calculated results to the printed page, which, if done manually and with the movable type of the day, is another great source of error. Babbage, therefore, proposed that the Difference Engine should be made to prepare mechanically the type or plates needed for printing. No mechanism for this was included in the first model but Babbage was carrying out independent experiments with such mechanisms at the same time.

The Project to Build the Difference Engine

Babbage recognized his model of 1822 to be just that, a model from which a final production machine could be developed, given the substantial resources in time, effort, and money that would be required. In that the manner of government support for research and development with which we are now familiar did not exist in Babbage's day, he commenced by communicating news of his model and the possibilities it opened to him to the scientific community, most notably in an open letter to Sir Humphrey Davy, president of the Royal Society.

Babbage's achievements brought him immediate acclaim. He was awarded the first Gold Medal of the Astronomical Society of London. Some of this acclaim must have been due to his ingenuity in reducing the mental task not just of arithmetic but of an extended sequence of arithmetic operations to a mechanical mechanism. Mostly, however, it was due to the perceived importance of the Difference Engine in the preparation of mathematical tables.

In the early nineteenth century tables were the only common aid to calculation—the Thomas de Colmar calculating machine was just starting production in 1822, and slide rules, with their limited accuracy, were rarely found outside such specialist applications as the calculation of excise duty on spirits. Any means to economize the production and, especially, ensure the accuracy of tables was of major importance. Nowhere was this so evident as in the preparation of the astronomical tables to aid navigation at sea. These tables had to be recomputed annually, and the consequences of errors in tables, translated into errors in navigation at sea, could be most serious. Therefore, Babbage's project was of major importance to a nation, such as Britain, that relied for much of its wealth on overseas trade.

Babbage's letter to Sir Humphrey Davy, and the evident importance of the Difference Engine as assessed by the scientific men of his day, led to support from the British government towards the development of the Difference Engine for the preparation of practical tables. The grant, initially fifteen hundred pounds but rising eventually to around seventeen thousand pounds, was never clearly formulated to embody the commitments and expectations of either Babbage or the government. It was probably seen by the government as an *ex gratia* grant-in-aid to Babbage, a grant without commitment or expectation, but was certainly seen by Babbage as a commitment to the construction project by the government.

This lack of a formal arrangement led to difficulties; Babbage considered that the government reneged on its agreement. The government gave no further support to the construction after 1833 when Babbage's relationship with the engineer Joseph Clement, who was building the Engine, reached an impasse. It is probably not coincidental that 1832 marked the passage of the Great Reform Bill and the first extension of the voting franchise in Britain. From that time, government patronage, of the sort that had supported Babbage, was no longer politically viable, though it was not until 1842 that the termination of government support was made explicit to Babbage.

Of Babbage's relationship with Clement we have less direct evidence. The construction of the Difference Engine was a very demanding piece of precision engineering for its day, though the existing portions of the calculating mechanism are proof that the necessary precision could be obtained by the development of appropriate and specialized tools and skill in their application. It seems, however, that precision was carried to extremes and applied in areas, such as the decorative finish of support columns, to which it was irrelevant. It seems also that Clement had grasped the potential for profit of an open-ended government job and Babbage felt exploited by this.

Babbage, on the other hand, treated Clement as his servant and seems not to have grasped that in the decade that the Difference Engine was being built it had declined from being the major part of Clement's work to one job among many of a successful engineering workshop. It is not surprising then that Babbage's demands that Clement relocate his workshop to better suit the Difference Engine project were countered by huge financial demands. This impasse stopped construction work on the Difference Engine in March 1833, and it was never resumed.

The demands for precision in the manufacture of the Difference Engine had a major influence in the development of the British machine tool industry. Joseph Whitworth, the leading machine-tool maker in the mid-nineteenth century, had been employed by Clement on the Difference Engine work. Whitworth's developments of standardized screw threads, for example, are traceable to Clement's work in the same direction for the Difference Engine. There seems much truth in the observation that "Babbage made Clement, and Clement made Whitworth." Late in Babbage's life the government received evidence from prominent engineers that the investment in the Difference Engine had been amply repaid by its spin-off into British industry.

It is a great pity that when work on the Difference Engine ceased it was close to completion. Henry Babbage later estimated that only a further five hundred pounds would have sufficed. Babbage could readily have found the funds; however his feelings and attitudes to both the government and Clement could not at the time have countenanced his doing so. Indeed, these feelings did much to form his embittered attitudes as an older man.

Within a year or two, Babbage's mind had moved a long way towards the much more complex and intellectually rewarding Analytical Engine. There was then no way he would have returned to the original Difference Engine design and brought it to completion, even had events made that feasible.

Plan and Side Elevation
of Difference Engine
1830

Figure 2.3. Elevation and plan drawings of Babbage's Difference
   Engine as planned about 1830. The calculating mechanism is on
   the left; the axes of figure wheels for the tabular value (far right)
   and six differences are clearly visible. The printing mechanism is
   on the right, and the moving table carrying the stereotype printing
   plate and the sector carrying the digit-type punches are visible in
   the center of both drawings.

The Design of the Difference Engine

The Difference Engine consisted of two major parts—the
calculating mechanism and the printing and control mechanism.
These are clearly seen in Figure 2.3, which shows the general
arrangement of the Difference Engine as planned about 1830. A
portion of the calculating mechanism was assembled in 1832 to
demonstrate to a committee of the Royal Society that the project was
proceeding satisfactorily. That portion, shown in Figure 2.4, is about
one-third of the height and one-half of the width, or about
one-seventh of the entire calculating mechanism. Almost all of the
parts of the entire calculating mechanism had been made, but not
assembled, when work on the project stopped early in 1833.

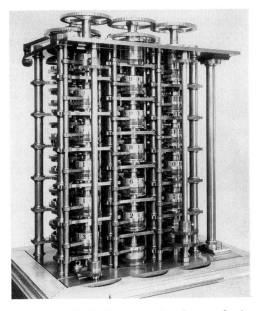

Figure 2.4. The portion of the calculating mechanism of the
   Babbage's Difference Engine assembled in 1832. Records of
   nearly a hundred functions tabulated by Babbage with this
   portion have survived.

Digits are represented in the Difference Engine by the rotational position of horizontal gear wheels. A number is made up of a series of these figure wheels rotating about a common vertical axis. The bottommost wheel represents units, the next tens, the next hundreds, and so on. (A user can imagine a decimal point located between any pair of figure wheels provided this is done consistently throughout the Difference Engine.) Babbage used the term *Axis* to mean a stack of figure wheels that together store a number as a collection of decimal digits. The entire Difference Engine consists of an axis for the tabular value of the function, another axis for the difference, a third axis for the second difference, and so on for as many orders of differences as are desired. These axes stand beside one another, as shown in Figure 2.3, with the axis of the tabular value nearest to the printing mechanism.

The Difference Engine is built on quite a large scale, with figure wheels about 6 inches (15 centimeters) in diameter spaced vertically about 3 inches (7.5 centimeters) apart on the axes. (These wheels are behind the numbered wheels visible in Figure 2.4.) No calculating machine before or since Babbage has used such large components. The large scale in Babbage's designs is possibly traceable to anticipated government expectations based on the proportions common in naval equipment. The large size probably did little to simplify the attainment of the desired accuracy of machined parts while adding considerably to the cost and manufacturing difficulties.

Each axis served not just as a number store but also as an adding mechanism. Addition occurred in two steps that will be explained with reference to adding the first difference to the tabular value.

Inside each first difference figure wheel there is a mechanism that is rotated through just as many steps as the value stored by the figure wheel. If the units figure wheel stands at 3, the mechanism will move through three steps. This motion is conveyed by gearing to the corresponding figure wheel of the tabular value axis. If the latter stood at 5 initially, it will be moved three steps to stand at 8. This process occurs simultaneously in the tens, hundreds, thousands, and other digit positions.

It may happen that addition to a figure wheel will generate a carry that must be propagated or added into the next higher digit position. If the units digit of the tabular value were initially 8 and 3 is added, it will move forward three places and come to stand at 1, but a carry must also be propagated into the tens figure wheel of the tabular value. Carry propagation is complicated by the fact that if the tens figure wheel already stands at 9 it will be moved forward by the carry to stand at 0 and a new carry will be propagated into the hundreds figure wheel. In the Difference Engine these consecutive carries may propagate, as on occasion they must, from the units up through the most significant figure wheel.

Each addition, therefore, consists of two distinct steps—the simultaneous addition of all figures of the first difference to the corresponding figures of the tabular value, and the consecutive propagation of carries from the units up to the most significant digits as required.

Tabulation of a function involves the repetition of this basic addition process for each of the orders of difference involved. As each axis is also an adding mechanism the tabulation of a cubic function from third differences, for example, requires six steps for each tabular value produced:

1. Addition of third difference digits to second difference digits

2. Carry propagation among second difference digits

3. Addition of second difference digits to first difference digits

4. Carry propagation among first difference digits

5. Addition of first difference digits to tabular value digits

6. Carry propagation among tabular value digits.

This process is shown schematically in Figure 2.5. Negative numbers may be handled with no additional mechanism by representing them as their ten's complements.

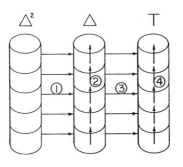

Figure 2.5. Tabulation of a cubic, showing sequential updating of the differences.

This scheme is readily extended to higher order differences. Tabulation from sixth differences, as planned for the Difference Engine, would require twelve steps for each tabular value produced. Babbage found a way to rearrange the calculation so that only four steps were required for each tabular value produced irrespective of the number of differences involved. This is characteristic of the sophisticated logical considerations underlying Babbage's designs.

Babbage observed that when the first difference is added to the tabular value, in steps five and six, both the third difference and second difference axes are idle. He could thus add the third difference to the second difference, steps one and two, at the same time as the first difference is added to the tabular value. Steps one and two overlap steps five and six. Thus only four units of time, for steps three to six, are needed for each tabular value produced. This rearranged manner of doing the calculation is shown in Figure 2.6. In modern terminology we would call the arrangement of hardware to perform a calculation in this way a *pipeline*.

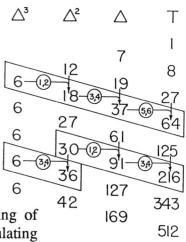

Figure 2.6. Tabulation of a cubic, showing the overlapping of updating used in the Difference Engine so that the calculating time is independent of the number of differences used.

The overlapping idea can be extended to higher differences and a new tabular value can always be produced in four steps. In general, all the even differences are added to the odd differences in two steps and all the odd differences are then added to the even differences (and the first difference is added to the tabular value) in two further steps. Not only does this rearranged form of the calculation save considerable time but it also makes the arrangements for driving the calculating mechanism much simpler.

The calculating mechanism of the Difference Engine is really quite straightforward as demonstrated by the early date at which Babbage produced his first demonstration model. Some complication is added by the (very necessary) apparatus that Babbage added to ensure that the machine would calculate accurately with great reliability. Although Babbage later found much simpler mechanisms for addition and carriage, the calculating part would have been perfectly successful if its construction had been completed as planned. The success of the portion shown in Figure 2.4 proves that.

There are among Babbage's papers a number of tabulations of short sections of the logarithm function with this small portion of the Difference Engine. These show that Babbage understood how to obtain rounded values for printing without any additional calculation.[1] Had the calculating part been completed, Babbage might well have discovered some new tabulation techniques because he always expected that there would be this kind of feedback on analysis once an automatic calculating machine was available. The twentieth century proved him right.

If the calculating mechanism of the Difference Engine is straightforward, the printing and control mechanism is not. Its sophistication and the considerable intellectual effort expended by Babbage on its refinement did much to lay the foundations for the Analytical Engine and make its very rapid development possible. It may also have delayed the completion of the Difference Engine to a fatal extent.

The Difference Engine was intended to print an entire page of tables automatically from the initial setting of the differences. Figure 2.7 shows a sample of seven-figure logarithm tables typical of those the Difference Engine was intended to prepare.

1550

No.	0	1	2	3	4	5	6	7	8	9	Diff.
1550	190 3317	3597	3877	4157	4438	4718	4998	5278	5558	5838	
51	6118	6398	6678	6958	7238	7518	7798	8078	8357	8637	
52	8917	9197	9477	9757	0036	0316	0596	0876	1155	1435	
53	191 1715	1994	2274	2553	2833	3113	3392	3672	3951	4231	279
54	4510	4790	5069	5348	5628	5907	6187	6466	6745	7025	1 28
55	7304	7583	7862	8142	8421	8700	8979	9259	9538	9817	2 56
56	192 0096	0375	0654	0933	1212	1491	1770	2049	2328	2607	3 84 4 112
57	2886	3165	3444	3723	4002	4281	4559	4838	5117	5396	5 140
58	5675	5953	6232	6511	6789	7068	7347	7625	7904	8183	6 167
59	8461	8740	9018	9297	9575	9854	0132	0411	0689	0968	7 195
60	193 1246	1524	1803	2081	2359	2638	2916	3194	3473	3751	8 223 9 251
1561	4029	4307	4585	4864	5142	5420	5698	5976	6254	6532	
62	6810	7088	7366	7644	7922	8200	8478	8756	9034	9312	
63	9590	9868	0145	0423	0701	0979	1257	1534	1812	2090	
64	194 2367	2645	2923	3200	3478	3756	4033	4311	45..		
65	5143	5421	5698	5976	6253	6531	6...				
66		7918	8195	8472	874..						
67	195 0690	096..									
68	..										

Figure 2.7. A sample of seven-figure mathematical tables laid out in a manner possible with the Difference Engine.

The full seven-figure logarithm is printed only for the first entry of the line. Other entries show only the four less significant digits. The three most significant digits are printed only if they changed during the preceding line (hence they appear on line 1553) or in the calculation of the first entry for the present line (line 1556). The columns and rows are not evenly spaced but rather an additional gap is left, after every fifth column and fifth row, to guide the reader's eye. All of these features could be obtained with the Difference Engine.

Each digit was printed by punching a type into a soft metal stereotype printing plate. The particular digits of the tabular function printed, and their number, was determined by selecting and counting wheels in the printing mechanism. Another counting wheel determined the number of table columns and their separations. This was actually a wheel of sixty positions, so that ten columns could be obtained by repeating the control pattern six times. By suitably programming this wheel, six, twelve, or fifteen columns, for example, could be obtained for the printing of trigonometric tables. A similar wheel controlled the spacing of columns, and it was possible to print table entries by columns instead of rows if desired. The printing of the leading three digits was controlled by a trip mechanism activated by the appropriate carry propagation in the tabular value axis.[2]

The printing and control mechanism underwent a major redesign about 1832, so that in the final design it would have been very much longer than shown in Figure 2.3. This redesign marks a major advance in Babbage's understanding of control ideas. In the earlier design the various counting wheels acted directly to carry out their program function themselves. In the later design they always put into gear a connection from the main drive to carry out the function. The control mechanism, therefore, transmits very little power and the weight of the mechanism to be driven does not limit the complexity of the control apparatus. This idea was extended to the control of the calculating mechanism (which was overlapped so far as possible with the printing), resulting in a design very similar to the barrels later employed in the Analytical Engine.

The Origins of the Analytical Engine

Despite the utility of the Difference Engine as a practical aid to table making it is, in the mathematical sense, an extremely limited instrument for it is only directly capable of handling polynomials. The powers of the engine are increased greatly if it is arranged so that the high-order differences can be effected by the tabular function or low-order differences. For example, the sine function satisfies the difference equation

$$\Delta^2 \sin(x) = - k \sin(x).$$

If we could make the second difference relate to the tabular value in this way, the sine function could be tabulated exactly, without the use of polynomial approximations.[3] Alas, the Difference Engine cannot carry out the multiplication required by the above formula.

In late 1822, after the completion of the first model of the Difference Engine, Babbage commenced exploring the sorts of feedback functions that could be calculated by the Difference Engine. These have definitions similar to

$$\Delta^2 u = units\ digit\ of\ u.$$

What motivated Babbage to explore these functions we do not know, but despite their analytic intractability they came to exercise a considerable fascination upon him. Two brief accounts of the functions were published by Babbage in 1822; the Difference Engine included additional transfer gearing to enable it to calculate such functions, and the model assembled in 1832 had additional facilities for this purpose. About fifty of these feedback functions, calculated with the model, are tabulated in Babbage's notebooks, and the concept provided the basis for his arguments about miracles in the *Ninth Bridgewater Treatise*.

When construction of the Difference Engine ceased in 1833, Babbage returned in earnest to feedback functions, such as the sine, which he characterized strikingly as "the Engine eating its own tail." Although Babbage's exact train of thought at this stage is unknown, it seems that he first realized that multiplication could be carried out by repeated addition if the ability to step numbers up or down on the axes (multiply or divide by ten) was provided. Division can be performed as repeated subtraction but it is a "tentative" process, for we need to be able to examine the result of one subtraction, whether positive or negative, before knowing what to do next. Babbage also found a substantially faster method of carry propagation, the Anticipating Carriage, that made carry propagation a parallel rather than a sequential process. The complexity of this new mechanism forced the abandonment of the arrangements of the Difference Engine where each storage axis is also an adder. In the Analytical Engine there is a separate "store" for numbers and a "mill," or arithmetic unit, where calculations are made.

Babbage's ideas developed very quickly, aided by the commanding knowledge of control mechanisms that he had gained from the printing part of the Difference Engine. By late-1834 the basic plans for the Analytical Engine had been formulated. The mill was separate from the store. Multiplication and division were carried out in the mill by combinations of simpler operations under the direction of one or more barrels. The sequence of operations ordered by the barrels included what today we call "loops" and by alternate sequences dependent on arithmetic results that arose during calculations (today known as "branching"). The calculation performed was directed by "super" barrels that initiated transfers of numbers between the store and mill and started the sequences of operations of the subsidiary barrels. The super barrels also included looping and branching capabilities. (In mid-1836 the super barrels were replaced by strings of Jacquard punched cards.) Within about a year of the cessation of construction of the Difference Engine, Babbage had formulated the basic design of a universal calculating machine. Most of the remainder of his life was spent in refining the details of this design.

The Analytical Engine

There was not one design of the Analytical Engine, but many. New insights of both a logical and mechanical nature continually opened up new possibilities to Babbage for his design, which was, therefore, in an almost continual state of flux.

Between 1834 and 1837 Babbage developed in outline form several possible arrangements of the basic storage and calculating units. Some of these were of considerable interest, such as one with two mills that could be used separately and in parallel for calculations on 30-digit numbers or linked together as a single mill for calculations on 60-digit numbers, but none were developed beyond a preliminary stage. However, by working with these early designs, Babbage gained the facility with logical design ideas that he was later to exploit so effectively.

Many-digit numbers are characteristic of Babbage's designs. Their use gives considerable accuracy, and also a large dynamic range for number values. Babbage did not consider the use of a floating point number representation, whose complexity the designers of early electronic digital computers also avoided.

By 1837 Babbage had settled on a straightforward arrangement, with a single mill and store, that is very similar to early electronic digital computers. This arrangement was altered little in the following years, but the design was refined and elaborated to a considerable extent. By 1847, when this design work ended, there was little doubt that an Analytical Engine could have been built had the necessarily considerable resources been available. Here we describe the design as it stood in the middle years between 1838 and 1840. It may be considered representative of Babbage's plans.

Figure 2.8 shows the general arrangement of Babbage's Plan 16, dated August 1840. The figure is actually a plan drawing of how the mechanism would have appeared from above. It also serves very effectively as a logical diagram of the functional parts of the mechanism and their interconnection. This has been emphasized in the figure.

On the right of Figure 2.8 is the store. This consists of figure wheels, similar to those in the Difference Engine, arranged on vertical axes on either side of a set of "racks" or toothed bars. The racks convey numbers between the store axes and the mill on the left of the figure.

Numbers consisted of forty decimal digits. Negative numbers, in a sign-and-magnitude representation, were indicated with a separate sign wheel on each store axis. In a mechanical calculating machine the binary number system has no especial advantage, whereas a decimal notation uses less apparatus and is easier for a human to interpret. Babbage carefully examined number bases between 2 and 100 at various stages in the design. The sign-and-magnitude representation is convenient for multiplication and division operations, but complicates addition and subtraction.

The Analytical Engine uses a much simpler mechanism than the

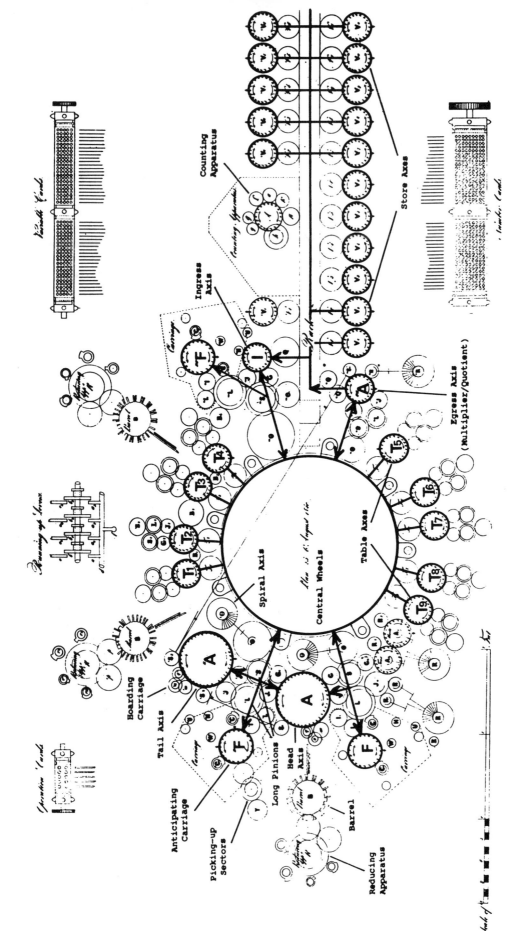

Figure 2.8. Babbage's Plan 16 for the Analytical Engine in August 1840. The original plan drawing of the mechanism has been annotated to show the functional relationships of the principal parts.

Difference Engine to store and read out numbers. To read a number each figure wheel is turned backwards to stand at its 0 position. In the process the wheel will rotate through just as many digit positions as the digit it originally stored, and this motion is conveyed via the racks to the mill. Number readout is therefore destructive, but the number read can be restored to the store axis, if desired, by leaving the store in gear with the racks as they are returned to their starting position at the end of the number transfer. In the mill the destructive readout has more complex effects and most number axes comprise a double set of figure wheels that are used alternately—one set receiving what the other set gives off.

The capacity of the store is unclear from the figure, as the racks may easily be extended further to the right. Babbage spoke at various times of from one hundred to one thousand numbers in the store. Because the Analytical Engine would have been fairly slow, one hundred numbers would probably have sufficed for all practical purposes. In that case the racks would have been about 10 feet (3 meters) long.

Babbage also proposed to have apparatus to read numbers from and punch numbers to Jacquard cards. The requisite apparatus would have communicated with the store racks, but the details are not known. Printing apparatus for making stereotype plates was also intended, but Babbage suggested that this might be a separate machine driven by punched number cards.

Quite long trains of gearing might be involved in the transfer of numbers from one place to another in the Analytical Engine. The necessary looseness and backlash in the gearing, required to ensure easy mechanical action, might have accumulated in these long transfers to such an extent as to make the operation of the machine uncertain. Babbage overcame this difficulty by a series of "lockings"—wedges that come between gear teeth to bring them accurately to their correct position. This is exactly analogous to the provision of amplification in electronic logic gates to ensure that the output voltage levels conform to a standard set of values irrespective of the particular logic circuit involved. Although the lockings added much mechanical complexity to the Analytical Engine, Babbage well understood that they were essential if the machine was to work reliably. This feature is characteristic of the sophistication of Babbage's designs and gives much confidence that the machine, if built, would have worked successfully.

On the left of Figure 2.8 is the mill, or central processing unit.

This consists of a number of axes of figure wheels arranged around a set of "central wheels." The central wheels are used to transfer numbers within the mill and play a role analogous to that of the racks in the store. The mill would have been about 6 feet (2 meters) in diameter and 15 feet (5 meters) high.

The ingress axis, I, and the egress axis, $"A$, are used as buffers for number transfers between the store and the mill. The head and tail axes, A and $'A$, together constitute a double-length (80-digit) accumulator to hold the product in multiplication and the dividend and remainder in division. A is also used as a single-length accumulator in addition and subtraction. The table axes, T_1 to T_9, are used in multiplication and division.

The axes F, $'F$ and $"F$ identify the three Anticipating Carry mechanisms incorporated in the Analytical Engine. As we saw, the Difference Engine used a sequential form of carry propagation. If the hundreds figure wheel, for example, stood at 9 and received a carry from the tens figure wheel, it would move forward one digit position to stand at 0 and propagate a carry to the thousands figure wheel. The thousands will not receive the carry until the hundreds figure wheel has actually moved forward. It is this delay that causes the carry propagation to be sequential and take considerable time.

The Anticipating Carry is so called because it anticipates this sequential action. The thousands may receive a carry for one of two reasons: either the hundreds figure wheel moved past 9 to 0 during the addition step and so generated a carry; or the hundreds figure wheel stands at 9 and so will propagate a carry received, by whatever cause, from the tens figure wheel. The anticipating carry incorporates a mechanism, the "carry chain," that directly implements these two logical alternatives. The anticipating carry mechanism can therefore determine, before any figure wheel is moved, which ones should receive a carry and all of these can be moved forward through one digit position simultaneously. The sequential and anticipating carry mechanisms are contrasted in Figure 2.9.

The anticipating carry was probably the idea of which Babbage was most proud. His autobiography contains a delightful story concerning its invention and describes how his principal draughtsman had thought Babbage had taken leave of his senses for even contemplating its possibility. Perhaps it was the base of the enormous confidence Babbage exhibited in developing the logical design of the Analytical Engine.

The carry chain of the anticipating carry would have demanded

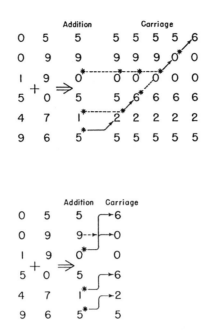

Figure 2.9. Babbage's two methods of carriage propagation in addition. The upper example shows the sequential carry mechanism used in the Difference Engine. Corresponding digits are first added simultaneously (units to units, tens to tens, and so on) and carriages warned, as shown by a star. The carriage propagation then proceeds sequentially from the units digit upward. The lower example shows the anticipating carriage used in the Analytical Engine. The addition process is unchanged, but all of the carriages are propagated simultaneously.

a very high degree of precision in its manufacture. But measurements made of parts built for the Difference Engine show that the requisite degree of accuracy had been obtained on a mass production basis by about 1830. There seems no basis for the common belief that Babbage's machines could not have been made with the technology available in his day, though doubtless it would have been expensive. Rather, it seems that after his bitter experience in attempting to build the Difference Engine, Babbage chose to concentrate on the intellectual issues raised in the design of the Analytical Engine and built only small trial models to verify his designs. Babbage's designs were very thoroughly developed and the mechanical issues carefully considered. They were much more than just pen and paper sketches of an idea.

The Methods Employed for Arithmetic Operations

The methods used for multiplication and division in the Analytical Engine are quite straightforward, although the amount of apparatus required is substantial and there are many technical refinements.

Multiplication commences by taking one of the operands from the store and repeatedly adding it to itself to form the first nine multiples, which are stored on the table axes T_1 to T_9. The multiplier is then taken one digit at a time, commencing with the units, and the corresponding multiple is selected from the table axes and added to the product, which is accumulated on the head and tail axes A and $'A$. The multiples on the table axes are all stepped up one digit position and the process is repeated with the next digit of the multiplier. The various actions are overlapped in such a manner that each whole step requires only a single addition time. The result is a double-length product that is returned to the store.

Division is similar. A table is first made of the nine multiples of the divisor. The two most significant digits of the remainder, on the head and tail axes, are compared simultaneously with the two leading digits of each of the multiples to estimate the next quotient digit. This guess will either be correct or one too large. The selected multiple is subtracted from the remainder and if this becomes negative the divisor is added back to give a new remainder. The new remainder is stepped one place and the process is repeated. In 1840 Babbage found ways of overlapping the actions so that division also took only a single addition (subtraction) time irrespective of whether the quotient digit had been correctly guessed initially.

Addition and subtraction are much more complex processes because of the sign-and-magnitude representation used in the store. In multiplication and division the signs of the operands can be ignored, the operands treated as unsigned, and the correct sign simply inserted into the result. A negative operand, however, turns an addition into a subtraction, and vice versa, and so the function performed in the mill must be changed by the sign.

Multiplication and division are slow, taking one to two minutes and one to four minutes respectively, so the overhead time in fetching operands and storing results is not important (although these are overlapped with other actions as far as possible). In addition and subtraction the fetching and storing, including the conversions from and to the sign-and-magnitude representation, take much longer than the two to three seconds required by the operation itself.

Babbage avoided these difficulties to a large extent by taking as his basic operation the addition or subtraction (in any mixture) of a whole set of operands. Any partial sums could be written to the store as required. In effect, Babbage provided residual storage in the mill (on the head axis A) of the partial sums in a complement number system. This is exactly the same as the practice in electronic digital computers, save that there the residual storage (in registers) is available for other types of operations as well.

Babbage organized addition and subtraction so that operands could be in different stages of processing simultaneously. This is shown in Figure 2.10. Each operand is first fetched from the store to the ingress axis. The value is then added or subtracted, as required, from the total on the head axis, A. This total is in a ten's complement representation. If the partial sum is to be written to the store, it is transferred to the egress axis and converted, in the process, to a sign-and-magnitude representation. Finally, the result is written to the store. The control is very ingeniously arranged so that the maximum possible throughput is achieved—the limitation being access to the store via the racks to fetch operands or store results. This was a stupendous achievement in logical design.

The Analytical Engine provided other arithmetic operations, but the complete set is not clear because Babbage did not list what we would now call the user instruction set. There were variants of multiplication and division for use when only a limited number of digits of the result were required. These were used, for example, in the early steps of finding a square root by iterative formulas. In earlier designs the square root operation had been implemented as an elementary operation. During the slow multiplication and division operations the ingress axis, I, and the anticipating carry, $"F$, could be used directly with the store as a difference engine. Possibly this was intended for calculating simple polynomial functions required by the main calculation, or sub-tabulation of functions between pivotal values calculated in the mill. It is a nice example of the use of functional parallelism.

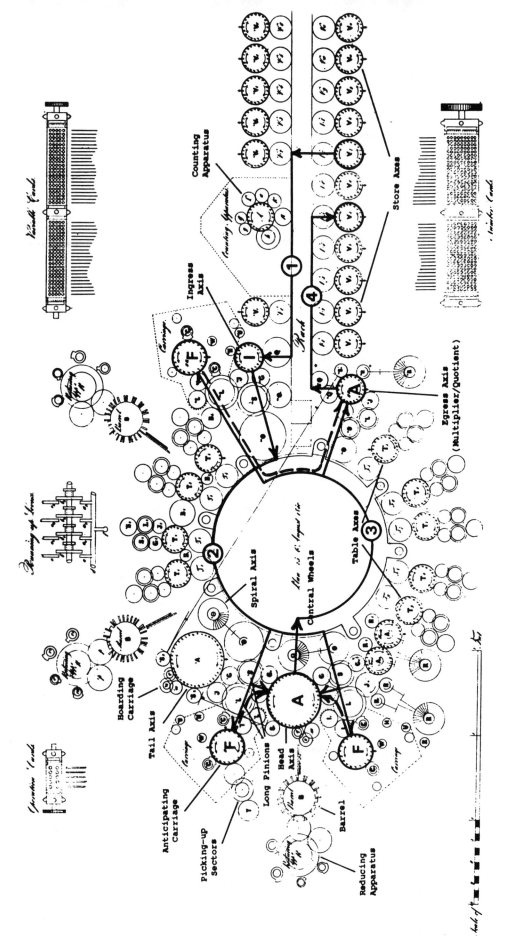

Figure 2.10. The arrangement of addition in the Analytical Engine. The four steps, which may be overlapped with one another for different operands, are described in the text.

The Control Mechanism

The algorithms used in the Analytical Engine, while simple enough in outline, are complex when examined in detail—for there are a large number of hardware components that must work together. Babbage achieved control of this machinery with a hierarchical system of mechanisms.

At the lowest level the control is exercised by "barrels" (Figure 2.11) similar to those employed in music boxes, barrel organs, and many automata familiar in Babbage's day. Studs may be screwed to the surface of the barrel in any desired pattern. When the barrel advances, by moving its axis sideways, one vertical row of studs acts by pressing against control levers in a pattern determined by the arrangement of the studs. The levers in turn engage and disengage the transmission of power from the main drive shaft to the various mechanisms of the Analytical Engine. One "vertical," or line of studs, determines the actions during one adding cycle. In practice, a barrel had from 50 to 100 verticals, each with as many as 200 studs.

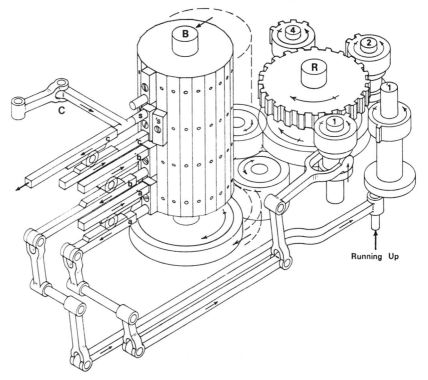

Figure 2.11. A barrel mechanism used in the Analytical Engine. The barrel may determine the sequencing between its own verticals by both the unconditional and conditional mechanisms shown here.

Some of the levers selected by the barrel control its rotation from one vertical to another. Some of these act unconditionally. Others establish a path by which a conditional event in the Analytical Engine, such as a carry propagation from the most significant digit position of a number (a running up), can move the barrel to another vertical. Thus, each vertical can determine which vertical will succeed it and which conditional events are to effect the choice. Interestingly, Babbage's arrangements provide only for what today we call "relative addressing"—i.e., a vertical can specify how far to go to the next vertical that is to act but cannot specify its absolute location. Babbage had no concept equivalent to the modern idea of the address of a word. A vertical may specify a return to a previous vertical and in this manner what we now call "loops" are provided.

Babbage's use of barrels was much more elaborate than this. There were, in general, several barrels—Figure 2.8 shows three but some designs had as many as seven. If these all turn together, the effect is nothing more than dividing up an inconveniently large barrel into a group of smaller ones. But in the case of addition and subtraction the barrels controlling the registers I, A, and $"A$ and associated mechanisms acted independently of one another, responding in part to local conditional events, yet cooperating together to implement the string of addition and subtraction operations. The whole arrangement is enormously sophisticated yet finely judged to best exploit the capabilities of the calculating mechanisms.

The barrels specify in detail how multiplication, division, addition, subtraction, and other arithmetic operations, are to be carried out. The user of the Analytical Engine would regard these arithmetic operations as basic and specify a calculation in terms of them as elementary functions. We have, therefore, a hierarchical arrangement of the control.

For the higher level of control, Babbage, in 1836, adopted the punched cards developed by Jacquard for pattern-weaving looms and used extensively since 1810 (Figure 2.12). A card is pressed against the ends of control levers so that the pattern of holes in the card determines which levers act. The action is entirely analogous to the studs comprising a vertical on a barrel. The Jacquard cards are strung together by narrow ribbons so that they comprise, in essence, a paper tape. It is possible, by mechanisms similar to those used to rotate the barrels, to move forward or backwards through a string of the Jacquard cards. In effect the string of Jacquard cards is equivalent to

Figure 2.12. A Jacquard pattern-weaving loom controlled by punched cards. Babbage adopted and generalized this mechanism for the user-level specification of calculations for the Analytical Engine. Courtesy Science Museum, London.

a barrel with an indefinitely large number of verticals. The adoption of the cards represents less a conceptual breakthrough than a pragmatic improvement on the earlier use of a super barrel to specify the steps of a calculation. Babbage made little of this development and its importance has been considerably over-romanticized by the analogy with modern uses of punched cards.

Programming the Analytical Engine

Although Babbage's mechanical technology is vastly different from modern electronics, it is relatively easy to find analogies that make his organization of the calculating units and storage and their control by the barrels and Jacquard cards familiar to modern computer users. It is only when we come to examine the facilities available for programming the Analytical Engine that Babbage's designs begin to look strange to modern eyes.

Two strings of Jacquard cards were needed to specify a

calculation to be performed by the Analytical Engine. One string, the "operation cards," specified the arithmetic operations to be performed. The second string, the "variable cards," specified the axes in the store that contained the operands and were to receive the results. These two strings cannot be regarded as separate parts of a single instruction, as are the operation and operand fields of an instruction in an electronic digital computer, because the operation and variable cards were intended to move and loop independently of one another under the direction of separate control mechanisms.

Babbage seems to have been led to separate the operation and variable cards on largely philosophical grounds stemming from his belief in the need to distinguish symbols for operation from those for quantity in mathematical notations. These views were probably reinforced when he considered the cards necessary for calculations such as the solution of simultaneous equations. There the pattern of operations required for carrying out row reductions is very simple and a straightforward loop of operation cards is readily found. No such simple loop structure exists for the variable cards, which can only specify single axes in the store. The loop structures that we now recognize concern rows of the matrix of coefficients of the equations and similar concepts related to the structuring of the data. As Babbage did not have the concept of a variable address in the store, neither was the Analytical Engine able to calculate the location of an operand in the store; there was no way in which the user programs could exploit this higher level structure in the data.

In reality, we know little of Babbage's programming ideas. There is nothing in the surviving papers in which this aspect of the machine is thoroughly discussed, e.g., nothing corresponding to a specification of a user instruction set. This is the more remarkable for it is the only aspect of the design that is discussed at length in a contemporary paper. In 1840, Babbage visited Turin in Italy and gave a series of seminars on the Analytical Engine. An account of these, by Menabrea, was translated into English by Ada Lovelace, who appended extensive notes prepared under Babbage's close guidance. These deal with the familiar modern ideas of flow of control in programs, particularly the formulation of simple loops and nested loops controlled by counters. However, the paper and notes carefully and deliberately skirt around any discussion of details of the means by which these are to be implemented.

Ada Lovelace has sometimes been acclaimed as the "world's first programmer" on the strength of her authorship of the notes to the Menabrea paper. This romantically appealing image is without foundation. All but one of the programs cited in her notes had been prepared by Babbage from three to seven years earlier. The exception was prepared by Babbage for her, although she did detect a "bug" in it. Not only is there no evidence that Ada Lovelace ever prepared a program for the Analytical Engine but her correspondence with Babbage shows that she did not have the knowledge to do so. Babbage seems to have deliberately employed independent persons to convey knowledge of the Analytical Engine to the wider public in exactly the same manner as, a decade earlier, he had used the well-known popularizer of science Dionysius Lardner to convey into print a detailed account of the purpose of the Difference Engine.

The conclusion seems inescapable that Babbage did not have a firm command of the issues raised by the user-level programming of the Analytical Engine. It would be quite wrong to infer that Babbage did not understand programming per se. The microprogramming of the barrels for multiplication and division show command of the basic branching and looping ideas and his skills in the microprogramming of addition and subtraction show complete virtuosity. It was from this base that Babbage explored the ideas of user-level programming. The issues of data structuring simply did not arise at the microprogramming level. There is some evidence to suggest that Babbage's ideas were moving in the directions now familiar in connection with the control mechanisms for loop counting in user-level programs. Had an Analytical Engine ever been brought to working order, there can be no doubt that Babbage's programming ideas would have been developed greatly.

Babbage realized that the Analytical Engine was a universal calculating machine in the sense that, given sufficient time, it could carry out any possible arithmetic calculation. The argument, clearly presented in simple terms in his autobiography, is based on three observations. First, arithmetic operations on numbers of more than forty digits can always be carried through by breaking them into 40-digit segments, so the limited number of digits on any store axis is no fundamental limit. Second, calculations can be specified by strings of operation and variable cards of unlimited extent, so there is no limitation to the size or complexity of programs. Third, numbers from the store can be punched onto number cards and later read back, and this provides a backing store of unlimited extent to overcome the limited number of axes in the store. This sophisticated argument has a very twentieth-century flavor. Babbage was not aware that there might be uncomputable numbers, a concept that derives from the brilliant work of Alan Turing in the 1930s.

Babbage's Later Calculating Engines

Work on the design of the Analytical Engine ended in 1847. At that time Babbage turned to the design of a Difference Engine No. 2, exploiting the improved and simplified arithmetic mechanisms developed for the Analytical Engine. The logical design was the same as for the earlier Difference Engine, but he employed simpler mechanisms for storing and adding numbers and carry propagation. The printing mechanism was simplified so that a whole number was impressed on a printing plate as a single action rather than in a digit-by-digit manner. A conventional print copy, using inked rollers, was made simultaneously. The control was arranged by a single barrel in a very straightforward manner. The design and a complete set of drawings was prepared by mid-1848. These Babbage offered to the British government, apparently to satisfy a commitment he felt existed in consequence of the failure of the project to build the first Difference Engine. The government showed no interest in the new design.

Babbage appears to have done no more work on calculating engines until the Scheutz Difference Engine (described in the next section) was brought to London in 1855. To the surprise of some, Babbage became an active and vigorous promoter of the Scheutzes and their machine.

Inspired, perhaps, by the Scheutzes' success, Babbage returned to design work on the Analytical Engine in about 1856 or 1857, when he was 65 years old. In this new phase of work Babbage was actively interested in building an Analytical Engine with his own resources. The logical design was somewhat simplified but, most importantly, far simpler and cheaper methods were proposed to implement the basic mechanisms. Babbage first experimented with sheet metal stamping and pressing for making gear wheels and similar parts. Later, he adopted pressure die casting for making parts—a newly invented technique that did not see extensive commercial use until the end of the nineteenth century. Babbage built many experimental models of mechanisms using these new techniques, and, at the time of his death in 1871, a model of a simple mill and printing mechanism was near completion. (Figure 2.13)

This last work of Babbage is poorly understood because of the disorganized and chaotic nature of the materials that remain. The impression is unavoidable that in this later work Babbage had lost the fine touch of genius exhibited in his earlier work, although his various

Figure 2.13. A model of the mill of the Analytical Engine that was under construction at the time of Babbage's death. The horizontal racks communicate numbers between the two number axes in the center and to the printing mechanism at the right. An anticipating carriage mechanism is located between the number axes. The calculating mechanism employs pressure die-cast metal components. Courtesy Science Museum, London.

experimental models still show much evidence of an ingenious and enquiring mind. In fairness, we must note that most of this later work was carried on when Babbage was between seventy and eighty years old.

Babbage's calculating machines and related materials were inherited by his youngest son, Major-General Henry P. Babbage, who had shown a strong interest in his father's work. Henry Babbage decided not to continue with the design of an Analytic Engine but instead to develop a manually operated machine for addition, subtraction, multiplication, and division (a four-function calculator), incorporating the mechanisms planned for the mill of the Analytical

Engine. Although eventually completed, when Henry was himself an old man, this machine appears never to have worked reliably. In any case, by the start of the twentieth century it had been rendered archaic by other developments of mechanical calculating machines, so that now it stands only as a scientific curio.

The Scheutz Difference Engine

The first successful automatic calculating machine was developed in Sweden in the 1840s by Georg Scheutz and his son Edvard. Their machine was a Difference Engine based directly on Babbage's design, which they learned about when George Scheutz translated Lardner's article into Swedish. In that Lardner's article contains only the most general descriptions of the mechanism of the Difference Engine (without drawings of the mechanisms) it is a small surprise that the Scheutz machine (Figure 2.14) looks very different from Babbage's (Figure 2.4).

Figure 2.14. The copy of the Scheutz Difference Engine built for the General Register Office, London. The pillar at the right moves across the front of the figure wheels to effect the carriage propagation. The printing mechanism is behind the calculating wheels at the left. Courtesy Science Museum, London.

In the Scheutz Difference Engine the figure wheels, as in Babbage's design, are horizontal wheels rotating about a vertical axis. However, the figure wheels for the tabular value are arranged in a row on a horizontal shelf, while the first- and higher-order differences are arranged on successive shelves below. There are five shelves, allowing up to fourth-order differences, and fifteen digits in all numbers. A sequential carry propagation is provided by "pillars" that travel the length of the mechanism in front of and behind the calculating wheels. As in Babbage's machine, the odd differences are updated simultaneously, then the even differences (and the tabular value) are updated together.

The printing mechanism punches stereotype plates, all digits of a number being impressed simultaneously after the manner of Babbage's later designs. The Scheutz Difference Engine prepares only a single column of tabular values. The page layout is made up manually from these strips. There is no attempt at an automatic mechanism for this purpose.

Construction of the Scheutz Difference Engine was completed in October 1853 with some assistance from the Swedish government. It was later taken to London where it, and Georg and Edvard Scheutz, were championed by Babbage. The machine was exhibited in the Paris Exhibition of 1855, awarded a gold medal, and widely acclaimed. The original machine was sold to the Dudley Observatory in Albany, New York, in 1856 to be used in preparing astronomical tables. A copy of the machine was made by Bryan Donkin & Co. for the General Register Office in England about 1858.

Three sets of tables were published that had been calculated, at least in part, by the Scheutz Difference Engine. A set of *Specimen Tables*, including a table of five-figure logarithms of the integers from 1 to 1000, was prepared on the original machine in 1856. That same year, a set of *Mountain Barometer Tables*, for assessing heights on mountains or depths in mines from simultaneous observations of barometric pressure and temperature, were prepared by the English copy of the Scheutz Difference Engine. The major production was the preparation of the *English Life Tables*, published in 1864, at the General Register Office.

Neither model of the Scheutz Difference Engine was found to be very satisfactory and the use of both was quickly abandoned. A number of factors contributed to this failure. The calculations were slow, largely because of the awkward carry propagation mechanism used. The machine depended on friction alone to keep the figure wheels in their correct position when a number was stored—there were no spring detents or other mechanisms equivalent to Babbage's lockings to retain the figure wheels in place. Without such provision it seems the figure wheels easily became displaced from their correct position and the calculation spoiled. Although this could be detected by examining the last value printed it was no doubt a source of considerable annoyance. The printing mechanism seems also to have been unreliable and errors of that sort would have been difficult to detect. In general, both machines were found to be delicate instruments that required considerable skill to manipulate and hence were ill-suited to routine use.

Later Difference and Analytical Engines

That the Scheutz Difference Engine possessed faults is scarcely surprising in view of its being the first completed machine of its type. It is regrettable that more experience had not been gained with the original machine before the English copy was made, when the opportunity might have been taken to eliminate the difficulties. Production of a reliable difference engine required the investment of new, inventive effort to build on the Babbage and Scheutz achievements. However, there were only two more developments in that direction in the nineteenth century.

In Sweden, Martin Wiberg had built a difference engine by 1860 and used it to prepare a set of interest tables for publication. The Wiberg Difference Engine was both smaller and simpler than the Scheutz, though it possessed the same arithmetic capability. The machine appears to have worked reliably and was used in the preparation of logarithmic and trigonometric tables that appeared in 1875.

In America, George Grant developed a small model of a difference engine in 1871 and exhibited a complete machine in 1876. But this machine soon faded into obscurity and appears not to have been put to any practical use.

In the twentieth century the use of difference engines in table making again received some prominence. In this case, however, the construction of special purpose machines was not attempted but ways were found to adapt the general purpose calculating machines then on the market to this special purpose. The best known work is that of

L. J. Comrie at the British Nautical Almanac Office in the 1920s and 1930s, using multiple register accounting machines manufactured by Burroughs and National Cash Register.

If little effort was made to develop difference engines, it is scarcely surprising that nothing substantial followed in the tradition of Babbage's Analytical Engine.

In Ireland an analytical engine was designed by Percy Ludgate about 1905. Initially this work was independent of Babbage's but later Ludgate came to know and be influenced by Babbage's ideas. The design, which was purely mechanical, contains some striking features. The mechanisms in which numbers were stored were physically transported from the memory when the number was read. A pseudologarithmic representation of digits was used to simplify both multiplication and division operations. A most interesting feature was the abandonment of Babbage's separate operation and variable cards and the adoption of control by a paper tape in which each instruction comprised an operation code and four address fields. Very little information on Ludgate's design has survived, and there is no evidence that he ever attempted to construct the machine.

Very interesting designs of analytical engines were made in Spain in the 1910s and 1920s by Leonardo Torres y Quevedo. Torres was a well-known engineer who vigorously exploited the new electromagnetic technologies in the development of control mechanisms. He is particularly well-known for two fully automatic chess playing automata for the ending of king and rook against a king. In 1920 Torres constructed an electromagnetic calculating machine that was driven by operands typed on a typewriter and delivered its results using the same device. Torres's ideas for an analytical engine were sufficiently well developed that there is no doubt that a successful machine could have been built in the 1920s had the need for such a machine been pressing.

The Importance of Babbage's Calculating Engines

In the designs of the Difference Engine and the Analytical Engine Babbage made the first major intellectual contributions towards the development of automatic digital computing machines although his ideas were not realized until over a century later. Two major questions remain about Babbage's work. Why were his machines not successfully constructed? And what influence did his ideas have on the subsequent development of automatic computers?

The present evidence suggests, quite strongly, that both the Difference Engine and the Analytical Engine could have been built successfully with the mechanical technology at Babbage's disposal. The calculating part of the Difference Engine came close to completion and the portion in the Science Museum, London, works superbly. The failure of that project seems traceable in part to Babbage's relationship with the British government over the funding of the project but especially to Babbage's relationship with the engineer Clement. The large physical scale of the machine and, particularly, the very high degree of precision attained in the manufacture of its parts and the concomitant expense seem to have been the root causes of the failure to bring it to completion.

The Difference Engine has a direct line of descendants through the Scheutz to the Wiberg and Grant difference engines. That these were not extensively used or developed, despite the apparent complete success of the Wiberg machine, indicates that the entire idea was not well judged. The sub-tabulation task, though laborious, was not the dominant mathematical task in the preparation of tables nor, with adequate organization and management, was it of overwhelming practical importance. Babbage's argument for the accuracy in typesetting made possible by machines (later strongly held by Howard Aiken) was not widely accepted, and Babbage's own logarithm tables are proof of the accuracy that could be obtained by manual techniques. When machine sub-tabulation was adopted by Comrie, it was in the context of a large-scale mechanization of table making in which the balance of effort in the whole project was not much changed.

Although the Analytical Engine could have been built, Babbage chose, for most of his life, not to attempt to do so. This is a natural response to his experiences with the Difference Engine and the enormous intellectual appeal of the questions raised by the Analytical Engine. Of great regret is the fact that Babbage never published a detailed account of any of his many ideas and mechanisms. The Menabrea-Lovelace paper deliberately concentrates on the mathematical principles embodied in the machine and completely avoids describing their mechanization.

Without a detailed description of the Analytical Engine its influence on later developments was quite limited. Certainly the idea of an automatic calculating machine was well-known in English and, to a lesser extent, American scientific circles and closely associated with Babbage's name. But only the most limited technical guidance was provided for later designers, who in effect worked independently of Babbage. The fruits of Babbage's considerable genius were therefore effectively wasted as far as practical influence is concerned. Only in the tapes of the Turing machine, and the idea of mechanization of computation used there, is there any strong echo of Babbage's ideas. Turing's place in the English intellectual tradition makes such a line of influence plausible if unproven.

In the practical field of making automatic calculating machinery it is even possible that Babbage's influence was counterproductive. What point was there in attempting to make an automatic machine when a man of Babbage's acknowledged genius had failed? Indeed, it is difficult to understand why machines were not built using electromagnetic technology early in the twentieth century. Torres's designs showed that it was certainly feasible to do so by 1914, and Stibitz's designs could have been implemented decades before they were.

Notes

1. The trick is to add 5 to the initial value of the tabular function in the most significant digit position beyond those to be printed (i.e., 1/2 in the least significant digit) and thereafter to simply truncate all values to be printed.

2. The difference table shown at the right of Figure 7 was not produced by the Difference Engine, and the row and column headings would have required further runs through the machine to insert them.

3. The use of feedback here is very similar to that employed in differential analyzers and analog computers (Chapter 5). What Babbage proposed is effectively a form of digital differential analyzer.

Further Reading

Babbage, H. P. *Babbage's Calculating Engines*. Los Angeles and Cambridge, Mass.: Tomash Publishers and MIT Press, 1982. The best edition of the contemporary writings of Babbage and others concerning his machines, collected and published by his son after Babbage's death.

Bromley, A. G. "Charles Babbage's Analytical Engine, 1838." *Annals of the History of Computing* 4(July 1982):196-217.

———· "The Evolution of Babbage's Calculating Engines." *Annals of the History of Computing* 9(1987):113-136. These two works by Bromley describe the design of the Analytical Engine in more detail.

Hyman, A. *Charles Babbage: Pioneer of the Computer*. Oxford: Oxford University Press, 1982. Babbage has become, in the last two decades, something of a cult figure and has generated considerable literature, much of it unreliable and unsubstantiated by careful examination of the primary sources. So far, the only trustworthy biography of Babbage is that of Hyman.

Lindgren, M. *Glory and Failure*. Vol. 9, Linkoping Studies in Arts and Science. Linkoping University Press, 1987. Reprinted by MIT Press, 1989.

Merzbach, U. C. *Georg Scheutz and the First Printing Calculator*. Washington, D.C.: Smithsonian Institution Press, 1977. The Scheutz Difference Engine and its successors are described in the Lindgren and Merzbach publications.

Randell, B. *The Origins of Digital Computers*. 3d ed. New York: Springer-Verlag, 1982. This reprint of selected papers discusses the machines of Ludgate and Torres, as well as of Babbage.

Stein, D. *Ada: A Life and a Legacy*. Cambridge, Mass.: MIT Press, 1985. This work assesses the role of Ada Lovelace.

Chapter 3

Logic Machines

Introduction

The popular conception of the computer is one of a giant calculator, a machine that can carry out millions of arithmetic operations at lightning-fast speeds. But if this were all that computers are, they would be unable to do most of the tasks they are commonly assigned. They could not sort or organize data, as they do each time we do word processing or use a database; they could not even carry out complex computations, because these involve making nonarithmetic decisions, e.g., deciding when to stop one arithmetic process and begin another. Computers are powerful because they are able to carry out long and complex sequences of logical as well as arithmetical operations and modify these sequences according to information presented to them, without any direct human intervention. Without the ability to make logical decisions, computers would have nothing more than an uncontrolled, raw arithmetic power, which would make them only slightly more useful than simple adding machines.

The computer was not the first calculating technology able to make logical decisions. Many punched-card systems, relay calculators, and electronic calculators of the 1930s and early 1940s (all of which are described in later chapters) had rudimentary logical capabilities. But there is an even earlier stream of development,

The author greatly appreciates the suggestions of Michael S. Mahoney and Linda M. Strauss in the preparation of this essay.

beginning around 1800, having as its central purpose the construction of machines capable of making logical decisions. This chapter traces the history of these machines built to solve problems of Aristotelian and symbolic logic, and shows how their development fits into a much older tradition of automata–devices and machines built to mimic mental and physical aspects of human behavior. This chapter also traces the growing understanding prior to the Second World War of the relationship between logic and the theory of computing, which is the foundation for computer science today.

The Automata Tradition

The automata tradition extends back into antiquity. In the Hellenistic period complex mechanisms were constructed to give the appearance of human animation. For example, around 200 B.C., Heron of Alexandria constructed a theater in which the god Dionysius would emerge and spray wine from his staff while the Bacchants danced in his honor. These Hellenistic mechanisms were powered in many different ways: by falling water, sand, or mustard seeds; heat; atmospheric pressure; and in one case by a primitive steam engine. The great civic clocks constructed in major European cities, beginning in the thirteenth century, also are part of this tradition. Human and other figures ornamenting the clocks became animated at the tolling of certain hours. For example, from the clock at Strasbourg the three Magi emerged and a cock crowed each day at dawn. Over time, in the late Middle Ages and the Renaissance, these clockwork automata became more elaborate and were built separately from the civic clocks.

Following the rediscovery and translation of Heron's writings, the great formal gardens of sixteenth- and seventeenth-century Europe were adorned with hydraulic automata. Elaborate nymphs, shepherds, and musicians were empowered by falling water. In eighteenth- and nineteenth-century France, miniaturized automata powered by spring mechanisms were produced in quantity and sold to the upper classes. Some of these works involved great craftsmanship: a girl able to sign her name, a flying bird with three hundred moving parts in its wing, a figure able to play the dulcimer.

Most of these automata modeled physical rather than mental processes. Of the latter variety were several attempts to construct

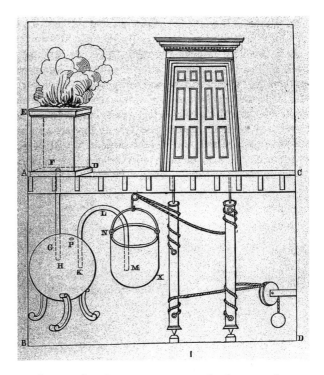

Figure 3.1. A pneumatic mechanism to open and close a door, designed by Heron of Alexandria.

Figure 3.2. The astronomical clock of Strasbourg, with its mechanical cock.

Figure 3.3. (a) Henry Maillardet's eighteenth-century autamaton that draws and writes in French and English. Courtesy Franklin Institute. (b) The Jaquet-Droz Writer of 1774. Courtesy Neuchatel Museum of Art and History. (c) The mechanism of the Jaquet-Droz Writer. Courtesy Neuchatel Museum of Art and History.

talking automata and perhaps more importantly van Kempelen's 1769 chess player, which though fraudulent (hiding a man inside the player) engendered a seventy-year debate over the possibility of mechanizing human thought processes. But the number of automata of this type on the Continent were few, especially in comparison to the number developed in England, where craftsmanship was not nearly so advanced. There are probably many reasons to explain why this is so, but one may have been philosophical rather than

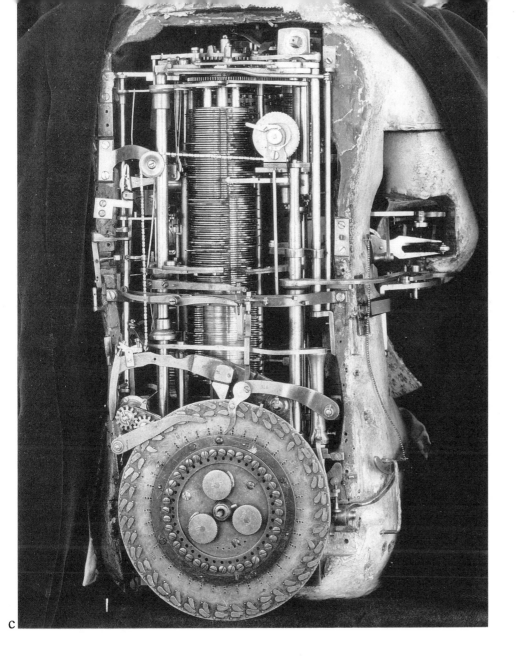

c

technological. Cartesian philosophy colored every aspect of Continental thought throughout the eighteenth century. Perhaps influenced by the elaborate clockwork automata of his time, Descartes explained even the most complex physical processes of the universe in terms of clocklike mechanisms. But he maintained a strict mind-body dualism, denying that mental processes can be explained in mechanical terms. This rationalist dualism was questioned, e.g., by Julien de La Mettrie in *Man the Machine* (1748) and by Baron d'Holbach in *System of Nature* (1770) as well as by the discussions surrounding van Kempelen's automaton, but the influence of Descartes' world view should not be underestimated.

The Development of Logic and Its Mechanization

Another line of development, sometimes closely intertwined with the automata tradition, was the effort to mechanize logic, historically regarded as the most central of the rational processes. In his *Ars Magna* the Spanish theologian Raymond Lull (1235–1315) used geometrical diagrams and primitive logical devices to try to demonstrate the truths of Christianity (Figure 3.4). He believed that each domain of knowledge involves a finite number of basic principles, so that by enumerating the permutations of these basic principles in pairs, triples, and larger combinations a list of the basic building blocks for theological discourse could be assembled.

Figure 3.4. The logical diagrams of Ramon Lull. Courtesy Martin Gardner.

Lull mechanized the process of forming these permutations by constructing devices with two or more concentric circles, each listing the basic principles around the circumference. The permutations could then be formed by spinning the dials so as to line up different permutations. One such device was used for studying the divine attributes. Each of two circles contained the fourteen accepted attributes (goodness, greatness, eternity. . .), and the device would give you the 196 (i.e., 14 x 14 = 196) permutations, e.g., "God is good and God is eternal," "God is eternal and God is great," etc. Similar devices were constructed for study of the soul and the seven deadly sins. Although these devices did not really offer labor savings or additional logical power, Lull's "great art" was admired by many Renaissance clerics and commented on by such noted scholars as Nicholas of Cusa, Athanasius Kircher (who is notable for his interest in automata, e.g., his plans for building a talking head), and Wilhelm Gottfried Leibniz.

Leibniz (1646-1716) was enamored with the power that algebraic symbolism and method had added to geometry during the previous century. In his *De Arte Combinatoria* (1666) and in later fragmentary works he described an "algebraico-logical synthesis" by which one could reason mechanically in all fields as one could reason in algebra. The first step was to devise a universal language, his "universal characteristic," for expressing thoughts in an unambiguous, symbolic way. Leibniz experimented with various linguistic schemes, e.g., representing primitive ideas by prime numbers and complex ideas by the product of these numbers. He also moved towards an algebra of logic by implicitly giving logical interpretations to the algebraic operators and relations +, x, −, =. But he never achieved substantial results, and this work became widely known only in the twentieth century when his fragmentary writings were first published.

The algebrization of logic, primarily the work of Augustus de Morgan (1806-1871) and George Boole (1815-1864), was important to the transformation of Aristotelian logic into modern logic and to the introduction of logic machines in the automation of logical reasoning. In his *Formal Logic* (1847) the British mathematician de Morgan began the algebrization process. He introduced quantification into logic. By using algebraic variables to represent the numbers of members of classes mentioned in a syllogism, e.g., there are a A's and b B's, he could strengthen a conclusion like "Some A's are B's" to "At least k A's are B's," where k is an algebraic expression involving a, b, and other variables that appeared in the premises.

In his *Mathematical Analysis of Logic* (1847) and *An Investigation of the Laws of Thought* (1854) the Irish professor of mathematics Boole rigorized logic by introducing algebraic symbolism and method. He let x, y, z represent classes, X, Y, Z individual members, 1 the universal class, 0 the null (empty) class, xy the intersections of classes x and y, $x + y$ the union of (disjoint) classes x and y, and $1 - x$ the complement of class x. He then presented in symbolic form, as the axioms of his logic, what he considered to be the basic "laws of thought." His axioms include, for example:

$x(1 - x) = 0$
   (The intersection of a set and its complement is null.)

$x(y + z) = xy + xz$
   (De Morgan's law on the distribution of intersection over union).

Boole could then formally deduce more complex "laws of thought" through algebraic manipulation.

These first efforts to reform Aristotelian logic were continued in the late nineteenth and early twentieth centuries by Charles Saunders Peirce, Gottlob Frege, Guiseppe Peano, Bertrand Russell, Alfred North Whitehead, and others. Their efforts further stimulated the mechanization of logic because machines could conduct or abet the algebraic manipulation that now represented logical reasoning.

Logic Machines

The first logic machine, the Stanhope Demonstrator, appeared prior to the algebrization of logic. Charles, third Earl of Stanhope, (1753-1816) was a politician and inventor of independent means. His scientific abilities were recognized early, leading to his induction into the Royal Society of London at the age of nineteen. Stanhope invented a microscopic lens, a hand printing press, a tuner for musical instruments, an improved system of canal locks, and an arithmetical calculating machine, as well as a theory of electricity. Stanhope's Demonstrator (Figure 3.5), refined over a thirty-year span, is a device able to solve mechanically traditional syllogisms, numerical syllogisms, and elementary probability problems. It consists of a 4" × 4.5" × 0.75" mahogany block with a brass top, having carved out of it a window 1" × 1" × 0.5". Slots were grooved in three sides of the block to allow transparent red and gray slides to enter and cover a portion of the window. On the brass face, along three sides of the window, integer calibrations from zero to ten were marked.

Figure 3.5. The face of Lord Stanhope's Logical Demonstrator.

To solve a numerical syllogism, for example:

Eight of ten *A*'s are *B*'s;
Four of ten *A*'s are *C*'s;
Therefore, at least two *B*'s are *C*'s.

Stanhope would push the red slide (representing *B*) eight units across the window (representing *A*) and the gray slide (representing *C*) four units from the opposite direction. The two units that the slides overlapped represented the minimum number of B's that were also C's. To solve a probability problem like:

Prob $(A) = 1/2$;
Prob $(B) = 1/5$;
Therefore, Prob $(A$ and B $) = 1/10$.

Stanhope would push the red slide (representing A) from the north side five units (representing five tenths) and the gray slide from the east two units (representing two tenths). The portion of the window $(5/10 \times 2/10 = 1/10)$ over which the two slides overlapped represents the probability of A and B.

In a similar way the Demonstrator could be used to solve a traditional syllogism like:

No M is A.
All B is M.
Therefore, No B is A.

The Demonstrator had obvious limitations. It could not be extended to syllogisms involving more than two premises or to probability problems with more than two events (always assumed to be independent of one another). Any of the problems it could handle were solved easily and quickly without the aid of the machine. Nonetheless, Stanhope believed he had made a fundamental invention. The few friends and relatives who received his privately distributed account of the Demonstrator, *The Science of Reasoning Clearly Explained Upon New Principles* (1800), were advised to remain silent lest "some bastard imitation" precede his intended publication on the subject. This publication never appeared and the Demonstrator remained unknown until the Reverend Robert Harley described it in the *Philosophical Transactions* in 1879. The Demonstrator was important mainly because it demonstrated to others, most notably to William Stanley Jevons, that problems of logic could be solved by mechanical means.

The second major figure was Alfred Smee (1818-1877), senior surgeon to the Royal General Dispensary and to the Central London Opthalmic Hospital. Also a Fellow of the Royal Society, he published a series of books on a field he called "electro-biology," the relation of electricity to the vital functions of the human body. Stimulated by the lectures of Herbert Mayo on the physiology of the brain, his laboratory work under John Frederic Daniell (inventor of the Daniell battery), and the prevailing theory of Luigi Galvani on the effect of electrical stimulation on nerves and muscles, Smee determined to study how the functions of the brain are related to the electrical stimulation of the nervous system.

In 1851, Smee published his most important book, *Process of Thought Adapted to Words and Language*, which, he stated, "is a deduction from the general system of Electro-biology." He planned to produce an artificial system of reasoning based upon natural principles, one that processes ideas in the same way that the human nervous system processes them. Little was known about the brain in 1850, and there were no good tools for its study. Smee had to rely on speculation rather than experimentation to gain his understanding of human thinking. The outcome of these speculations was to be demonstrated in his electro-biological machine.

According to his theory, each idea is determined by the presence or absence of certain properties (redness, roundness, etc.), and each property is represented in the brain by the electrical stimulation of a nerve fiber. Thus, for Smee, an idea consists of a collection of electrically stimulated nerve fibers. One might envision Smee building an elaborate electromechanical machine with artificial nerve fibers and cortex. But consistent with the technology of 1850, the machines Smee conceived were entirely mechanical. His Relational Machine, so called because it represented the relationship between the various properties that comprise an idea, was intended to represent one thought, idea, or mental image at a time. One version of it was constructed from a large piece of sheet metal, repeatedly divided into halves by metal hinges. Half of the metal would represent the presence, the other the absence, of a property. The metal flaps, representing absent properties, would be folded out of sight until all that remained was a piece of metal representing the collection of properties that formed the idea.

Smee designed a second machine to compare ideas. This Differential Machine consisted of two Relational Machines linked together by an interface able to compare the properties represented by each Relational Machine and then to judge whether the ideas agree, probably agree, possibly agree, or disagree. Representation of ideas and judgments about them, the tasks his machines were designed to do, comprised the entire rational thinking faculty for Smee.

Smee was confident his machines could model human thought. He was concerned, however, about the feasibility of constructing his machines because of the elaborate mechanical engineering involved and the problem of scale. He wrote in *Process of Thought* that

> when the vast extent of a machine sufficiently large to include all words and sequences is considered, we at once observe the absolute impossibility of forming one for practical purposes, inasmuch as it would cover an area exceeding probably all London, and the very attempt to move its respective parts upon each other, would inevitably cause its own destruction.

Although Smee may have built small scale models of his machine (even this is doubtful), he realized that his hope for a machine that could represent the natural processes of thought and judgment was beyond his reach. Nevertheless, his books were popular in mid-nineteenth-century Britain and spread his conviction of the possibility of mechanized thought.

Stanhope's work inspired William Stanley Jevons to construct his "logic piano," the best known logic machine of the nineteenth century. Jevons (1835-1882) was professor of logic and political economy at Owens College, Manchester, and later at University College, London. His scientific interests were broad, and while working as an assayer in Australia early in his career, he made important contributions to anthropology, natural history, meteorology, and chemistry. His research in logic was encouraged by his teacher, Augustus de Morgan. Today, Jevons is perhaps best known for his unfortunate theory of the correlation between sunspots and economic cycles.

In his 1869 logic textbook, *Substitution of Similars*, Jevons announced the construction of the logic piano (Figure 3.6). It was the culmination of a long series of inventions and aids to the calculation of syllogisms: logical alphabet, logical slate, logical stamp, and logical abacus–all tools to write quickly the lines of a truth table in a logical argument.

The logic piano was a box approximately three feet high. A faceplate above the keyboard displayed the entries of the truth table. Like a piano, the keyboard had black-and-white keys, but here they were used for entering premises. As the keys were struck, rods would mechanically remove from the face of the piano the truth-table entries inconsistent with the premises entered on the keys.

A truth-table for n proposition requires 2^n entries. The table for

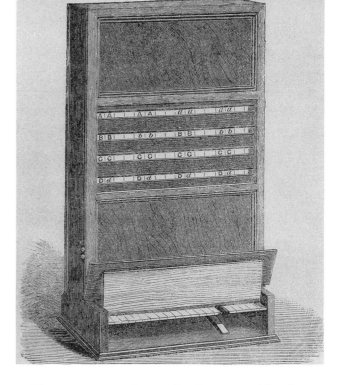

Figure 3.6. The logic piano designed by William Stanley Jevons.

$n = 4$ is as follows, if we represent the truth of a proposition by an upper case letter, and its falsity by the same letter in lower case:

Table 3.1. Truth-table for n = 4

PQRS	PQRs	PQrs	PQrs
PqRS	PqRs	Pqrs	Pqrs
pQRS	pQRs	pQrs	pQrs
pqRS	pqRs	pqrS	pqrs

The proposition "if P, then Q," is true just in case P is false or Q is true. If this proposition were entered on the keyboard of the logic piano, the face would show:

Table 3.2. Truth-table for the proposition "if P, then Q" is true in
case P is false or Q is true, when n = 4

PQRs	PQRs	PQrs	PQrs
			(second line removed)
pQRS	pQRs	pQrs	pQrs
pqRs	pqRs	pqrs	pqrs

As propositions were entered on the keyboard, representing additional premises that must be satisfied simultaneously, other inconsistent entries would disappear from the face.

The machine was limited to solving problems involving four or fewer propositions, although these could easily be handled manually. Jevons once planned a ten-term machine, but abandoned the project because the proposed machine would have occupied an entire side of his study. As the philosopher Francis Bradley pointed out, the action of the logic piano did not result in a conclusion stated in the form of a proposition, but only in the truth table entries consistent with the conclusion. Jevons worked unsuccessfully to resolve this problem, which he termed the "inverse problem" and which he somewhat misleadingly associated with the process of mathematical induction. And, as his adversary John Venn noted, the logic piano has no practical purpose, for there are no circumstances in which difficult syllogisms arise or in which syllogisms must be resolved repeatedly enough to justify mechanization of the process. Jevons countered that it was a convenience to his personal work and useful in his logic classes.

The Reverend John Venn (1834-1923) was lecturer in moral science and fellow of Gonville and Caius College, Cambridge. He published on moral science, history, probability, and logic. His *Symbolic Logic* (1894) was the most widely used logic textbook of its day. In it he presented his famous technique for diagramming logical arguments, described a logical diagramming machine, and discussed the general purposes and possibilities of logic machines.

Diagramming of logical arguments has a long history. In the Middle Ages diagrams were devised for remembering various forms of the Aristotelian syllogism. In the seventeenth and eighteenth centuries, the mathematicians Gottfried W. Leibniz, Leonhard Euler, and J. H. Lambert all had developed systems for diagramming logic. The first practical system of diagramming was announced by Venn in an 1880 article in *Philosophical Magazine*. It described his method of Venn diagrams, which is only a slight variation on the method of intersecting circles still taught in schools today.

Venn also designed a diagramming machine for logical arguments involving four propositions. (Venn diagrams treat at most three.) This is somewhat surprising because of Venn's belief that logic machines are both useless and unworthy of the name "logical." Like Jevons, Venn first developed other laborsaving devices: a rubber stamp of his intersecting circles and a puzzle board in which each piece of the intersecting circles could be removed separately. Then he developed the machine, with four intersecting ellipses hung on pegs by strings such that each section, attached by a separate peg, represented one of the sixteen possible logical combinations. To exclude a combination, the appropriate peg would be released, allowing the section it held to fall below its normal level. The keyboard consisted simply of the sixteen pegs to be individually manipulated. No device was added by which a number of pegs could be removed at once. Thus, it is more properly categorized as a diagram than a machine.

The last major figure in the development of nineteenth-century logic machines was Allen Marquand (1853-1924). After studying at Johns Hopkins University with C. S. Pierce, who probably taught him about logic machines, Marquand was appointed tutor of logic at the College of New Jersey, as Princeton University was then called. Marquand soon abandoned logic to become professor of art and archeology. Besides important work on classical Greek art and archeology, he contributed to the algebra of logic and built several logic machines.

Marquand improved upon Jevon's logic piano. He constructed a crude version in 1881, and a Princeton colleague, Charles Rockwood, followed the next year with a more elaborate version. It measured $12" \times 8" \times 6"$ and used a mechanical action, with rods and levers connected by pins and catgut strings (Figure 3.7). Marquand

Figure 3.7. Allen Marquand's logic machine.

proposed a third version that would have changed the action of the machine from mechanical to electromechanical, but difficulties with the new electrical technology prevented him from advancing beyond building a prototype from a hotel annunciator.

Marquand's machine was designed for syllogisms involving four propositions. The front of the machine displayed pointers representing the sixteen possible logical combinations. The pointers would turn to indicate the consistency or inconsistency of the logical combinations with the premises. Marquand improved upon Jevons' keyboard for entering premises, opening the possibility of constructing a machine capable of handling many more propositions. However, both machines were limited in the complexity of argument they could handle, and both produced only logical combinations consistent with the concluding proposition rather than the proposition itself.

In 1936 Benjamin Burack, a psychologist at Roosevelt College in Chicago, constructed the first electrical logic machine (Figure 3.8). It was packaged in a small suitcase and powered by batteries. The bottom of the case contained wooden blocks representing propositions. These blocks held metal contacts, and when the blocks were moved to certain positions, circuits would be activated showing whether a syllogism was valid or which of seven categories of fallacies occurred. Burack's machine offered little advantage over manual checking and was generally unknown until it was described in the literature in 1947.

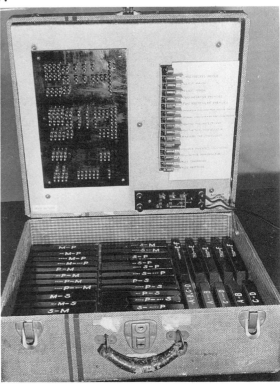

Figure 3.8. Benjamin Burack's portable electical logic machine. Courtesy Martin Gardner.

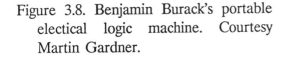

Better known was a logic machine built in 1947 by Harvard University undergraduates William Burkhardt and Theodore Kalin. Their machine was essentially an electrical version of Jevon's logic piano, capable of handling syllogisms with as many as twelve terms. Logical premises were entered by setting switches that established an electrical circuit logically isomorphic to the premises. Lights indicated the lines of the truth-table consistent with the premises. Use of the Burkhardt-Kalin machine was much faster than checking the syllogisms manually. And, unexpectedly, their machine could establish the well-known indeterminacy of truth value of the logical paradoxes by lights that alternated true and false. (An example of a logical paradox is "this statement is false." It is easy to establish that the statement in the quotation marks is true if and only if it is false.)

After the Second World War, it became apparent that general-purpose stored-program computers could achieve the same results as any of these special-purpose logic machines. Subsequently, all major logic machines have been programmed on computers. The first such effort was made by Hao Wang in 1960. He programmed an IBM 704 computer to test the first 220 theorems of the propositional calculus as presented in Bertrand Russell and Alfred North Whitehead's *Principia Mathematica*. The process was completed in less than three minutes, at least a thousand times faster than could be done manually. Since 1950 a number of computers have been programmed to act as logic machines. They have been used either to try to discover new logical results or to investigate the general principles by which computers can be used to prove theorems.

Logic and Computing

The logic machines described here did not have any practical significance. They did not provide meaningful control of the daily information flow in the factory or business office, nor did they enable scientists to solve problems they could not otherwise easily solve by hand. Although logic machines were occasionally used as didactic aids, their chief importance was theoretical. They demonstrated that logical processes could be mechanized. Thus, it should come as no surprise that their principal role in modern computing is also theoretical. The existence of logic machines reinforced the relationship between logic and computing, and helped

Figure 3.9. Claude Shannon, who discovered the isomorphism between switching circuits and the propositional calculus. Courtesy AT&T Archives.

to set the context in which two theoretical papers of the 1930s were written, papers that provided the underpinning for the modern theory of computing.

In a 1938 paper based upon his master's thesis at MIT, Claude Shannon demonstrated how relay and switching circuits could be expressed in the logical symbolism of the propositional calculus, and vice versa. Some examples of the correspondence he discovered are:

logic	circuit
true	closed
false	open
and	serial
or (inclusive)	parallel

Similar circuit interpretations can be given for the logical connectives not, nand (not both), exclusive or, and equivalence. This isomorphism between propositional calculus and relay and switching circuits became a powerful new design tool. Inspired by Shannon's paper, Burkhardt and Kalin employed it in the design of their special-purpose electrical logic machine. A more important application was to electrical circuit design for computers. Complex circuits could be more readily simplified by simplifying the corresponding Boolean expression; and in many cases it was easier for a circuit designer to express his design in a logical expression and only later translate that into a circuit design. Hundreds of papers followed Shannon's, building this fundamental isomorphism between logic and computing into a theory of switching circuits and a practical design methodology.

Shannon was not the first to suggest this isomorphism. The idea had been suggested in the Russian literature in 1910 by Paul Ehrenfest and followed up in 1934 by V. I. S. Sestakov. It also appeared in a 1936 Japanese publication by Akira Nakasima and Masao Hanzawa. However, none of these received the wide attention of Shannon's paper, mainly because his paper was published in English and presented a detailed account of the isomorphism in a way that highlighted its value to circuit design theory.

The other important theoretical paper of the 1930s was Alan Turing's "On Computable Numbers" (1937). Turing characterized which functions (or, as he equivalently considered, which numbers) in mathematics are effectively computable. By this he understood functions that can be computed in a mechanical fashion by a well-defined algorithm that requires no human intervention during the course of the computation. Turing's paper was one of the original contributions to the area known as recursive function theory, a subject in vogue then because of the interest in the methods used in Kurt Godel's famous incompleteness results, concerns about the constructivist foundations of mathematics, and other independent research in logic.

Turing phrased his characterization in terms of theoretical machines, known today as Turing machines. He defined a mathematical function to be effectively computable just in case it could be calculated by one of his machines and demonstrated that one of his machines, the Universal Turing Machine, was able to simulate any of his other machines. Thus, by Turing's criteria, a mathematical function is effectively computable if and only if it can be computed by the Universal Turing Machine.

Figure 3.10. Alan Turing, whose characterization of effectively computable functions gave the first theoretical description of the stored-program computer.

A Turing machine consists of an infinite tape, broken into cells, and a mechanical device capable of scanning the tape and performing a few basic read and write operations. At any moment, depending on the internal state of the machine and the symbol in the cell being scanned, the machine may move the tape one square left or right, or print or erase a symbol in the scanned cell. Function arguments are entered as a coded sequence of 0s and 1s on consecutive cells. Function values are read off as another coded sequence of 0s and 1s when the machine completes its activity. If the activity never ceases, the function is not effectively computable for that argument. The universal machine represents essentially a function of two variables, one being the number of a particular Turing machine it is to simulate and the other being the function argument.

The importance of the Universal Turing Machine to computer science becomes clear once it is recognized that it is a theoretical model of a digital, stored-program computer. Instructions programming the operation of the machine, as well as data, are entered on the tape. The tape serves the dual function of input-output medium and memory—similar to magnetic tape in computers (which is used, however, only as a secondary storage medium). Information is stored, processed, and transferred digitally. Central processing takes place at the read-write mechanism, which is able to carry out logical and arithmetic operations on the scanned cell and those adjacent to it—whether they represent instructions, input data, or intermediate results. Many programming features, like conditional and unconditional branching and recursive loops, have their Turing machine equivalents.

Just as Shannon's paper served as the starting point for the theory of switching and relay circuits, Turing's paper opened the field of automata theory—the theoretical study of the computing capabilities of well-defined information processing automata—whether they be natural, physical artifact, or theoretical. This provided an abstract model and formal description for what was occurring in computer design.

Turing's methods, and the methods of recursive function theory more generally, were also employed in another area of theoretical computer science, the theory of complexity. This field considers the complexity of information-processing problems in terms of the amount of time, cost, storage space, or other computational resources that are required to compute a solution to the problem. Turing had demonstrated the existence of a class of problems too complex for solution by his machines. The most important of these was the halting problem: given the number describing to the universal machine a particular Turing machine and a given input, decide whether the machine will ever halt its computation. Turing demonstrated that the halting problem is computationally undecidable, that no Turing machine can make this decision. This placed a theoretical limit on what is mechanically computable and on our practical abilities to predict computation lengths and systematically diagnose programming errors. Working within the bounds set by Turing, many other researchers have developed finer meshes for ascertaining computational complexities of problems.

It has been a long and sometimes tenuous line of development from the logic machines of Stanhope and Jevons to modern computer science theory. But today logic is the foundation for automata theory, switching theory, and other theoretical areas of computer study; and the computer is a tool much more capable of logical processing than any of the special-purpose machines of the past.

Further Reading

Aspray, W. "The Scientific Conceptualization of Information." *Annals of the History of Computing* 7(1985):117-140. A historical survey of the contributions of Shannon, Turing, and some of their contemporaries.

Bedini, Silvio A. "The Role of Automata in the History of Technology." *Technology and Culture* 5(1964):24-42. A standard account of the history of automata.

Bolter, J. David. *Turing's Man*. Chapel Hill: University of North Carolina Press, 1984. A social and philosophical examination of the meaning and results of Turing and others to modern society.

Chapuis, Alfred and Edmond Droz. *Les Automates*. Neuchatel: Edition du Griffon, 1949. A classic and heavily illustrated work on the history of automata.

Davis, Martin. "Mathematical Logic and the Origin of Modern Computers." In *Studies in the History of Mathematics*. Edited by Esther R. Phillips. Washington, D.C.: Mathematical Association of America, 1987. A logician explains the role of logic in the development of modern computing.

Gardner, Martin. *Logic Machines and Diagrams*. 2d ed. Chicago: University of Chicago Press, 1982. The standard survey of logic machines and diagrams.

Hodges, Andrew. *Alan Turing*. New York: Simon and Schuster, 1983. An authoritative biography, but accessible to a general audience.

Kline, Morris. *Mathematical Thought From Ancient to Modern Times*. New York: Oxford University Press, 1972. The best survey history of mathematics available today.

Kneale, William and Martha Kneale. *The Development of Logic*. Oxford: Oxford University Press, 1962. A standard account of the history of logic.

MacKay, D. "Mindlike Behavior in Artefacts." *British Journal for the Philosophy of Science* 2(1951):105–201. A philosopher examines attempts to model human thinking.

McCorduck, Pamela. *Machines Who Think.* San Francisco: W. H. Freeman, 1979. A popular history of artificial intelligence.

Price, Derek de Solla. "Automata and the Origins of Mechanism and Mechanistic Philosophy." *Technology and Culture* 5(1964):9–23. An influential essay setting the history of automata in a larger intellectual context.

Shannon, Claude. "Symbolic Analysis of Relay and Switching Circuits." Master's Thesis, MIT Cambridge, Mass., 1940. The thesis which established the fundamental connection between logic and switching theory.

———· "Computers and Automata." *Proceedings of the London Mathematical Society* 10(October 1953):1234–41. A brief survey of the connections between computers and automata by one of the leading participants.

Tarjan, Rudolf. "Logische Maschinen." In *Digital Information Processors.* Edited by Walter Hoffmann. New York: Wiley Interscience, 1962, 110–59. A useful survey of logical machines.

Turing, Alan. "On Computable Numbers, with an Application to the Entscheidungsproblem." *Proceedings of the London Mathematical Society*, Series 2, 42(1937):230–65. This famous paper introduced the Turing machine.

Vartanian, Aram. *La Mettrie's L'Homme-Machine.* Princeton: Princeton University Press, 1960. A good edition, with scholarly historical analysis, of La Mettrie's famous book.

Von Boehn, Max. *Puppets and Automata.* Translated by Jean Nicoll. New York: Dover Publications, 1972. A popular account of automata.

Chapter 4

Punched-Card Machinery

Introduction

From quite early in the twentieth century, until the advent of moderately priced electronic computers in the late-1950s, the bulk of the automatic data processing needs of commerce was met by punched-card machines. There were two main strands in the development of these machines, which are described in this chapter.

The first strand was the development of census machinery in the United States. Beginning in the early 1880s, Herman Hollerith (1860–1929) developed a range of equipment for the mechanical tabulation of the 1890 United States census; this machinery saw several improvements in the censuses of 1900 and 1910. From this point, however, the Bureau of the Census increasingly adopted the commercially manufactured punched-card machines it had helped to originate.

The second strand was the commercial development of punched-card machinery. Hollerith realized, from an early date, the statistical and accounting possibilities of his machines in commerce and incorporated a company to develop and supply suitable equipment. From this beginning, between the two world wars a large-scale industry developed that came to be dominated by IBM. The machines themselves evolved in complexity out of all recognition from the original census machines, and applications blossomed in statistics, accounting, and science.

Finally, with the advent of the stored-program computer in 1945, punched-card machine technology underwent a twenty-year transformation, during which the products of the industry were turned into electronic data processing computers.

The Development of Census Machinery

The Census Problem

The first United States decennial population census took place in 1790, when the recorded population was a little under four million. The early censuses were comparatively simple affairs: only a few inquiries were made of the head of each family, and the published census reports were modest in scope. By 1850, however, the population had increased by more than a factor of five and many more inquiries were made of every citizen; furthermore the number of tabulations, as measured by the size of published reports (1,605 pages in 1850), had grown considerably.

In the 1850 census, for the first time, the tabulation was performed by the method of "tallying." In essence, tallying involved examining each questionnaire (or schedule) returned for a census district and recording a mark on a tally sheet for each fact, or combination of facts, to be tabulated. Totals for larger sections of the population were then determined by adding the counts from individual tally sheets. At first this process was entirely unmechanized. In the latter part of the 1870 census, and in the 1880 census, a very limited degree of mechanization was provided by the Seaton device. This simple contrivance enabled several tally sheets, combined on one length of paper, to be brought conveniently close together. Notwithstanding the help of the Seaton device, the 1880 census took about seven years to process. Given the influx of immigrants that was then occurring—it was expected that the population of America would perhaps double in the next decade—it was evident that in the next census either the scope of the inquiry would have to be curtailed or a method of mechanical tallying introduced.

Herman Hollerith, then employed at the Census Bureau, thus became aware of the population census problem. Hollerith, a graduate of the Columbia School of Mines, New York, had been engaged in the collection of industrial statistics since joining the bureau in the fall of 1879. In 1882, he resigned from the Census Bureau, spending a year as an instructor in mechanical engineering at MIT followed by a short period as an examiner in the United States Patent Office, after which he became an independent patent agent. During these years he worked on both a tabulating system and railway braking systems. A patent application was made in 1884 for an early form of tabulating system based on a punched paper tape, and patents for a card-based system were filed in 1887. Conflicting accounts of the origination of the idea of using a punched-card medium appear in the literature. The idea may have been suggested by a senior member of the bureau staff, J. S. Billings; alternatively, Hollerith may have derived the idea from the Jacquard loom, or the method of punching a physical description of a railroad passenger in his ticket (Hollerith in fact used a conductor's punch to perforate cards in early trials of the system). In any event, the development of the idea was entirely due to Hollerith.

From 1887 a number of trials of the system were made, compiling mortality statistics for Baltimore and other cities and medical statistics for the Office of the Surgeon General of the Army. The major trial for the tabulating system came in 1889 when the director of the census, Robert P. Porter, organized a competition to select a tabulation system for the 1890 census. Three competitors submitted entries: in addition to Hollerith's system, there was another system based on paper "slips" and another based on cardboard "chips." Both of the systems of Hollerith's competitors involved the transcription of schedule entries on to paper slips or cards, which were then repeatedly sorted and counted by hand, quick identification being facilitated by color coding. The contest involved the recording and tabulation of the schedules for the St. Louis district from the 1880 census, representing something in excess of ten thousand individuals. The Hollerith system was a convincing winner: the recording of data was significantly faster than either of his competitors, and tabulation was up to ten times as fast. The reason for the speed of the Hollerith system was that, unlike the other systems, once a card had been punched, all manual tallying and sorting was eliminated.

The Hollerith Electric Tabulating System

The Hollerith Electric Tabulating System consisted of several pieces of apparatus in addition to the tabulating machine itself. The tabulation of the census involved three distinct processes: the recording, tabulation, and sorting of data.

```
1  2  3  4 | CM UM | Jp | Ch Oc | In | 20 50 80 | Dv Un | 3  4 | 3  4 | A  E  L | a  g
5  6  7  8 | CL UL | O  | Mu Qd | Mo | 25 55 85 | Wd CY | 1  2 | 1  2 | B  F  M | b  h
1  2  3  4 | CS US | Mb | B  M  | O  | 30 60    | 0  2  | Mr | 0  15 | 0  15 | C  G  N | c  i
5  6  7  8 | No Hd | Wf | W  F  | 5  | 35 65    | 1  3  | Sg | 5  10 | 5  10 | D  H  O | d  k
1  2  3  4 | Fh Ff Fm | 7  1 | 10 40 70 90 | 4  0 | 1  3 | 0  2 | St I  P | e  l
5  6  7  8 | Hh Hf Hm | 8  2 | 15 45 75 95 | 100 Un | 2  4 | 1  3  4 | K  Un | f  m
1  2  3  4 | X  Un Ft | 9  3 | i  c | X  R  L  E  A | 6  0 | US Ir Sc | US Ir Sc
5  6  7  8 | Ot En Mt | 10 4 | k  d | Y  S  M  F  B | 10 1 | Gr En Wa | Gr En Wa
1  2  3  4 | W  R  OK | 11 5 | l  e | Z  T  N  G  C | 15 2 | Sw FC EC | Sw FC EC
5  6  7  8 | 7  4  1  | 12 6 | m  f | NG U  O  H  D | Un 3 | Nw Bo Hu | Nw Bo Hu
1  2  3  4 | 8  5  2  | Oc O | n  g | a  V  P  I | Al Na | 4 | Dk Fr It | Dk Fr It
5  6  7  8 | 9  6  3  | O  | p | o  h  b | W  Q  K | Un Pa | 5 | Ru Ot Un | Ru Ot Un
```

Figure 4.1. Form of the 1890 census card.

Each schedule returned in the census contained the information for a complete family. From this schedule one card was punched for each person.

Figure 4.1 illustrates the form of the card: each $6^5/8$" × $3^1/4$" card had 288 punching positions and was corner-clipped to ensure the correct orientation. The leftmost 48 punching positions contained the four-digit code of the census "enumeration" district; because a complete batch of schedules for a district was punched together, the district number was "gang punched" identically on each card. The gang punch (Figure 4.2) was a lever-operated device in which the pattern of holes was set up by an arrangement of metal slugs, and up to six cards could be perforated in one stroke.

Figure 4.2. Gang Punch. Courtesy Smithsonian Institution. Photo No.
64550.

The data for an individual was recorded in the right-hand 240 punching positions of the card. Data items were recorded in a number of irregularly shaped regions, or fields, on the card, starting at the top left and moving approximately clockwise around the card. The third field, for example, recorded the racial type of the individual (Japanese, Chinese, Octoroon, Indian, etc.). The fourth field recorded gender (male, female). The fifth field recorded the five-year period in which the age of the subject fell (0-4, 5-9, 10-15 . . . 100-plus) and the sixth field the unit within the five-year period. The seventh field recorded "conjugal condition" (unmarried, married, divorced, widowed). And so on round the card for a total of twenty-one fields.

The data was recorded using the pantograph punch (Figure 4.3). The punch had a drilled guide plate bearing an image of the card to the front and a carriage for a blank card to the rear; by depressing an index pin into a hole in the guide plate, a hole was punched with accurate registration in the corresponding position in the card. It is interesting to note that, unlike later card-punching practice, data was

Figure 4.3. Pantograph punch. Courtesy Smithsonian Institution.
Photo No. 64551

not transcribed literally onto the card but had to be interpreted by the operator. Thus, an age of 57 (say) would be recorded as a hole in the corresponding five-year period (i.e., 55-59) and a second hole in the additional units (i.e., 2). Similarly, the place of birth was recorded as a two-letter code in fields 10 and 11, for which a code list was supplied (e.g., "Ag" for Connecticut, "Ka" for Germany—the codes had some, but not much, mnemonic significance). Because the order of fields clockwise around the card was the same as the order of the schedule inquiries, the punching operation was quite smooth flowing and operators averaged seven hundred cards per day. In the 1890 census, plain manilla cards were used, so that a "reading board," bearing a printed image of the card (as in Figure 4.1) enabled cards to be read back for verification by another person.

The tabulating machine (Figure 4.4, left) was used to count the number of holes, in selected positions and in selected combinations, of a batch of cards passed through it. The machine contained a maximum of forty clocklike counters, each capable of registering up

Figure 4.4. Hollerith electric tabulating system. Courtesy Smithsonian Institution. Photo No. 64563.

to 9,999. Cards were sensed by a hand-operated press that bore 288 spring-loaded pins: when the "pin-box" was brought down onto a card a pin encountering a hole would pass through, dip into a mercury cup, and complete an electrical circuit; but if the pin met solid card, it would simply be pressed back and no circuit would be completed. A counter included in the circuit would thus be incremented by one, or not, depending on the presence or absence of a hole.

The simplest operation the tabulating machine could perform was to count the number of holes in selected positions in a batch of cards. Thus, in principle, if one counter was wired to register males and another to register females, the effect of passing a batch of cards through the machine would be to obtain the total number of males and females represented. Invariably, actual counts were much more complex so that as much information as possible could be extracted in a single passage of the cards through the machine. For example, in the first count of the census, the male and female populations were classified by "color-nativity" and tenure for different age groups using the full forty counters.[1] Each combination was achieved by wiring relay circuits. For example, one counter was required to register the total number of native-white persons aged 45-plus; therefore, the counter was wired into a relay circuit that passed a current if one of the holes 45, 50, 55 . . . 100-plus was punched, the citizen was white, and both parents were born in the United States.[2]

A counting operation would begin by resetting all the counters and then reading the cards for an enumeration district one-by-one with the press. When all the cards had been passed through the machine a supervisor would record the totals and reset the counters, and the operator would begin the next batch of cards. Impressively fast speeds could be obtained by a skillful operator, and even an average operator managed eight to ten thousand cards a day.

The tabulating machine had several measures to ensure accuracy. For example, when the cards of a given enumeration district were tabulated, sensing the correct district code caused a bell to ring; failure to ring indicated that a card from another enumeration district had been put into the pack. A contemporary reporter described the sound of the dozens of machines as "for all the world like that of sleighing." The tabulating machine would also record the grand total of cards read; this value would then be cross-checked with the subtotals of the different classifications, although discrepancies of one or two units were usually tolerated.

After the first count, succeeding counts determined finer statistics for smaller divisions of the population. For example in the second count, for conjugal condition, it was required to determine, for each sex of the seven racial types, marital status classified by age. First the cards had to be sorted into the seven racial groups. This sorting process was achieved using the sorting box, as a by-product of the first count.

The sorting box (Figure 4.4) consisted of approximately two dozen compartments each having an electrically operated lid, normally kept closed. By an appropriate relay circuit, of an identical type to that used for the counters, a combination of holes could be used to select a compartment whose lid would fly open when a card of the right type was sensed. The operator would drop the card into the offered compartment and close the lid. The fact that only one lid opened eliminated the possibility of the operator placing the card in the wrong compartment; closing the lid with a deft tap took almost no time.

The Hollerith tabulating system achieved its superiority over a manual system in a number of ways. First, it enabled as many as forty complex combinations to be counted in a single handling of the cards; this was far more than was possible in a manual system and was the most decisive advantage of the census machine. Second, the Hollerith system eliminated a great deal of the physical sorting and counting of records of a manual system; thus the sorting box was always used alongside the tabulating machine, presorting cards for a subsequent count with the minimum cost in time and handling. Third, the Hollerith system was inherently more accurate than a manual system because the possibilities of incorrectly sorting and counting were greatly reduced.

Further Census Developments

The tabulation of the 1890 census was a technical and financial triumph for Hollerith. It was well reported in the press, appearing for example as the main article in the August 30, 1890 issue of *Scientific American* (Figure 4.5). Within six weeks of the start of the census, the rough count of the population was complete (total 62,622,250 citizens). This achievement was only a partial vindication of the Hollerith system because the rough count was produced not by using punched cards but by registering family counts directly into the tabulating machines using a simple keyboard. After the rough count, the detailed tabulations began for which nearly sixty-three million cards had to be prepared, one for each citizen. Altogether, seven counts were made involving several hundred million card passages through the census machines. The census was completed in a little over two years, a great improvement on the previous census, and much more complex and refined tabulations were produced (the published reports of 10,220 pages were nearly twice the length produced for the previous census). Approximately one hundred

Figure 4.5. Cover of the *Scientific American*, August 30, 1890. This evocative engraving shows scenes from the 1890 U.S. population census. *Bottom*: The incoming completed schedules are received and assembled for onward processing. *Top right*: Schedules are punched onto cards using the pantograph punch. *Top left*: Using the census machine, the cards for an enumeration district are tabulated and deposited one by one into the sorting box. *Center*: Using a special keyboard, family head counts are entered for the rough count. Courtesy Smithsonian Institution. Photo No. 47941.

SCIENTIFIC AMERICAN

[Entered at the Post Office of New York, N. Y., as Second Class Matter. Copyrighted, 1890, by Munn & Co.]

A WEEKLY JOURNAL OF PRACTICAL INFORMATION, ART, SCIENCE, MECHANICS, CHEMISTRY, AND MANUFACTURES.

Vol. LXIII.—No. 9.
ESTABLISHED 1845.

NEW YORK, AUGUST 30, 1890.

[$3.00 A YEAR.
WEEKLY.

ELECTRICAL TABULATING MACHINES

SPECIAL RETURN CARD

PUNCHING SPECIAL RETURN CARDS

CENSUS BUILDING 6 & 2d STS

SCIENTIFIC AMERICAN

ELECTRICAL COUNTING MACHINES

ENUMERATORS SCHEDULES

ASSORTING AND TIEING ACCORDING TO SUPERVISORS DISTS

THE NEW CENSUS OF THE UNITED STATES—THE ELECTRICAL ENUMERATING MECHANISM.—[See page 132.]

census machines were used and several hundred pantograph punches, all of which were maintained by Hollerith and his assistants. The machines evidently needed regular repair and maintenance, but it is possible that the faults were not entirely mechanical:

> Mechanics were there frequently . . . to get the ailing machines back in operation. The trouble was usually that somebody had extracted the mercury (which made the necessary electrical contacts) from one of the little cups with an eye-dropper and squirted it into a spittoon, just to get some un-needed rest.[3]

While the preparations for the 1890 census were underway, Hollerith received several inquiries from European countries that led to the adoption of the system for the 1890 censuses of Austria and Norway, and also for Canada nearer to home. Hollerith made several trips to Europe during the mid-1890s consolidating the use of his machines in European censuses. His reputation was quickly established both in the United States and in Europe, where he was awarded several honors and academic distinctions. In 1896, Hollerith incorporated his business as the Tabulating Machine Company. But it was not until the twelfth United States census of 1900, for which Hollerith was awarded the contract by Director of the Census W. R. Merriam, that his machines saw large-scale use again.

The 1900 population census relied for the most part on the census machines used for the 1890 census, although their number was increased considerably. An apparently simple improvement, the automatic feeding of cards, was made to some of the tabulators, which eliminated the hand feeding of cards and the manual closing of the press. Although automatic feed was used to only a limited extent in the 1900 population census, when it was used it made a several-fold improvement in the speed with which cards could be processed. Automatic card feeding eventually was provided in all punched-card machines.

The most significant change of punched-card machine use in the 1900 census occurred with the tabulation of the census of agriculture, which required the accumulation of quantities (such as the number of bushels of wheat produced on each farm). This necessitated a card capable of storing numerical quantities, and an "integrating" (as Hollerith termed it) tabulator. In fact, Hollerith had already developed a suitable multicolumn card format and a small reliable integrating tabulator that was then in use with the New York Central Railroad Company (see next section). A new punching machine, the key punch, was introduced for the punching of the agricultural census cards. This device was a great improvement on the pantograph punch in that cards could be punched far more rapidly using the calculator-style key pad (Figure 4.6). The keypunch was manufactured in essentially the same form for more than half a century. The cards were summarized by large, hand-fed integrating tabulators provided with ten adding units. The 1900 agricultural census also saw the introduction of another important advance, the electrical sorting machine. This machine enabled sorting to be carried out as an independent operation, and not merely as a by-product of regular tabulation with the census machine. Prior to the advent of the electric sorter, sorting could only be achieved by "needle sorting"—an awkward operation that entailed poking a blunt needle through the holes in a stack of cards, to isolate groups of cards with common hole punchings.

Once again the census, completed in approximately two and a half years, was a technical and financial success for Hollerith. The Tabulating Machine Company supplied over three hundred tabulating machines and more than sixteen hundred pantograph and key punches. The company, however, was not awarded the contract for the 1910 census, because Hollerith was unable to agree on financial terms with the new director of the census, S. N. D. North.

Figure 4.6. Hollerith key punch used for the 1900 U.S. census. Courtesy Smithsonian Institution. Photo No. 64549

In 1905 Hollerith severed his connection with the Bureau of the Census and from that point put all his energies into developing the commercial application of punched-card machines.

In the meantime, Director North established a census machine shop to improve and develop new equipment for the forthcoming 1910 census. The most notable improvement to the system was the incorporation of printing counters in the tabulators; these eliminated the copying down of the counter dials, which was both time consuming and a potential source of error. In 1907 a mechanical expert, James Legrand Powers, was employed to improve the key punch. The result was an entirely new device (figure 4.7) that

Figure 4.7. Powers key punch, 1910 U.S. census. Courtesy ICL Historical Collection.

was electrically powered and had an automatic feed which resulted in much faster operation; a complete card was set up prior to the punching operation so that corrections could be made without repunching an entire card. The new punch also had gang punching and simple sorting facilities. Powers was also involved in making substantial improvements to the sorter that Hollerith had supplied for the 1900 census. Hollerith sued the Bureau of the Census for patent infringement, but the case was not clear-cut and after two years the action was dropped by mutual agreement. In 1911, Powers left the employ of the Bureau of the Census to establish the Powers Accounting Machine Company, an organization which proved to be a serious competitor for the Tabulating Machine Company.

Commercial Development of Punched-Card Machinery

Development of the Punched-Card Machine Industry

During the early years of the Tabulating Machine Company, which Hollerith had incorporated in 1896, the company operated in a comparatively small way on two fronts. First, it supplied census machinery to the United States Bureau of the Census and to the census organizations of other countries, particularly in Europe. Second, it attempted to supply tabulating machinery for commercial use. The cyclical nature of the census business—censuses were taken in the first or second years of the decade almost everywhere—meant that Hollerith needed to look for other, noncyclical, uses for his tabulating machines in order to stabilize the revenues of his business.

Initially, the commercial use of tabulating machines was on a very small scale—a few machines were supplied for the compilation of insurance and railroad statistics. Hollerith was not able to interest a large-scale user, the influential Pennsylvania Steel Company, until 1904. Following the loss of the Bureau of the Census contract in 1905, commercial work became the mainstay of Hollerith's company; the machines themselves evolved rapidly and their use increased greatly, particularly by railroad companies. By 1908, the Tabulating Machine Company had about thirty customers, including railroads, utilities, manufacturers, and government agencies. Thereafter the revenues (and therefore the customer base) grew at the rate of about 20 percent every six months.

By 1911 the Tabulating Machine Company had expanded to a size that exceeded Hollerith's ambitions. Aged 51 and not in strong health, he stepped down as general manager and allowed the company to be acquired by a well-known business promoter, Charles Flint. American business was then caught up in one of its periodic merger waves, and Flint formed a new organization, the Computing-Tabulating-Recording Company (C-T-R) by consolidating three principal concerns. These were a manufacturer of computing scales (i.e., machines that weighed an article and calculated the cost in one operation), the Tabulating Machine Company, and a manufacturer of time recorders (i.e., machines used for recording the "clocking on" and "clocking off" time of employees). Each of these companies was recognized by one word of the new title: Computing-Tabulating-Recording. C-T-R expanded rapidly, achieving some economies of scale both in selling costs and in manufacturing, and it also had the greater security resulting from diversification. Hollerith remained a director for a year or two, and a technical consultant until 1921, when he retired.

In 1911, the year in which C-T-R was formed, James Powers incorporated the Powers Accounting Machine Company. The company developed a range of commercial punched-card machinery considerably superior to that offered by C-T-R, in particular offering a printing tabulator that was far better suited to commercial applications. For the first time, machines competitive with the Hollerith system had appeared on the market.

It is fair to say that there were three key figures in the development of the punched-card machine industry: Herman Hollerith, James Powers, and Thomas J. Watson. Watson (1874-1956), who became president of C-T-R in 1914, was a man of a completely different mold from Hollerith and Powers; he considered himself foremost a salesman. He had already had a meteoric career with the National Cash Register Company, and brought much of its sales-oriented culture with him to C-T-R. Watson immediately realized that the tabulating machine division was the most promising part of the company, but that its products were inferior to those of the Powers company. A research department was set up under E. A. Ford—Hollerith's principal coinventor—whose staff would soon include such outstanding inventors as J. W. Bryce, C. D. Lake, B. M. Durfee and F. M. Carroll. Products to match the competition soon followed. Under Watson's leadership the company had trebled in size to well over three thousand employees by 1924, when the name was changed to International Business Machines (IBM).

As in the United States, the punched-card machine industry in the rest of the world was based on the exploitation of, and competition between, the Hollerith and Powers patents. In Europe for example, the British Tabulating Machine Company (BTM) was formed in 1907 in London with an exclusive right to manufacture and market Hollerith machines in Great Britain and its Empire.[4] In 1913, the Accounting and Tabulating Machine Corporation of Great Britain was formed to market the Powers machines; the British Powers company soon became independent of the American parent and developed many of its own machines. Competition between the two British companies was intense. Continental Europe also had a thriving tabulating machine industry: in Germany the Deutsche Hollerith Maschinen Gesellschaft (usually known as *Dehomag*) was formed in 1910; this company developed several important patents that C-T-R acquired when it took a 90 percent stake in the company in 1923. C-T-R also established a French sales organization, Société Internationale des Machines Commerciales (later IBM France). In both of these countries, as in other European countries, the Hollerith and Powers lines competed. Europe also had its own indigenous manufacturers: Machines Bull in France, and Soviet Russia also produced machines. By the mid-1920s, IBM, Powers, or BTM outposts were to be found beyond Europe and the United States in most developed corners of the globe. Even so, although punched-card machines were important and pervasive, the industry was quite a small one and quite minute by comparison with the present day computer industry. For example, by the end of the 1920s IBM had only about three thousand customers in America—this has to be compared with the hundreds of thousands of computer installations it has today; again, IBM's annual revenues were then only about twenty million dollars compared with about fifty billion dollars in the mid-1980s; similarly, its head count has risen perhaps one hundred times from the three thousand it had in the late 1920s.

The Powers Accounting Machine Company of the United States was itself the subject of a merger in 1927, when it was acquired by the Remington Rand Corporation. As a result of the fierce competition between IBM and Remington Rand the machines developed very rapidly: the tabulating machines produced in the 1930s contained several thousand precision components, and were among the most complex of manufactured devices.

In spite of the Great Depression of the 1930s, the punched-card

Figure 4.8. Evolution of the punched card: (a) 45-column TMC card, (b) 80-column IBM card, (c) 90-column Remington Rand card.

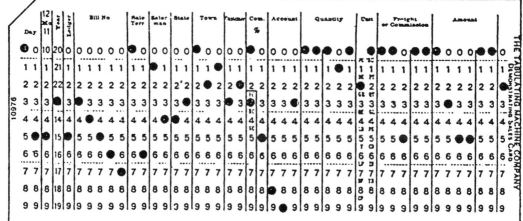

a

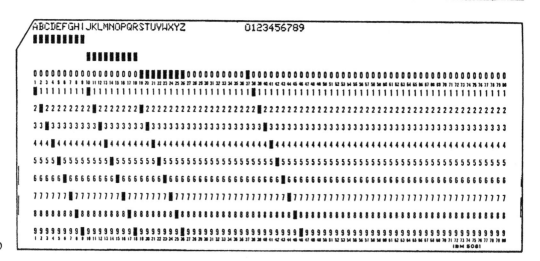

b

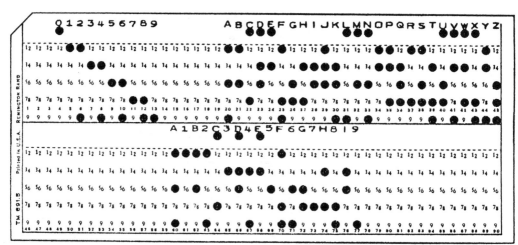

c

machine industry largely held its ground, expanding again vigorously in the second half of the 1930s with the demand for government office mechanization created by the Social Security Acts of 1935, and the general increase in the size and operations of the federal government from the time of the New Deal. By the end of the decade, IBM had grown to about twelve thousand employees; it had several manufacturing plants, and large educational and research divisions at Endicott, New York. In addition, the company had marketing and manufacturing operations in most major countries (excluding the British Empire).[5]

Development of the Machinery

The most important early development of the Hollerith tabulating system occurred in connection with the tabulation of statistics for the New York Central Railroad in the mid-1890s. This commercial application had the important requirement of needing the accumulation of quantities, such as route-miles, the weight of shipments, and monetary amounts. Hollerith created for this application the multicolumn card in which numerical data could be recorded in fields of several adjacent columns (Figure 4.8).[6] To accumulate the numeric quantities Hollerith introduced a small integrating tabulator.[7] This machine, similar to that shown in Figure 4.9, used the hand-feed pin-box reading mechanism of the original census machine; selected numeric fields were added into counters of which up to four were provided.

Figure 4.9. Integrating tabulator. Courtesy ICL Historical Collection.

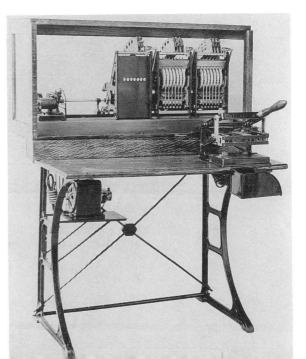

The early 1900s, during which the Tabulating Machine Company had some success in placing machines in commercial applications, saw Hollerith and his assistant E. A. Ford make several improvements in the range and versatility of the machines. Most notably, during 1905-1907, they improved greatly the tabulator, which took on the familiar appearance of the floor-standing electrically driven machine. Figure 4.10 shows punched-card machines in use in a typical small office of the early 1900s. The new model incorporated automatic feed, which enabled it to tabulate cards at the rate of 150 per minute; this was many times the speed achievable in the hand-fed machines, and much less fatiguing. Another important improvement was the incorporation of a plugboard so that the machine could be more rapidly reconfigured to tabulate data from one card format to another; this was a great step forward on the physical rewiring that had formerly been necessary. The punched card itself went through some evolution in size and the number of columns, eventually standardized at a forty-five column, twelve-row card of dimensions 7 3/8" × 3 1/4" and corner-clipped. The automatic sorter, first introduced in 1901 for the agricultural census, was reengineered as the vertical sorter, operating at a speed of 250 cards per minute. For any card column selected by the operator the sorter would distribute cards into thirteen receiving compartments, one compartment for each of the twelve possible punching positions and a thirteenth for unpunched cards.[8] The vertical arrangement of the sorter was chosen to minimize the space occupied in a crowded office (Figure 4.10). This turned out to be an unfortunate decision, for the sorter became known as the "back-breaker," on account of the amount of stooping needed to collect the sorted cards, and it was not popular with operators.

After incorporating the Powers Accounting Machine Company in 1911, Powers and his assistant W. W. Lasker began to develop their range of machines for commercial use. The Powers machines, although functionally similar to the Hollerith machines and using the same card format, operated on different mechanical principles: in place of the electrical sensing and relays of the Hollerith equipment, the Powers machines used mechanical pin sensing and were entirely mechanical in operation, electric motors supplying nothing more than motive force. (There was some advantage in the mechanical sensing at first, as the machines were not affected by any conducting metal impurities in the cards; in the long-term, however, mechanical operation was inherently less flexible than electrical.) The new equipment included a horizontal sorter that was less tiring for

Figure 4.10. Punched-card office of the Retail Hardware Mutual Fire Insurance Company, Minneapolis, circa 1920. Note the key punch on the table at left, the vertical sorter at center rear, and the tabulator at the right of the room. Courtesy ICL Historical Collection.

machine operators than the C-T-R vertical sorter, because they no longer had to stoop to remove the cards. The Powers printing tabulator was a far superior device to that offered by C-T-R. First, the machine had a printing head that enabled it to list cards and print totals. And second, it was fitted with a "connection-box" that enabled it to be reconfigured for a new application in a matter of seconds, compared with the much longer time needed to replug the C-T-R machine. The first card punch (the so-called slide-punch) produced by Powers was less satisfactory, and it was quickly replaced in 1916 by an electrically driven key punch of a similar pattern to the hand-operated Hollerith punch.

By 1919, C-T-R was able to announce that it too had developed a printing tabulator, which was marketed the following year. The new design, due to C. D. Lake, in addition to printing had an "automatic-control" device. On previous tabulators it had been necessary to manually insert "stop-cards" to cause the machine to halt so that totals could be copied down—now both copying and stop-cards were eliminated, because automatic control detected the change in a group number. C-T-R also developed, in the early 1920s, an electrically operated keypunch and a four-hundred-cards-per-minute horizontal sorter that rivaled those of Powers.

In its turn, the Powers organization achieved what was probably the single most important development between the wars—the introduction of alphabetic equipment in 1924. Letters of the alphabet were encoded in a single column of the card by means of a special code, the 45-column cards being otherwise identical to those used on the numerical equipment. Both an alphabetic tabulator and an alphabetic keypunch were provided. The introduction of alphabetic equipment opened up entirely new areas of commercial application that had not been possible with the numerical-only machines. IBM subsequently brought out its own, rather more flexible, alphabetic equipment. In 1928, IBM introduced the familiar 80-column card with slotted holes (Figure 4.8b), which gave a great increase in capacity over the 45-column card. Remington Rand followed suit in 1930 with a 90-column card, in which two characters were punched in each of 45 columns (Figure 4.8c).

This pattern of development—each of the two manufacturers bettering the offerings of the other—is one that, in broad terms at least, characterized the development of punched-card machinery between the two world wars. The development of punched-card machines illustrates, in microcosm, the accelerating trends in automatic control and operation that swept across the developed world during that period. Over the years hundreds of improvements were made by each manufacturer to its products and equally large numbers of patents were taken out. Of the many improvements only a handful were really fundamental, but the cumulative effect of hundreds of minor improvements was to transform the machines. Increasingly, the machines required less and less operator intervention and became more sophisticated in their operation. For example, the introduction of "major-minor" automatic control enabled two levels of subtotalling to be performed automatically, and eventually three levels.[9]

In the early 1930s, IBM introduced a range of 80-column machines that were a high point in the interwar development of

Figure 4.11. IBM punched-card machines of the 1930s: (a) alphabetic duplicating printing punch, (b) horizontal sorter, (c) alphabetical accounting machine (Tupe 405). Courtesy ICL Historical Collection.

a

b

c

punched-card machinery (Figure 4.11). The leading machine of the series was the model 405 alphabetic electric accounting machine.[10] The new accounting machine inherited all the improvements of the previous decade—three levels of automatic control were provided, a replaceable plugboard enabled an application to be changed in seconds, paper feed mechanisms enabled standard sized continuous stationery to be used for the print out, and full subtraction facilities were provided; cards could be totalled at the rate of 150 per minute, or listed at a speed of 75 cards per minute. The 405 was a very flexible machine that required a significant training period to learn to use successfully and represented a great increase in complexity and sophistication over the tabulators that preceded it. Series 400 accounting machines, based closely on the original model 405, remained in production until punched-card machines ceased to be manufactured in the late-1960s.

The 1930s were the heyday of the punched-card machine industry and the number and power of the products of both manufacturers increased considerably. Punched-card machines may be classified by three broad functions: recording, sequencing, and processing. For recording data, the simple electrically powered key punch was supplemented by floor standing models with full alphabetic keyboard, gang punching, and program control; verifiers with similar facilities were also provided. The reproducing punch enabled decks of cards to be duplicated and reformatted, and the interpreter printed the contents of a card along its top edge. The most important sequencing machine, the card sorter, achieved a typical speed of six hundred cards per minute. The sorter was supplemented by the collator, which could merge two ordered decks of cards to produce a single-sequenced card file. A valuable adjunct to the accounting machine was the summary punch by which an updated card file could be produced simultaneously with tabulation; this would then serve as the new master file the next time the application was run. Probably the most complex punched-card machine to be developed before World War II was the multiplying punch, the most important of which was the IBM model 601, announced in 1931.

Applications: Commercial and Statistical Computations

The earliest uses of punched-card machines were statistical; it was not until the Tabulating Machine Company's second decade that accounting applications began to dominate. This trend accelerated markedly with the appearance of printing tabulators that had automatic control in the early 1920s and the later appearance of alphabetic equipment. Accounting machines were not designed with mathematical computation in mind, but their use in this context was an important link between the prewar world of mechanical computation and the postwar world of electronic computers.

Although Hollerith made a little progress in the commercial field during the early years of the Tabulating Machine Company, it was not until he was able to offer an integrating tabulator with automatic feed and vertical sorter that major accounting operations could be undertaken. The first of these was for the Pennsylvania Steel Company in 1904 and the second was a sales analysis application for the Marshall Field retailing organization. Punched-card machinery was expensive to rent and consequently was only used, at first, by very large organizations that could make good use of its ability to make short work of a large volume of transactions; the needs of small businesses could be met adequately by less automatic but lower-cost bookkeeping machines, such as those made by Burroughs. The Hollerith machines, however, arrived at a critical period in the development of large-scale American enterprise; it was during this period in the late nineteenth and early twentieth centuries that much of modern business accounting practice came into existence, particularly cost accounting in manufacturing. The Hollerith business grew rapidly on the strength of this new wave of increasing business scale. As large-scale business became more and more the norm, the use of the machines became quite widespread, so that by 1913 a journalist was able to report

> the system is used in factories of all sorts, in steel mills, by insurance companies, by electric light and traction and telephone companies, by wholesale merchandise establishments and department stores, by textile mills, automobile companies, numerous railroads, municipalities and state governments. It is used for compiling labor costs, efficiency records, distribution of sales, internal requisitions for supplies and materials, production statistics, day and piece work. It is used for analyzing risks in life, fire and casualty insurance, for plant expenditures and sales of service, by public service corporations, for distributing sales and cost figures as to salesmen, department, customer, location, commodity, method of sale, and in numerous other ways. The cards besides furnishing the basis for regular current reports, provide also for all special reports and make it possible to obtain them in a mere fraction of the time otherwise required.[11]

Sales analysis, first undertaken for Marshall Field in about 1907, was a very common commercial application, and it illustrates well the use to which punched-card machines were put. Sales transactions were recorded onto cards, different fields recording the salesman number, the value of the transaction, the value of the commission, the product code, and so on. (Fig. 4.8a shows a typical early sales card.) To total up the commissions for each individual salesman during an accounting period, for example, the cards would be sorted by salesman number, which would put all the transactions for each salesman into juxtaposition. Blank stop-cards would then be inserted to separate the cards for each salesman from the next. Finally, the cards would be run through the tabulator; as each stop-card was encountered the tabulator would halt, so that the total commission for the salesperson could be copied into a ledger for subsequent payment.[12] The same sales cards could also be used to provide other analyses. For example, to examine stock movement during a period, the total sales of each product would be required. This could be quickly obtained by sorting the sales cards into product code order and performing another tabulation. A great point was made by tabulating machine salesman of the "unit record" principle: that a single record could serve a variety of purposes by the simple process of sorting and tabulation.

The demands of commercial applications were a prime stimulus to the production of new tabulating equipment. For example, the introduction of alphabetic equipment was a direct response to the need for names and addresses and alphabetic descriptions on tabulator listings; and the provision of several levels of automatic control enabled very sophisticated customer statements and management reports to be produced. Accounting machines only added and subtracted, so that utility companies, for example, who charged customers on unit-cost-times-quantity basis had to perform the necessary multiplication prior to the punching operation. The multiplying punch introduced in the early 1930s was designed to satisfy this need.[13]

Just as the needs of commerce were a spur to the development of the punched-card machine industry, the technology also helped to shape the organization of business. Thus, the highly centralized accounting systems of industry were very much geared to what was technically achievable with the commercially available machines, and a generation of accountants between the two world wars grew up on a diet of the standard textbooks on mechanized accounting. When computers became available in the 1950s and 1960s, they tended to be used at first as glorified electric accounting machines and were simply absorbed into old-fashioned accounting systems. It took a new generation of accountants, and much trauma, to exploit the potential of the computer, particularly its capability for dealing with transactions in real time.

Applications : Scientific Computation

In the 1930s the two principal means of performing digital computation were using desk calculators or punched-card machines. Though the use of desk machines was very widespread (see Chapter 1), there existed just a few centers using punched-card machines. In volume terms, the number of punched-card machines used for digital computation before World War II was quite insignificant, but they were important in creating an awareness of their computational possibilities within the scientific establishment and within the punched-card industry itself.

The first person to make use of punched-card machines in scientific computation was L. J. Comrie, superintendent of the Nautical Almanac Office, Greenwich, England. Comrie was, in principle, opposed to the construction of special-purpose computing equipment and had already established his reputation by adapting commercial accounting machines to scientific ends. Comrie first used punched-card machines in connection with Brown's Tables of the Motion of the Moon in 1929, which he described in a classic paper published in 1932. Comrie subsequently resigned from the Nautical Almanac Office to form his own company, Scientific Computing Services (SCS), in 1937. SCS became a leading center for digital computing and, before the war, it was the only British computing service to make use of punched-card machines. It is perhaps indicative of the scale of computational activity of the day that SCS could not justify the cost of acquiring machines but mainly used the bureau service of the British Tabulating Machine Company.

In the United States, astronomical computation also provided a motive for using punched-card machines for digital computation. Wallace J. Eckert (1911-1976), an astronomer at Columbia University, learned of Comrie's activities in England and began in 1933 to do similar work using the punched-card machines housed in the Columbia University Statistical Bureau in New York.[14]

In 1934, Eckert became director of the Scientific Computing Bureau at Columbia, which was the first American center for punched-card computation, using machines donated by IBM; in 1937, the laboratory was renamed the Thomas J. Watson Astronomical Computing Bureau. The computing bureau accepted a wide range of computational tasks, such as harmonic analysis, the integration of differential equations, and the construction of astronomical tables.

Table 4.1. Punched-card machine tabulation of $y = x^2 + 2x + 1$

Argument x	Function y	First difference	Second difference
0.00	1.00		
		0.21	
0.10	1.21		0.02
		0.23	
0.20	1.44		0.02
		0.25	
0.30	1.69		0.02
		0.27	
.	.	.	.
.	.	.	.
.	.	.	.
etc.			

One of the most elegant and simple of Eckert's techniques, the tabulation of a function by the method of differences, illustrates punched-card computing nicely. Suppose it was required to tabulate the function $y = x^2 + 2x + 1$ for $x=0$ to 1 in steps of 0.10 (Table 4.1). The process would begin by recording the constant second difference on a total of ten cards, using the gang punch and placing a card containing the top value of the first difference column at the front; i.e., the deck would contain the value 0.21, 0.02, 0.02, 0.02. . . . The cards would then be run through the tabulator and successive totals recorded on cards using the summary punch. The top value of the function column would then be placed at the front of the new card deck, which would now contain the values 1.00, 0.21, 0.23, 0.25. . . . Finally, a last run through the tabulator of this card deck would produce a listing (and a card deck if required) containing the values 1.00, 1.21, 1.44, 1.69. . . , the required table. In practice, the process was a little more complicated than this.

Some of Eckert's more complex calculations—notably the

integration of differential equations—required the use of a multiplier, a tabulator, and a summary punch acting in concert. Eckert commissioned a "calculation control switch" that enabled a sequence of arithmetic operations to be performed during a single card passage; this was one of the earliest examples of automatic sequence control. Eckert later developed these ideas in the IBM Pluggable Sequence Relay Calculator (see Chapter 6) and the Selective Sequence Electronic Calculator (Chapter 7).

Postwar Development

After the many technical developments of the 1930s, the war years saw relatively little advance in punched-card machine design due to the supervention of other wartime research priorities. The manufacture and use of the machines, however, increased considerably. IBM, for example, emerged from the war with nearly twice the employees it had when the war began.

The two most important wartime developments were the application of electronics and the development of sequence-controlled calculators. A prototype electronic multiplier was available within IBM by the end of 1942, although it was not until 1946 that it became commercially available as the model 603; operating at one hundred cards per minute, it was about ten times faster than the electromechanical 601. During the last year of the war, IBM developed the Pluggable Sequence Relay Calculator. This machine, which was capable of performing a sequence of up to fifty arithmetic steps, was specified by W. J. Eckert and designed and built by a team led by C. D. Lake and B. M. Durfee.

In 1948 these two developments were brought together in the IBM 604 electronic calculating punch—a machine with 1,400 electronic tubes and a capacity of sixty program steps. More than 5,000 of these calculators were sold during the next ten years. The other punched-card machine manufacturers quickly followed IBM's lead by introducing electronic multipliers and calculating punches in the next few years. The IBM 604 was the main computing element in a very important development, the Card-Programmed electronic Calculator (CPC). The CPC was a popular transition machine that sold in hundreds until reliable, moderately priced, stored-program computers became available in the mid-1950s.

The introduction of electronics into punched-card machines was, in a phrase of the period, "evolutionary not revolutionary"; that is to say, the functional characteristics remained unchanged and the new technology merely enhanced the speed and reliability of the machines. It is obvious in retrospect that by the early 1950s punched-card machines were a declining technology, that they would eventually be superceded by electronic computers. The speed with which this happened, however, is often exaggerated. Electronic computers were for several years expensive and unreliable alternatives to traditional tabulating equipment, and could only be justified by the largest and most prestigious data processing users; for prudent business people, tried and trusted electronic accounting machines were generally a more sensible choice. During the 1950s some very competitive new punched-card machines were introduced that occupied "that ill-defined boundary which divides computers from calculators." For example, in 1958 IBM announced its model 628 calculating punch, which used second generation transistor electronics, had a small magnetic core memory, and could be plugged with up to 160 program steps. Another second generation calculating tabulator, the Univac 1004 (Figure 4.12), was introduced by Sperry Rand in about 1962, and many hundred were sold in the United States and Europe. Even as late as 1959 there were less than four thousand

Figure 4.12. The Univac 1004 calculator, also sold in the United Kingdom and Europe as the ICT 1004, shown here, by International Computers and Tabulators (ICT, the descendant of the British Tabulating Company). Courtesy ICL Historical Collection.

computers in the United States, compared with several thousand punched-card machine installations. It was probably not until the launching of the IBM 1401 in 1959, outstandingly the most successful early data processing computer, that this began to change.

By the late 1960s traditional punched-card machines had effectively gone out of production, although punched cards themselves continued to be the dominant input-output medium for electronic computers. IBM flirted briefly with a new 96-column card in 1969 for its small System/3 range of computers, and included an off-line sorting machine, but it was not a commercial success. During the 1970s even this vestigial use of punched cards declined with the increasing use of direct data entry on visual display units. By the late 1980s punched cards had all but vanished.

Notes

1. Color-nativity is the racial type and country of birth. Tenure equals farm or home ownership. The overt interest of the Bureau of the Census in statistics of race is sociologically interesting, but beyond the remit of this chapter.

2. The relay circuits we now recognize as simple AND and OR logic functions, but such a formalism did not exist until the late 1930s.

3. G. Austrian, *Herman Hollerith: Forgotten Giant of Information Processing* (New York: Columbia University Press, 1982), 72.

4. Although BTM derived the full benefit of IBM's research and development, it was required to pay a 25 percent royalty for the privilege. This onerous royalty rate frustrated the growth of BTM; and because it also lacked Watson's charismatic leadership, it never prospered to anything like the extent of IBM in America. It never became more than about one-twentieth the size of IBM, in spite of having a sales area of one-third of the developed world.

5. Comparative data for IBM and the Remington Rand Tabulating Machine Division are hard to come by. Although Remington Rand had overall revenues comparable with IBM, the bulk of its

revenues were derived from typewriter sales and other office products. According to contemporary sources, IBM had about an 80 percent share of the American tabulating machine market and Remington Rand about 20 percent.

6. Apart from the population census, where the old form of card persisted, the multicolumn format of cards was universally adopted; Figure 4.8a shows an example dating from shortly before World War I.

7. Hollerith had in fact experimented with an earlier integrating tabulator for the Office of the Surgeon General in 1899 and for the Agricultural Census in 1893. All types were based on a Leibniz stepped-wheel adding mechanism (see Chapter 1).

8. Because the card sorter only operated on a single column, to sort a field of n digits, cards had to be passed through the sorter n times, starting with the most significant digit. An analogous sorting technique in computer programming is known as the bucket or radix sort. See D. E. Knuth, *The Art of Computer Programming*, vol. 3 (1973), 382-84.

9. It is interesting that a vestige of this old accounting machine control mechanism remains in the RPRG programming language, which in fact evolved as a simulator of punched-card accounting machinery.

10. Gradually the term *electric accounting machine* or *EAM* had come to be preferred to *tabulator*, reflecting the shifting domain of application.

11. S. G. Koon, "Hollerith Tabulating Machinery in the Business Office," *Machinery* 20(1913):25.

12. The insertion of stop-cards and the copying down of totals were time-consuming operations that were entirely eliminated in the printing tabulators with automatic control of the 1920s.

13. Before the arrival of the multiplying punch, an ingenious technique known as "progressive digiting" enabled cumulative products to be computed using only a tabulator and a sorter; this

method was devised in the 1920s to compute ton-mile statistics for railroad companies but largely fell into disuse when multiplying punches became available. See J. C. McPherson's introduction to the Charles Babbage Institute Reprint Series edition of W. J. Eckert's *Punched Card Methods in Scientific Computation* (1940).

14. The Columbia Statistical Bureau was one of several statistical units, established in American universities and government departments in the 1920s and 1930s, that used punched-card machines for large-scale statistical research. Another well-known center was at Iowa State College. During World War II many more statistical laboratories came into existence for operations research and statistical investigations.

Further Reading

Austrian, G. *Herman Hollerith: Forgotten Giant of Information Processing*. New York: Columbia University Press, 1982. An authoritative biography of Hollerith that includes a good account of early tabulating machine developments.

Belden, T. G. and M. R. Belden. *The Lengthening Shadow: The Life of Thomas J. Watson*. Boston: Little, Brown and Co., 1962. The official biography of Watson, which is less sanitized than one might expect, and which includes useful data on the development of IBM.

Chandler, Alfred D. *The Visible Hand*. Cambridge, Mass.: Harvard University Press, 1977. A magisterial work that enables the reader to appreciate the American business context in which punched-card machines developed.

Comrie, L. J. "The Application of the Hollerith Tabulating Machine to Brown's Tables of the Moon." *Monthly Notices of the Royal Astronomical Society* 92, no. 7(1932):694-707. Comrie's classic account of the first use of punched-card machines for scientific computation.

————· *The Hollerith and Powers Tabulating Machines*. London: Office Machinery Users Assoc., 1933. A difficult to obtain but unrivaled description of the punched-card machines of the day.

Connolly, J. *History of Computing in Europe*. IBM World Trade Corp., 1967. Detailed account of European punched-card machine and computer industries.

Eckert, W. J. *Punched Card Methods in Scientific Computation*. New York: Columbia University Press, 1940. Reprinted with an introduction by J. C. McPherson as Vol. 5 in the *Charles Babbage Institute Reprint Series for the History of Computing*. Los Angeles and Cambridge, Mass.: Tomash Publishers and MIT Press, 1984. A detailed description of the use of punched-card machines in the T. J. Watson Scientific Computing Bureau at Columbia University.

————· "The IBM Pluggable Sequence Relay Calculator." *Mathematical Tables and Other Aids to Computation* 3(1948):149-61. A useful description by the designers.

Engelborg, S. *International Business Machines: A Business History*. Ph.D. diss., Columbia University, New York, 1954. Reprinted by Arno Press, New York, 1976. A pioneering study of IBM, when it was still a relatively small company.

Goldstine, H. H. *The Computer: From Pascal to von Neumann*. Princeton University Press, 1972. An excellent account of punched-card computation is given in Chapter 11.

IBM Computers—The Story of Their Development." *Data Processing* 2(1960):90-101. An excellent account of IBM equipment during the transition from punched-card machines to computers.

Koon, S. G. "Hollerith Tabulating Machinery in the Business Office." *Machinery* 20(1913):25-26. Particularly good account of the early commercial use of punched-card machines.

Martin, T. C. "Counting a Nation by Electricity." *Electrical Engineer* 12(1891):521-30. A charming and well-illustrated semi-popular account of the Hollerith Electric Tabulating System.

Murray, F. J. *Mathematical Machines 1: Digital Computers*. New York: Columbia University Press, 1961. A good account of latter day punched-card machines.

Phelps, B. E. "Early Electronic Computer Developments at IBM." *Annals of the History of Computing* 2(1980):253-66. Includes a discussion of the development of IBM 603, 604, and CPC.

Randell, B. *The Origins of Digital Computers*. 3d ed. New York: Springer-Verlag, 1982. Contains a chapter on the development of tabulating machines, and a bibliography of other readings.

Sheldon, J. W, and L. Tatum. "The IBM Card Programmed Electronic Calculator." In *Review of Electronic Computers: Proceedings of the Joint AIEE-IRE Computer Conference, December 1951*. New York: American Institute of Electrical Engineers, 1952, 30-36. Provides a description of the CPC.

Truesdell, L. E. "The Development of Punched Card Tabulation." In *The Development of Punched Card Tabulation in the Bureau of the Census, 1890-1940*. Washington, D.C.: GPO, 1965. A definitive account of the origins and development of census machinery and the use of commercial punched-card machines for census work.

Chapter 5

Analog Computing Devices

Introduction

Imagine that you are standing on the bank of a small river. On the opposite bank, on a small rise inaccessible to you, is a tall building whose height you would like to determine. Fortunately, you have with you a protractor, or similar angle measuring device, that enables you to sight the angle above the horizontal of the foot and top of the building. Then, turning, you carefully pace a convenient distance away from the building (the ground also being conveniently flat) and repeat the angle measurements. You now have sufficient information to determine the height of the building.

But how do you do the actual calculation? One method is to use trigonometry—develop the formulas that apply in this situation and use a pocket calculator to evaluate them substituting your observed angles and distance paced for the unknowns. An alternative approach would be to do a careful scale drawing (Figure 5.1) from which the height of the building could simply be measured without any knowledge of trigonometry.

The first method of calculation uses a *digital* technique. The quantities involved are represented by numbers (strings of decimal digits—hence the name), and the numbers are manipulated in an abstract manner independent of the original problem.

The second method of calculation uses an *analog* technique. The

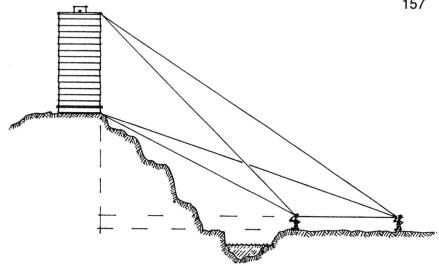

Figure 5.1. A graphical solution to the surveying problem described
in the text.

quantities in the problem are represented by a direct proportion (or analog) of the length of lines and the angles between them. Unlike the digital technique, the accuracy of the analog technique is limited by how carefully and accurately the drawing is made and the result measured. On the other hand, the analog technique is generally quicker to apply and less prone to error, as the whole problem is set before you as a picture. Its adaptability is clear if you were to subsequently ask how far away is the building, or how high is the rise on which it stands?

Analog methods of calculation have a very old tradition and many are still in common use. For example, in artillery surveying, digital (computer) techniques are used for the basic calculation and a graphical analog device is still commonly used as a check against error. In World War II, graphical devices were the basic technique. Figure 5.2 shows a plotter used in antiaircraft defense. From an observation post the direction (bearing), angle above the horizon (altitude), and distance to the aircraft (range) can be measured. These are set up on the plotter instrument, and the aircraft's height can then be read off and its position over the ground marked on the map.

Simple direct analogs, such as those just discussed, are very common. There are more sophisticated approaches in which it is not the problem itself that is modeled. Rather, the equations describing the problem are derived and are then modeled in such a way that the original problem is much less evident. It is this approach that is discussed in this chapter.

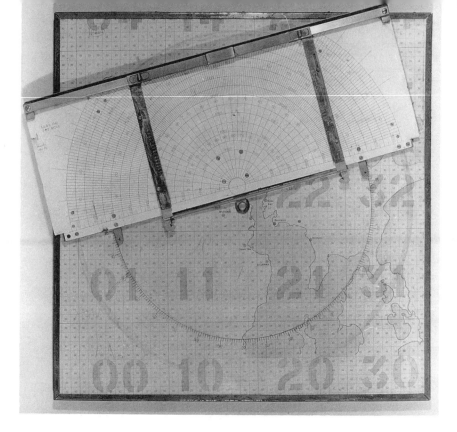

Figure 5.2. An antiaircraft plotter. The vertical triangle, from which the height and horizontal range can be determined from the slant range and altitude angle, is solved by the gridded chart that has been laid flat onto the map.

Simple Analog Devices

We start with some simple examples of analog devices. Figure 5.3 shows a more refined example of a plotting instrument for antiaircraft defense. The altitude angle and range are entered by positioning the angular arm that represents the line of sight to the aircraft. By manually setting the vertical arm the height and horizontal range can be read off.

Figure 5.4 shows a more elaborate mechanism, called a *resolver*, for converting from polar to rectangular coordinates. This mechanism works automatically and is a component part of many of the devices described later. They are found in naval gunnery computers from World War I, and a simpler form occurs in Kelvin's harmonic analyzer in the 1870s and in numerous other harmonic analyzers from the turn of the century onwards.

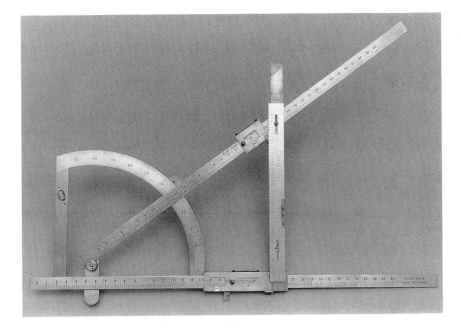

Figure 5.3. A more sophisticated mechanism for solving the vertical
triangle in antiaircraft gunnery. Here each of the elements of the
triangle is represented by a metal bar that can be rotated or slid
to place it in correct relative physical relationship to the elements
of the original problem.

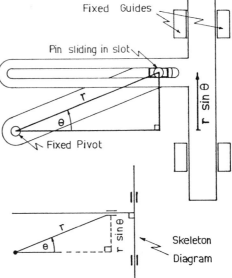

Figure 5.4. A mechanical resolver for converting from polar to
rectangular coordinates. An arm is rotated through an angle θ.
Sliding radially on the arm is a block carrying a pin whose
distance from the center is r. Together r and θ represent the
hypotenuse of a right-angle triangle. The pin moves in a
horizontal slot in an arm constrained by guides to slide vertically.
The vertical movement of the arm is therefore $r \sin \theta$. A similar
arm, with a vertical slot, sliding horizontally will yield $r \cos \theta$.

A multiplying mechanism can be constructed using similar triangles, as shown in Figure 5.5. One slide input rotates an arm about a fixed pivot for the first operand. A second slide input positions a slider on the rotated arm for the second operand. The vertical position of the slider on the rotating arm yields the product on an output slide. This multiplier mechanism also appears in World War I gunnery computers, but antecedents are found in some of the more elaborate integraphs of the late nineteenth century.

Figure 5.5. Skeleton diagram of a multiplying linkage. Since the triangles *ABC* and *ADE* are similar,

$$BC/AB = DE/AD,$$

so

$$BC = [DE \times AB]/AD = a \times b$$

if *AD* is taken as unit length.

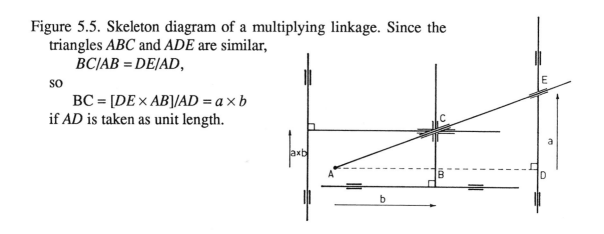

The Powles *Calliparea*, patented about 1870, is a more mathematically sophisticated device. It was designed to measure directly, without calculation, the cross-sectional area of a wire for determining its resistance to electric current. The instrument, shown in Figure 5.6, may have been a prototype model. It was probably not extensively manufactured because the same accuracy in area could be obtained with ordinary callipers and a slide rule, the use of which could also allow the inclusion of the resistivity of the wire and its length in the calculation. The mathematical principle underlying its operation is shown in Figure 5.7.

An important basic analog mechanism is the differential, which adds two independent motions. Several forms of this mechanism are shown in Figure 5.8, which indicates how the common bevel gear differential might be understood from simpler forms. Here it is not the linear position of a slide, but the angle though which a shaft rotates, that provides the analog of a quantity in the original problem.

Figure 5.6. Powles Patent Calliparea (ca. 1870) for directly
measuring the cross-sectional area of round wire.

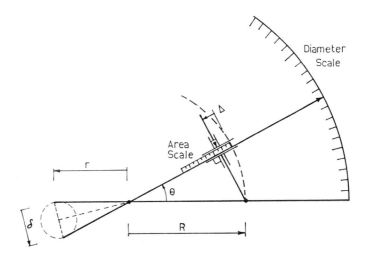

Figure 5.7. The mathematical functions performed by the Powles
Calliparea. From the figure,

$\delta = 2r \sin (\theta/2)$,

$\Delta = R(1 - \cos \theta) = 2R \sin^2 (\theta/2)$

by the trigonometric identity,

$\cos \theta = 1 - 2 \sin^2 (\theta/2)$

in the instrument $r = 2$ inches and $R = \pi$ inches, where

$\Delta = 2R(\delta/2r)^2 = \pi/8 \; \delta^2 = 1/2(\pi\delta^2/4)$

Thus the difference δ represents the cross-sectional area of a circle
with diameter δ to a linear scale of 0.5 inch to each square inch
of area.

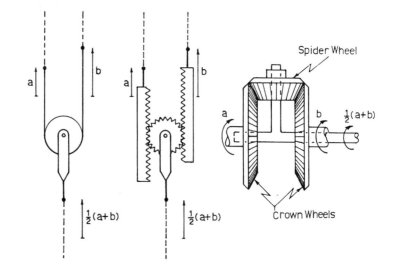

Figure 5.8. Three forms of differential mechanism for adding two independent quantities. If either suspension rope of the pulley at the left is raised, the pulley is raised by half that amount, and the two ropes may be manipulated independently. In the center the same effect is obtained by replacing the ropes by toothed racks and the pulley by a gear wheel. If the racks are bent to form circular crown wheels, as at the right, the same mathematical function is obtained with all linear motions replaced by circular motions of (possibly) unlimited extent. The latter is the common automobile form of differential that ensures that the number of revolutions made by the engine (connected to the spider shaft) is equal to the mean of the number of revolutions made by the driving wheels (connected via half-axles to the crown wheels).

Although a differential mechanism occurred in antiquity (the Antikythera Mechanism, described below), it was not reinvented until the mid-seventeenth century. Its first use in calculating machinery was in the naval gunnery computers of World War I, but a simpler form was used in Kelvin's tide predictors (1870s) and harmonic synthesizers.

All of the devices thus far described are theoretically exact in their action. Aside from "noise" introduced by the limited accuracy in machining the parts, the mechanisms do not introduce any structural error due to the geometry of the mechanism being inexact. Frequently, however, the mathematical description of a problem is simplified so that it can be solved by a more straightforward analog device if the error thus introduced is of no importance to the user.

Astronomical Clocks, Orreries, and Planetariums

The motions of the heavenly bodies, and particularly the planets or "wandering stars," have held a fascination for people since antiquity; this fascination is enshrined in the scientific knowledge of astronomy and the speculative knowledge of astrology. Mechanical models representing the heavens, either to show the present positions of bodies or to "calculate" their positions at an earlier or future epoch, have been known for at least two thousand years.

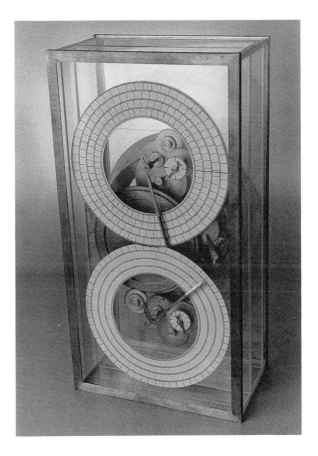

Figure 5.9. The first working modern reconstruction of the Antikythera Mechanism, made by the author. The case is approximately 12"× 6"× 3" (320 × 160 × 80mm). In the original, the case was of bronze and wood, with opening doors like a triptych. The whole was covered by inscriptions in Greek explaining the use of the mechanism.

The earliest extant example of an astronomical computer is the Antikythera Mechanism, from 80-50 B.C., recovered from an ancient wreck in 1901 and interpreted from X-ray images by the historian Derek de Solla Price. Figure 5.9 is a photograph of a modern reconstruction made to a recent reinterpretation of its mechanism and function by the author. The input is turned once per day and drives a dial showing the age of the moon—the 29.53 day cycle from new moon through full moon and back to new moon. This in turn drives dials that show the positions of the sun and the moon among the stars and the eighteen-year cycle of lunar and solar eclipses. Figure 5.10 shows schematically the arrangement of the mechanism which includes thirty-nine gears and is the only example of a differential gear mechanism known before the mid-seventeenth century.

Figure 5.10. The logical organization of the Antikythera Mechanism. The heart of the mechanism is based on the Metonic Cycle: 254 Sidereal Months of 27.32 days (for the moon to return to the same place relative to the fixed stars) takes approximately 235 Synodical Months of 29.53 days (from new moon back to new moon) or 19 Sidereal Years of 365.26 days. The eclipse indication is based on the Saros cycle—the pattern of eclipses repeats after 233 Synodical Months, or nearly 18 years. The boxes show the gear ratios of the various sections of the gear train.

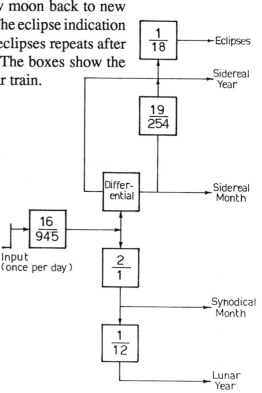

Planispheric astrolabes, which show star and planetary positions in altitude and azimuth coordinates, as seen from the earth's surface, appear to have originated in Hellenic times and Islamic examples are known from the ninth century. Astrolabes were practical tools of navigation and also served as aids to astrological divination and prediction.

With the development of mechanical clocks in the thirteenth century, wheelwork was adapted for directly indicating the motions of heavenly bodies. From the design of Giovanni de Dondi in 1364 the design of astronomical clocks was progressively refined and elaborated. The cathedral clock at Strasbourg (1842) is probably the best known and that of Jens Olsen (Copenhagen, 1955) is arguably the finest. The development of smaller clocks of this type was strongly supported in the eighteenth-century French courts.

Orreries, models showing the heliocentric motions of the planets, are named for one produced for the Earl of Orrey in 1712. They became very well known in the nineteenth century as aids in popular lectures on astronomy. The main element in the design of these instruments was the calculation of geared wheelwork to approximate the astronomical periods involved.

The development of the planetarium in 1919-1923, by Walter Bauersfeld of the Carl Zeiss optical works in Jena, is the most important modern contribution to analog astronomical devices. In this instrument, the firmament and planets are represented by optical projections on the inside of a large hemispherical dome. This instrument has seen considerable elaboration through the twentieth century and features the geocentric representation of planetary motions.

The principle embodied in planetary projection is shown in Figure 5.11. The earth and another planet, say Mars, are represented by the motions of points on circles of a size and inclination to represent the planetary orbits to scale. A rod or similar mechanism joining these two points carries an optical projector for the planetary image on the dome. The planetary orbits, though nearly circular, are in reality ellipses, so the motions are not correctly represented by uniform circular motions. The deviation of the fixed radius of a circle from the ellipse is not of great importance, but the nonuniform motion of the planet in the ellipse, because it accumulates from day to day, cannot be neglected. The linkwork shown in Figure 5.11 is used to approximate the nonuniform planetary motion. Note that this mechanism is not theoretically exact and possesses structural errors.

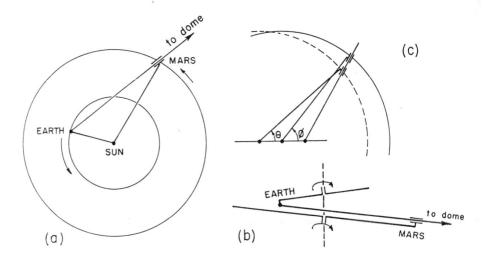

Figure 5.11. The principle employed in locating projected planetary images on the dome of the Zeiss Planetarium. The mechanism models the relative positions of the earth and a planet in space. At (c) is shown the simple link mechanism used to approximate the nonuniform motion of a planet in its elliptical path, ø, from a uniform circular motion, ϴ.

Its justification lies solely in the adequacy of its precision to the task at hand.

The art of approximating complex functions by simple mechanisms was elaborately developed during World War II by Antonin Svoboda (who later played a leading role in postwar developments of computers in Czechoslovakia). The purpose was to find very simple mechanisms that would produce solutions to complex problems in ballistics and gunnery sufficient for use in military equipment. Commonly, these did not attempt to simplify the mathematical description of the problems but attempted to fit approximate formulas to their solutions.

Planimeters

All the analog devices described thus far have been essentially geometric in nature. The output is dependent only on the present state of the inputs. Previous values of the inputs do not effect the output, and the devices therefore exhibit no memory of past events. We are well aware, however, that much of the power of digital computers stems from their memory. The same is true of analog devices, much of whose power stems from the discovery in the first half of the nineteenth century of mechanical embodiments of the mathematical function of integration—effectively involving a form of memory of past inputs.[1]

Integrating devices arose first as planimeters—instruments for measuring directly, by tracing the perimeter, the area enclosed by an irregular closed curve such as the boundary of a parcel of land on a map. The idea seems to have been first discovered by the Bavarian engineer Hermann in 1814 and was rediscovered by Tito Gonnella in Florence in 1824, but neither succeeded in having a satisfactory working model made. A further rediscovery by the Swiss, Oppikofer, led to successful manufacture by Ernst in Paris about 1836. In these instruments the integrating wheel moves on the surface of a cone, a principle rediscovered by Sang in 1851 and widely reported in the English literature.

Wetli in Zurich, in 1849, substituted a disc for the cone of the earlier planimeters, making the integration of negative-valued functions possible. The disc-and-wheel integrating mechanism used by Wetli, shown in Figures 5.12 and 5.13, was extensively used in Differential Analyzers in the 1930s and 1940s. In fact, any continuously adjustable, variable-speed drive mechanism can act as an integrator, so a wide variety of different forms exist. Wetli planimeters were manufactured by Starke in Vienna and later improved by Hansen in Gotha.

Figure 5.12. The principle of operation of the Wetli disk-and-wheel integrating mechanism. The dependent variable, y, determines the distance of the integrating wheel from the center of the disk. If the disk is rotated through an angle, Δx, then the integrating wheel is turned by

$\Delta z = [y\Delta x]/r.$

Hence, after a period of action,

$z = 1/r \int y \, dx.$

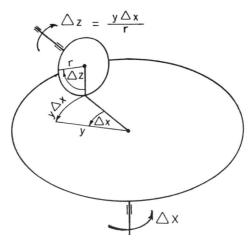

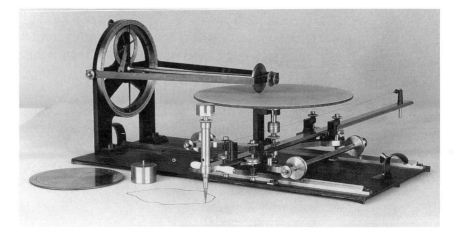

Figure 5.13. A Wetli planimeter (1849). In this planimeter a movement of the tracing point in the x-direction causes the disk to be rotated by means of a flexible wire. Movement in the y-direction causes the disk to be moved on a carriage with the tracing arm so that the integrating wheel is, in effect, displaced from the center of the disk. Courtesy Science Museum, London. Negative No. 3293.

A major step forward was the invention of the polar planimeter in 1856 by Jacob Amsler, then a student at Königsberg. In the Amsler planimeter the integrating wheel moves, by a combination of rolling and sliding motions, over the paper on which the area to be measured is drawn. The principle is shown in Figures 5.14 and 5.15. The simplicity, ease of use, and low price of the Amsler planimeter soon drove all older forms from the field and led to the manufacture of many thousands of the instruments in the nineteenth century—over twelve thousand by Amsler alone by 1884. Amsler-type planimeters are still being manufactured for their traditional uses in surveying, architecture, and engineering design. An important common usage was in the analysis of indicator diagrams to determine the efficiency of steam engines.

Although theoretically exact in its function, the Amsler planimeter is susceptible to faults that limit its precision in practice. From about 1880, several forms of "precision planimeters" were manufactured, particularly by Coradi in Zurich, to reduce these

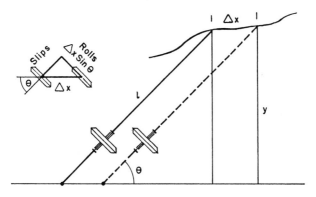

Figure 5.14. The principle of Amsler-type Planimeters. When the ordinate is y, the arm of length l is inclined at an angle $\theta = \sin^{-1}(y/l)$ to the x axis. If the arm translates a distance Δx in the direction of the x axis parallel to itself, the integrating wheel will turn about its axis and slide parallel to its axis. The turning will be through an angle

$$\Delta z = [\Delta x \sin \theta]/r = [y\Delta x]/[lr].$$

The total rotation of the integrating wheel in tracing around a closed curve will therefore be just

$$z = 1/[lr] \int y\, dx.$$

The integrating wheel will also be turned as the arm rotates about its pivot, but in tracing completely around a closed curve the arm will return to its initial position so the net effect of this will be zero. The path that the pivot follows is unimportant and in the Amsler planimeter is just a circle.

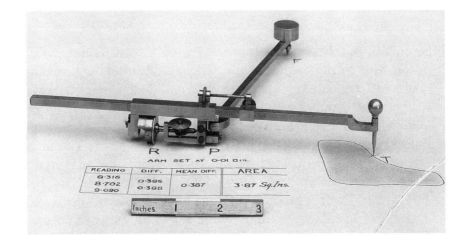

Figure 5.15. An Amsler planimeter. The arm length may be adjusted to alter the scale of units in which the record is made by the integrating wheel. Courtesy Science Museum, London. Negative No. 82.

errors, especially those arising from the motion of the integrating wheel over the unprepared paper surface. Most of these devices were superseded by the invention by Lang in 1894 of the compensating planimeter. In this form, the arms of the Amsler planimeter can be disposed in two roughly mirror-image ways when tracing an area. Averaging measurements made in these two configurations mitigate many of the errors.

A particularly simple and inexpensive form of planimeter, the Hatchet planimeter (named from its resemblance in one form to a hatchet), was developed from 1887. The principle is shown in Figure 5.16.

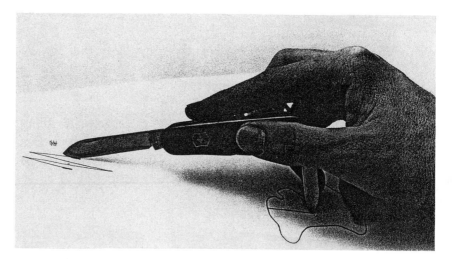

Figure 5.16. A serviceable planimeter of the hatchet type can be made with an ordinary penknife. The long blade is pressed to make an indentation in the paper. The outline of the irregularly shaped area is traced while keeping the short blade vertical and allowing the long blade to slide in the direction of its edge. The long blade is then pressed to make a second indentation. The area traced is just the length between the blades times the arc length moved sideways by the long blade. A scale for area can be engraved on one blade for measuring between the two indentations made in the paper. While eminently serviceable, the Hatchet planimeter is not a precision instrument. The mathematical analysis is complex and the result is not theoretically exact. The errors are minimized if the area is small, tracing starts near its center of gravity, and the results of clockwise and anticlockwise tracings are averaged.

An important generalization of the Amsler planimeter is the moment planimeter. An ordinary planimeter measures the area within a closed curve. By introducing additional integrator wheels that are geared so that their axes are rotated through two and three times the angle moved by the integrator arm, it is possible to measure the moment of inertia and other higher order moments of the area.[2] These moments are of considerable engineering importance, and the devices were widely used, particularly in ship design. Figure 5.17 shows a moment planimeter employing precision sphere and wheel integrators.

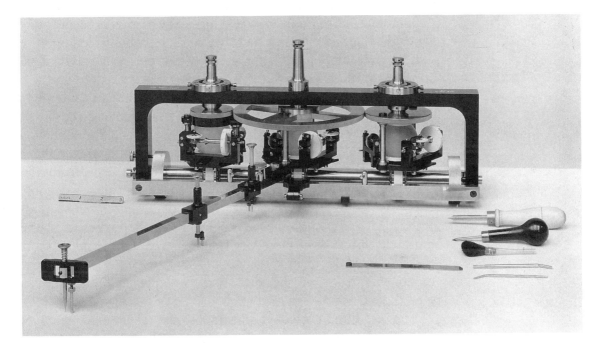

Figure 5.17. Moment planimeter designed by Hele-Shaw and manufactured by Coradi in Zurich. Integrating wheels moving over the paper are replaced by wheels moving over glass spheres for greater precision. Courtesy Science Museum, London. Negative No. 786.

The Work of Lord Kelvin

Although planimeters and their derivatives were of considerable practical importance, the importance of the mechanization of integration to other areas of mathematics was not immediately realized. It was William Thomson, later Lord Kelvin, who, in the 1870s, first grasped their wider significance. Most twentieth-century analog devices can be seen as realizations and direct developments of Kelvin's ideas.

Kelvin was led to the study of analog computing machinery from the need to predict tide heights in ports—an essential requisite to navigation in an era when dredging of channels was uncommon and in countries, such as England, where the tidal variation in water height is considerable and maritime trade was of such economic importance.

The tides are caused, primarily, by the periodic gravitational influences of the moon and the sun in their relative motions around the earth. The basic influences are diurnal, due to the earth's rotation, but additional influences of longer periods arise from such causes as the eccentricity of the earth's orbit around the sun and the inclination of the earth's axis. These basic influences are modified by the shape of the continental shelves and coastal estuaries. From the mathematical work of Fourier it was realized that the tide height could be represented by a series of sine functions of the appropriate periods for the lunar and solar influences, together with their harmonics. The amplitude and phase of these sine functions can be determined from the analysis of the records of tide gauges at each port. Once these components are known, the height of the water at any future time can be predicted.

The prediction process is simple in principle. A resolver mechanism (Figure 5.4) is set for the required amplitude and phase and driven at the appropriate rate for each component. The outputs of these are then added together, by a form of differential mechanism, to give a continuous record on a paper chart of the water height as a function of time. From this chart the times and heights of high and low water can be tabulated.

In Kelvin's *harmonic synthesizer* (Figure 5.18) the summation is performed by a wire and pulley system. Because the wire is not everywhere vertical the sine functions are slightly distorted, but the error introduced by this is small enough to be unimportant. Kelvin's *tide predictor* was completed by 1876. A second one was constructed

Figure 5.18. Kelvin's tide-predicting machine. Gearing from the drive handle is used to drive resolver mechanisms, which are set to generate sine functions of the required amplitude, phase, and periods. The components are added by a wire-and-pulleys system, and the resultant water height is recorded as a continuous curve on the paper roll. Tide tables are then prepared by reading the heights and times of maxima and minima of the curve. Courtesy Science Museum, London. Negative No. 86.

for the Indian government, and similar devices remained in use by all major maritime nations until recent times.

The determination of the amplitudes and phases of the components from the tide height records is more difficult and involves the evaluation, for each component, of integrals of the form

$$\int h(t)\, s(t)\, dt$$

where $h(t)$ is the record of tide height against time and $s(t)$ is a sine or cosine function of the period of the component sought. The evaluation of these integrals is a lengthy and tedious process by hand.

Kelvin used this principle as the basis of a harmonic analyzer in which he employed a form of integrator (the details of which are unimportant) devised by his brother James. The mechanism of this tide analyzer, completed in 1879, is shown in Figures 5.19 and 5.20. The integrating wheels are displaced by following the recorded tide height on a chart the forward motion of which is synchronized to the oscillation, backwards and forwards, of two discs representing sine and cosine functions for each required periodic component. The amplitude and phase of the component can be found from the final integrals shown by the integrating wheels. Kelvin's instrument has eleven integrators for five basic periodic components and the constant term. The harmonics are found by repeating the analysis with the chart record moved at one-half, one-third, and one-fourth of its normal rate.

In 1876, at the same time that he designed the harmonic analyzer, Kelvin discovered that integrator mechanisms could be used for the solution of differential equations.

In Kelvin's analysis any linear second order differential equation may be reduced to the form

$$d/dx \,(1/P(x)\ du/dx\,) = u.$$

If u_i is any function of x approximating the solution to the differential equation, then

$$u_{i+1} = \int P(x)\ (C - \int u_i\, dx)\, dx$$

is a closer approximation to a solution of the differential equation. This iterative formula, Kelvin realized, had basically the same form as the products in the tidal analysis and could be carried out by two

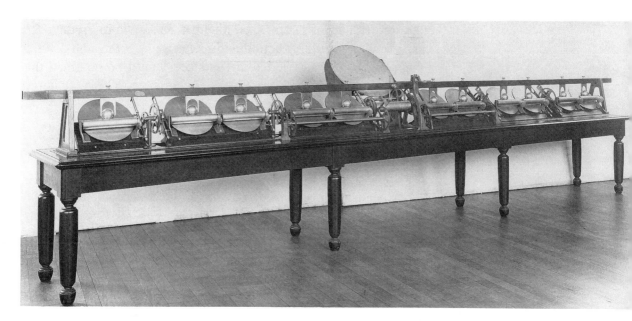

Figure 5.19. Kelvin's Harmonic Analyzer for Tides. Courtesy Science
Museum, London. Negative No. 86.

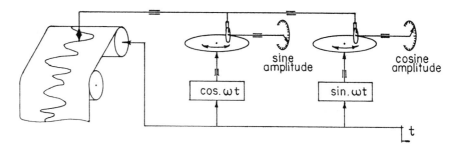

Figure 5.20. The principle of Kelvin's Harmonic Analyzer for Tides.
Kelvin converted the integral to the form
$$\int h(t)\, d\left(\int s(t)\, dt\right),$$
where the integral
$$\int s(t)\, dt$$
is just another sine or cosine function. These functions are easily
produced by resolver mechanisms, which rotate the disks of two
integrators backward and forward with the period of each tidal
component sought. The integrating wheels (balls in Kelvin's
design) are displaced by the recorded tide height, which is
obtained by tracing a chart record. The integrating wheels then
indicate the sine and cosine amplitudes, from which the amplitude
and phase of the component are easily found.

integrator mechanisms connected together, as shown in Figure 5.21. Thus, given any initial function and having it pass through a series of these mechanisms, a series of functions would be obtained that converge to a solution of the differential equation. The next step is best told in Kelvin's own words:

> So far I had gone and was satisfied, feeling I had done what I wished to do for many years. But then came a pleasing surprise. Complete agreement between the function fed into the double machine and that given out by it.... The motion of each will ... be necessarily a solution of [the differential equation]. Thus I was led to a conclusion which was quite unexpected; and it seems to me very remarkable that the general differential equation of the second order with variable coefficients may be rigorously, continuously, and in a single process solved by a machine.[3]

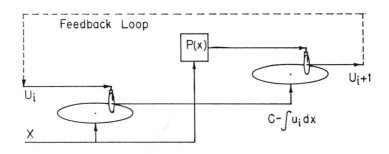

Figure 5.21. Kelvin's method for solving a linear differential equation of the second order. Given some approximation to the solution, the mechanism produces a closer approximation and the process can be applied iteratively, commencing with the newly found approximation. However, if the output and the input are connected together to form a feedback loop, the mechanism produces an exact solution to the differential equation in a single pass.

Kelvin here had discovered the basic feedback principle by which integrator mechanisms can be applied to the solution of differential equations. Although he generalized the principle to the case of any differential equation of any order, his mechanism could not be realized at the time. The basic difficulty is that the torque output from the wheel of an integrator is very slight and is inadequate to drive further integrating mechanisms. Kelvin's ideas had to wait another fifty years before they were realized by Vannevar Bush in his Differential Analyzer, which we discuss below.

In 1878, Kelvin also invented a machine for solving simultaneous equations, essentially similar to a machine developed by Wilbur in 1934, which we will also discuss shortly.

Scientific Instruments in the Twentieth Century

Kelvin's ideas on harmonic analysis and synthesis were widely copied, and many synthesizers were built following his general plan for both tidal and general harmonic work. Coradi of Zurich manufactured a harmonic analyzer similar in style to the moment planimeter in Figure 5.17, and a number of adaptations of conventional planimeters for this purpose were also made, but no more specialized devices similar to Kelvin's analyzer appear to have been built.

An important application of the harmonic synthesizer to finding the roots of polynomials was made and embodied in a special-purpose machine, the Isograph, at Bell Telephone Laboratories in 1937—a method copied on other harmonic synthesizers, including those used in the design of electrical filters.[4]

Kelvin had proposed in 1878 a method for the solution of sets of simultaneous linear equations that was implemented by Wilbur at MIT in 1934. Such equations arise in many areas of engineering design, and one application envisaged by Babbage for the Analytical Engine had been the determination, by their means, of the orbital parameters of comets. The relative magnitudes of the variables are represented in the machine by the angles through which metal plates are turned about horizontal axes. A system of wires and pulleys is used to constrain the motions of the plates for each equation in the set, as shown in Figure 5.22. This system is repeated for each equation in the set and the plates can then only take up relative positions that represent the solution. If an approximate set of solutions is found by the machine, they may be used to find a more accurate set by an iterative process using the same machine settings except for the constant terms. The machine is, in practice, therefore capable of providing almost any desired degree of accuracy in the solutions.

Electrical technology was also used in a limited way in analog

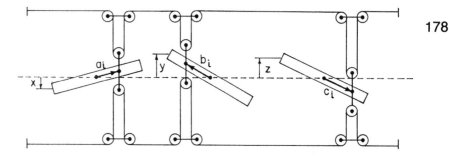

Figure 5.22. The principle of the Kelvin/Wilbur machine for solving
simultaneous linear equations. The two wires running over the
system of pulleys constrain the movement of the tilting plates so
that $a_i x + b_i y + c_i z = 0$. An exactly similar arrangement is used
to constrain the plates for the other equations in the set. When all
the constraints are present, the relative tilts possible for the plates
give a solution to the set of equations.

computing devices from World War I, but before World War II little
progress had been made in abstracting these devices to the
representation of mathematical functions. Rather, electrical circuits
were assembled in direct analogy to the system under study—each
component of the system was modeled by an electrical component
that had the same functional behavior in the electrical domain as the
component in the original system domain.

An important series of machines of this type were the Network
Analyzers developed by General Electric and Westinghouse for the
simulation of electrical power supply networks. The DC (Direct
Current) Network Analyzer of 1925 used only resistive components
and could, therefore, only model steady-state behavior. The AC
(Alternating Current) Network Analyzer of 1929 used reactive
impedances and could be used to study both phase and magnitude in
alternating current power networks. Later machines could also
exhibit the transient (short-term) behavior of a network in response
to a surge due to equipment switching or failure. Similar electrical
components and circuit techniques were used by Mallock in an
electrical instrument for the solution of simultaneous equations in
1933.

Another important technique in the 1930s and 1940s was the use
of electrolytic tanks, resistive papers, and elastic membranes to model
continuous two-dimensional systems. In particular they were used to
determine the electrical field potentials in the vicinity of the complex
grids and electrodes in vacuum tubes as an aid in their design. These
tubes, precursors of transistors and other modern electronic devices,

were widely used in radio and radar equipment. The height at any point of an elastic rubber membrane, for example, would represent the electrical potential at the corresponding point in the tube. Anodes, cathodes, and other electrodes would be represented by bars and rods that fixed the height of the membrane in the appropriate places. The path followed by a small steel ball rolling on the membrane would then represent the path followed by an electron in the tube. These techniques suffered the disadvantage, however, that they could not easily model the space charge effect on the potential distribution created by other electrons in motion in the space between the electrodes.

Although there were many other developments in the first half of the twentieth century akin to those we have just described, they were all of an ad hoc nature and did not lead to any general synthesis or to the emergence of a general class of machines, except for the Differential Analyzer and the Gunnery Computers to which we now turn.

The Differential Analyzer

Vannevar Bush at MIT was concerned through the late-1920s and the 1930s with the development of machines to aid the calculations with continuous functions required by design engineers. (The Wilbur machine for solving simultaneous equations was part of this work.)

Bush's first machine, an Integraph used for the integration of the product of two functions, was described in 1927. The functions are entered by following curves with pointers attached to linear potentiometers—variable resistances whose voltage or current output is proportional to the movement of the potentiometer. The integral of the product of the outputs from the two potentiometers is formed by a commercial electrical watt-hour meter. The result of this integration is followed up by a relay and servomotor system and is used to plot the integral as a continuous curve. In this way the machine can evaluate integrals of the form

$$F(x) = \int f(x)g(x)\, dx,$$

a special case of which are those same integrals for Fourier analysis as handled by Kelvin's harmonic analyzer—ones of great practical importance in electrical engineering.

Bush realized, as Kelvin had, that by making one of the inputs follow the output (i.e., by adopting a feedback or "back coupling" principle) the machine could solve differential equations which are equivalent to

$$f(x) = \int f(x)g(x)\, dx.$$

The capabilities of the machine were extended by adding a linkage multiplier (similar to Figure 5.5) and a second integrator of the disc and wheel type (Figure 5.13) with a relay and servomotor follow-up. This machine was capable of solving most second-order differential equations of practical importance to an accuracy of 1-2%.

Bush's generalization of his integraph to the solution of a wide range of differential equations depended on the adoption of the capstan type of torque amplifier developed by Nieman for power steering in motor vehicles. The principle of this device is shown in Figure 5.23. The use of torque amplifiers meant that the small torque available from the friction wheel of a Wetli disc-and-wheel integrator

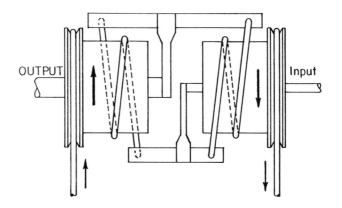

Figure 5.23. The Nieman capstan type of torque amplifier. The two drums are rotated continuously in opposite directions by an electric motor. Whenever the input shaft moves, its arm tightens the band on one drum and loosens it on the other so that the friction on the drum causes the output to be turned with the input but with a much greater torque. In the Differential Analyzer the output drives the input of another torque amplifier to give a total torque amplification of about 10,000 times.

could be used to drive a substantial load of other calculating machinery. It was the absence of any form of torque amplifier that had prevented Kelvin from making further progress in this direction.

Bush's Differential Analyzer, as the new machine was called, consists of a set of integrators, input and output tables for tracing and plotting continuous curves, and a very flexible system of shafting—the bus shafts—arranged to enable the input of any mechanism to be connected to the output of any other, as required by the problem being solved. Gearing could be included to give any prescribed ratio between bus shafts, and differential gears (Figure 5.8) enable shaft rotations to be added and subtracted. One bus shaft is driven by a motor to represent the independent variable. A typical Differential Analyzer is shown in Figure 5.24.

Figure 5.24. A Differential Analyzer, similar to Bush's original design, developed in the Courtaulds Laboratories. The integrators are on the left with a two-stage torque amplifier and a handle for setting the initial conditions into the integrators. On the right are the input and output tables. The bus shafting is in the center. Courtesy Science Museum, London. Negative No. 272/74.

To understand how the machine was used let us consider the solution of the differential equation for an object projected into the air in a constant gravitational field and with an air resistance proportional to its velocity. The differential equation is

$$d^2y/dt^2 + k \, dy/dt + g = 0.$$

Suppose the rotation of one bus shaft represents

$$d^2y/dt^2$$

and the independent variable shaft represents t. With one integrator we can produce an output on another bus shaft of

$$\int d^2y/dt^2 \, dt = dy/dt$$

and integrating this again we produce

$$\int dy/dt \, dt = y.$$

The constant g can be represented by a shaft, appropriately preset, while the constant k is introduced by an appropriate gear ratio. Writing the differential equation in the form

$$d^2y/dt^2 = - [\, k \, dy/dt + g \,]$$

exhibits the feedback relationship necessary to complete the setup shown in Figure 5.25.

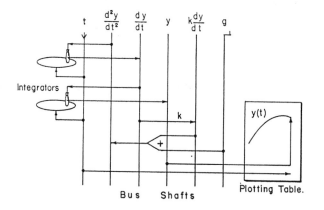

Figure 5.25. Sample setup of the Differential Analyzer for solving
  the differential equation
    $d^2y/dt^2 + k \, dy/dt + g = 0.$

The equation just described can be solved by analytical methods. If, however, the gravitational field is a function of height, $g(y)$, and the air resistance is a general function of velocity, $f(dy/dt)$ known only empirically, then no analytical solution can be found. However, the differential equation is still readily solved on the Differential Analyzer as shown in Figure 5.26.

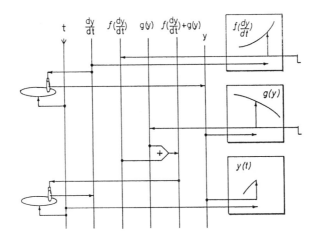

Figure 5.26. Differential Analyzer setup for solving the equation
$$d^2y/dt^2 + f(dy/dt) + g(y) = 0$$
in the form
$$dy/dt = - \int [f(dy/dt) + g(y)] \, dt,$$
with the functions f and g provided from input tables.

In that the Differential Analyzer can be set up to solve any arbitrary differential equation and this is the basic means of describing dynamic behavior in all fields of engineering and the physical sciences, it is applicable to a vast range of problems. In the 1930s, problems as diverse as atomic structure, transients in electrical networks, timetables of railway trains, and the ballistics of shells, were successfully solved. The Differential Analyzer was, without doubt, the first general-purpose computing machine for engineering and scientific use.

Bush's original Differential Analyzer provided six integrators, three input tables, an output table, and a manually operated multiplier. It could achieve an accuracy near 1 in 10^3 (0.1%). Bush's ideas were soon copied, first by Douglas Hartree in Manchester. Hartree made a demonstration model using mainly components from the Meccano construction toy system, which yielded an accuracy of about 1 in 10^2 (1%) and proved surprisingly useful in calculations of atomic structure, before embarking on the construction of a large-scale and more accurate machine. In total, about nine major Differential Analyzers were in operation before World War II, and at least as many again were constructed during the 1940s.

Much of the art in using the Differential Analyzer lay in molding the equations to suit the forms available on the machine. This led, in particular, to demands for additional integrators for a variety of auxiliary purposes. In the setup of Figure 5.25, for example, the constant k is introduced as a gear ratio. If it were desired to investigate the dependence of the solution on this constant, it would be necessary to change the gear ratio before each run of the machine. A much more convenient approach would be to set the constant k on a bus shaft and to use an integrator as a constant ratio drive that is simply varied between runs.

A more profound application arises when multiplication occurs. Instead of using a special multiplying mechanism, two integrators, connected as suggested by the formula

$$uv = \int u dv + \int v du,$$

can often be employed. It was a great strength of the Differential Analyzer, not found in later electronic analog computers, that integration could be performed with respect to any variable represented by a shaft in the setup.

In a similar manner, a sine or cosine function, perhaps for use as a forcing function when studying the behavior of a car suspension on a rough road, can be introduced by solving the auxiliary differential equation

$$d^2z/dt^2 = -kz$$

as part of the setup. Much ingenuity was expended in finding simple and economical setups for a wide variety of functions occurring in differential equations.

Hartree successfully extended the use of the Differential Analyzer to problems involving a time-delayed function (by having an input pointer trace an output curve somewhat behind the output pen) and, with more limited success, to the solution of some partial differential equations arising in heat flow and similar problems.

Bush had the last word in performance of Differential Analyzers when, in 1942, a new Differential Analyzer was produced at MIT. In this machine an accuracy of 1 in 10^5 in the components was sought to achieve better than 1 in 10^4 (0.01%) accuracy in the solution of differential equations—about ten times greater accuracy than possible with any other machine. Variables were transmitted in this system not by shaft rotations but by electrical signals derived from capacitive encoders on the integrating wheels, which were reconstituted to mechanical motions by servomotors as required. The interconnection of the components was determined by a system of relays, themselves controlled by information read from punched tapes. The setting of initial conditions in the integrators, etc., was also controlled by punched tape so that no manual actions were required to set a problem into the machine. It was even possible to run separate problems simultaneously in different parts of the machine. The setup task which had previously taken hours or days now required only minutes, for the preparation of the tapes could be carried out away from the machine. In this way, the throughput of the Differential Analyzer was greatly increased.

Despite the sophistication of Bush's second Differential Analyzer, simpler, fully mechanical machines similar to his first design continued to be made into the 1950s because of their much lower cost. Differential Analyzers were finally superseded by electrical analog computers of generally lower precision, and later by digital computers, because the precision mechanical work required in the construction of a Differential Analyzer made them prohibitively expensive. But the mathematical flexibility of the Differential Analyzer was never matched by electrical analog computers and originally only with difficulty by digital computers. Figure 5.27 shows an ingenious postwar development in which mechanical components are interconnected by flexible steel tapes rather than bus shafts.

Figure 5.27. An experimental flight simulator for the Viscount aircraft (ca. 1950). Mechanical analog computing components are interconnected by flexible steel tapes running over pulleys to combine the accuracy of mechanical computation with the flexibility of interconnection of electrical analog systems. Courtesy Science Museum, London. Negative No. 306/73.

Gunnery Computers

Differential Analyzers have considerable historical importance as the first general-purpose automatic computing devices for scientific and engineering work. However, because of their cost, they were never very common nor their use widespread.

In terms of practical use, mechanical analog computing devices played their most dominant role in military applications, particularly for the aiming of guns and other weapons from moving platforms or at moving targets. Although inherently special-purpose in nature, gunnery computers reached a high degree of sophistication because of the mathematical complexity of gunnery problems and the urgent military need. Most importantly, the need to solve these problems continuously in real time, with a delay no greater than a small fraction of a second, made other forms of calculation of little use and provided a secure niche for analog computers until well into the 1970s.

Military analog computers had their origin before World War I in naval gunnery to control the aiming of guns against moving targets. Because the speed of ships is small compared with the velocity of shells, simple linear approximations generally suffice, and the main task of the mechanism is to continuously keep track of the range and bearing of the target. Such computing mechanisms were developed in England by Pollen and Dreyer. In America, Hannibal Ford introduced in his gunnery computers an integrator employing two balls squeezed between an integrator disc and an output cylinder. Because no sliding movement is required in its operation the components of this integrator can be squeezed together with substantial pressure, so the torque output is much greater than that of a Wetli disc-and-wheel integrator and is adequate for most purposes without torque amplification. Although the accuracy of the disc-and-ball integrator is not high, it formed the basis of most military applications because of its simplicity, robustness, and convenience.

Rapid development of gunnery computers occurred in the 1920s in response to the substantial military threat from aircraft, as demonstrated in the final years of World War I. In essence, the antiaircraft gunnery problem is straightforward. The aircraft is tracked with instruments to determine its present position. From a continuous series of observations the course and speed of the aircraft can then be found. The course is extrapolated for the time of flight of the shell, assuming the course and speed to remain constant, to give the aircraft's future position when the shell reaches it. A feedback loop is involved because the time of flight of the shell depends on the future position of the aircraft.

The problem is made difficult by practical considerations. The shell must be aimed, and timed by a fuse mechanism, to explode within about 30 feet (10 meters) of the aircraft, which, if flying at high altitude, might travel 1 mile (1.6 kilometers) or more during the flight of the shell. No very effective range-finding instruments were available until the introduction of radar at the start of World War II.

The time to locate the aircraft, set up the calculation, and start firing the guns was short—about thirty seconds—and thereafter the computer had to continuously provide updated firing data to the guns.

Figure 5.28. (a) and (b) The Vickers antiaircraft gun Predictor (ca. 1930).

The first successful antiaircraft gun computer, the Vickers Predictor (Figure 5.28), was developed by the English armament manufacturing firm of Vickers in 1924 and entered service in 1928, well before the invention of the Differential Analyzer. The general arrangement of the mechanism, which uses polar coordinates to achieve the necessary accuracy, is shown in Figure 5.29. Linkage mechanisms (like the resolver of Figure 5.4) were extensively used in the design, and disc-and-ball integrators drove the balance dials. Operators were required to enter deflections to keep the dials, and hence the equations, balanced and to enter ballistic data by following curves on drum charts. These operators acted, in effect, as servomechanisms, and the action of the predictor was entirely

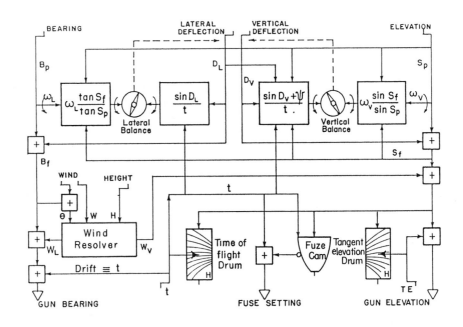

Figure 5.29. General arrangement of calculation in the Vickers antiaircraft gun, Predictor. The calculations were done in polar coordinates to achieve the required accuracy, but the basic equations the Predictor was required to solve were then quite complex:

$$\sin D_L / t = \omega_L \, [\tan S_f / \tan S_p]$$

and

$$[\sin D_V + \psi]/t = \omega_V \, [\sin S_f / \sin S_p],$$

where

$$\psi = (1 - \cos D_L) \sin S_p \cos S_f.$$

mechanical, even to the extent of employing a clockwork gramophone motor to drive the integrator discs. An antiaircraft gun predictor employing Cartesian coordinates was introduced by Sperry Gyroscope Co. in the early 1930s, and similar devices were developed for naval purposes. Some five to ten thousand such instruments were used in World War II.

The evolution of gunnery computers seems to have been completely independent of the evolution of civilian Differential Analyzers until near the outbreak of World War II. During the war the Differential Analyzers were taken over for military purposes, principally for the solution of the differential equations of shell trajectories in the preparation of ballistic firing tables. Development of gunnery computers in World War II rapidly responded to the greatly improved capabilities of aircraft. This involved the use of much more sophisticated mathematical principles in the gunnery computers, such as the autobalance mechanism sketched in Figure 5.30, and the extensive use of servomechanisms to reduce the requirements for manual operators and increase the accuracy of the results. These developments were influenced by the mathematical techniques used in designing setups for Differential Analyzers and in turn influenced further such developments after the war.

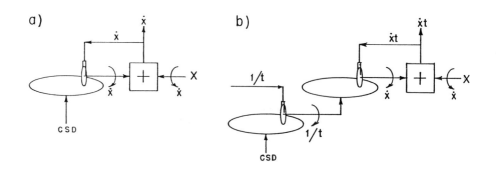

Figure 5.30. The principle of the auto-balance mechanism employed in the Sperry Predictor. In diagram (a) is shown the interconnection of an integrator to act as a differentiator. The input is a shaft position representing a position coordinate, x, of the aircraft. This shaft turns at a rate x as shown by the curved arrow annotation. If the integrating wheel is displaced from the center of the disk driven from a constant speed drive (CSD) by an amount x, then the integrating wheel will rotate at a rate x. The input and the output from the integrating wheel are subtracted in a differential. If the two rates are not equal, the output of the differential will move the integrating wheel across the disk to restore the balance. This mechanism does not respond instantaneously to a change in the input rate but approaches it exponentially with a time lag dependent on the gear ratios and other constants of the mechanism. By driving the disk at a rate $1/t$, where t is the time of flight of the shell, the output is made xt as shown in the diagram (b).

Many other types of mechanical analog computing mechanisms were developed for military uses in World War II. Most common were the bomb sight computers used in aircraft for aiming at ground and ship targets, and the computers for directing defensive guns on bombers against attacking fighter aircraft. The linkage computing mechanisms, of very simple construction but very sophisticated design, developed by Svoboda at MIT (described above) deserve particular mention.

After World War II, designs of mechanical gunnery computers were greatly elaborated and their use expanded to many military applications. They continued to be developed into the 1960s and beyond, and remained in active military service well into the 1970s. Some, such as the 1943 mechanical analog computers directing the heavy guns of the USS *Ohio*-class battleships, are still in active service. Later devices were frequently a hybrid of mechanical and electrical analog devices, particularly in avionics applications.

Analog computers yielded only slowly to electronic digital devices. The exact pattern is difficult to follow because of security restrictions, but until recent times the major applications of digital computers appear restricted to command post and other tactical control systems, rather than direct weapon control. The major reason for the demise of analog systems was the gradual replacement of guns by missiles and other self-guided weapons, for which no accurate aiming system was necessary, although the missiles themselves frequently contained analog guidance systems.

Thus, although mechanical analog computing devices played only a small, but important, role in scientific developments in the twentieth century, they played a dominant role in military computing for fifty to sixty years and were very extensively applied.

Electrical Analog Computers

World War II produced remarkable technological advances in many areas of human endeavor but in no area were the consequences so profound as in electronics. In analog computation the war resulted in the emergence of an electrical computing technology to rival the earlier mechanical technology.

This was stimulated in no small part by the scarcity of the skilled labor required to manufacture and maintain precision mechanical systems. The military, for example, was largely satisfied with existing mechanical gunnery computers. It was not until near the end of the war that electronic or hybrid analog devices began to offer functional advantages over their mechanical predecessors, with the replacement of human operators by more reliable servomechanisms and the gradual direct coupling of inputs from radar systems.

One single project, the development of the M-9 antiaircraft gunnery computer by the Bell Telephone Laboratories, shaped the future of electrical analog technology in a way even more significant than the ENIAC did for digital technology.

The basic computing elements of the M-9 were nonlinear potentiometers made by winding fine resistance wire on nonlinear formers. With these the output voltage is not directly proportional to the position of the input but can be made proportional to geometric or ballistic functions occurring in the gunnery problem. By making the height of the former proportional to the derivative of the desired function any reasonable monotonic function can be generated. This idea can be traced back to experimental antiaircraft gunnery computers in the last years of World War I. The principle was rediscovered in the Bell Labs about 1940.

The use of potentiometers as computing elements suffers one great fault that had made previous devices unsuccessful. If the output of the potentiometer drives other circuitry, the current drawn distorts the function generated by the potentiometer so that the accuracy of the computation is seriously compromised.

This difficulty was overcome in the M-9 by having each potentiometer drive an amplifier with high-input impedance to isolate the output of the potentiometer from the input of succeeding circuits. These amplifiers were of high gain (about 10,000 power) but connected in a feedback arrangement so that the output of the amplifier was continuously compared with its input. In this way the output was made insensitive to any fluctuations in the gain of the amplifier. This arrangement is called an "operational amplifier" and was developed by Lovell at Bell for the M-9. The same idea had been independently discovered by Philbrick in 1938. A similar feedback loop was used to control the servomotors that drive the inputs of the potentiometers.

An operational amplifier can be used to perform a wide range of computing functions by suitably arranging the feedback circuit. Some simple arrangements typical of those used in the M-9 are shown in Figure 5.31. After the war operational amplifiers became the basis of

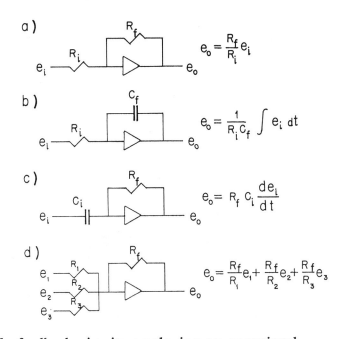

a)

$$e_o = \frac{R_f}{R_i} e_i$$

b)

$$e_o = \frac{1}{R_i C_f} \int e_i \, dt$$

c)

$$e_o = R_f C_i \frac{de_i}{dt}$$

d)

$$e_o = \frac{R_f}{R_1} e_1 + \frac{R_f}{R_2} e_2 + \frac{R_f}{R_3} e_3$$

Figure 5.31. Simple feedback circuits employing an operational amplifier as (a) and isolating amplifier and scale changer; (b) an integrator; (c) a differentiator; and (d) an adder. Differentiation is normally avoided because of its sensitivity to noise in the input. More elaborate functions can be obtained with more complex feedback circuits.

electrical analog computers and were interconnected, as shown in Figure 5.32, to solve differential equations in an analogous manner to the setup of Differential Analyzers. However, although Differential Analyzers required a high-precision shafting system for interconnection and high-precision mechanical components, the operational amplifiers could be simply and inexpensively interconnected by wiring. Because of their low cost, and despite their generally lower accuracy, electrical analog computers became enormously popular in the 1950s for solving the wide range of engineering and scientific problems that were suitable for the Differential Analyzer. One logical deficiency of electrical analog computers that needs mention is the fact that integration and differentiation can only be performed with respect to time, so that many of the techniques for setting up equations on the Differential Analyzer are inapplicable.

Figure 5.32. An electrical analog computer setup, analogous to the
  Differential Analyzer setups of Figs. 5.25 and 5.26 for solving
  the differential equation
  $$d^2y/dt^2 + k\, dy/dt + g = 0$$
  in the form
  $$dy/dt = -\int [k\, dy/dt + g]\, dt.$$

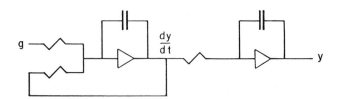

As in the M-9, electrical analog computers used potentiometers
for generating complex functions. These potentiometers were moved
by servomotors directed by electronic amplifiers. Multiplication of
two variables is a typical function normally performed in this way.
Much ingenuity was expended on ways to utilize electrical analog
computers most effectively.[5]

Although the direct current type of electrical analog computer just
described became the standard type for laboratory use in the 1950s
and 1960s, it had serious competition from alternating current devices
in military and aviation applications. AC has some technical
advantages. For example, trigonometric functions can be readily
generated by the inductive coupling of one coil turned at an angle to
another as shown in Figure 5.33.

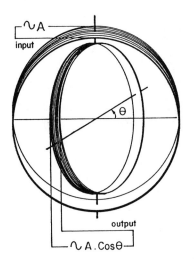

Figure 5.33. The principle of the AC electrical resolver.

Motorlike devices well suited to this purpose had been widely developed during World War II for the remote transmission of shaft angles under the name of Selsyns or Magslips. Analog computer systems assembled from such components were relatively small and light and were extensively used in the 1950s and 1960s in military and civilian aircraft systems. Frequently they were hybridized with some mechanical analog computing components. As noted above, many such systems remained in use well into the 1970s.

Conclusion

There are two fundamentally different ways in which a numerical value can be represented in a calculating device. In an analog device a direct proportion is established between the quantity represented and the position of a sliding or rotating part in a mechanical system or the voltage in an electrical circuit. Conceptually, the mechanism can take on any value in a given range. In a digital device each part can take on one of only a finite set of states, and a group of similar devices is necessary to represent a number as a string of digits in some number system.

Any mechanical or electrical device is, in practice, subject to disturbing influences, conveniently called "noise." If a digital device is disturbed by a small amount, no error in its indication will arise. In a mechanical device a spring detent will restore a wheel to its correct position. In an electronic circuit an amplifier, such as is present in the output of any logic gate, will restore any disturbed voltage to defined and well-separated discrete ranges. Digital systems can, in practice, be made immune to the effects of noise and a number can be represented to any arbitrarily high precision by a large enough group of similar digital devices.

An analog device, in contrast, has no noise immunity. If its state is disturbed, the new state represents a perfectly valid value of the variable, and the mechanism can in no way distinguish the new state from the original. The precision that can be achieved in an analog computer is, therefore, entirely limited by how small the noise can be kept. High precision, whether in the machining of mechanical parts, the manufacture of electronic components, or the isolation of a circuit from external electromagnetic influences, is always difficult and expensive to obtain. Therefore, although a precision near 1 part in 10^3 (0.1%) is, with care, readily enough obtained in an analog device, 1 in 10^4 (0.01%) is difficult and expensive, and 1 in 10^5 (0.001%) is rarely obtained. As an example, a simple 25 centimeter, straight slide rule yields a precision of about 1 in 300, but to achieve 1 in 10^4 a scale length of about 10 meters and an elaborate construction, such as the Fullers helical slide rule or the Thatchers grid iron slide rule, is necessary.

Counterbalancing the limited precision of analog devices is their general simplicity of form and consequent economy of manufacture. In a digital device, a large group of parts is needed to represent a number. Only addition of numbers is commonly available as a digital function. To calculate a sine, for example, we must usually evaluate a power series—with the multiplications this implies—carried out, in effect, by a series of additions. Evaluation of a sine function in a digital system is, therefore, both complex and relatively very slow compared with an analog system (Figures 5.4 and 5.33).

In practice, two further characteristics distinguish analog and digital devices, although a few exceptions can be found. Digital devices, such as a mechanical calculator or an electronic digital computer, are usually general-purpose devices that can readily be adapted to carry out a wide range of tasks. If a digital device can calculate a sine function, for example, it is usually easy to adapt it to calculate a logarithm or Bessel function. An analog mechanism for the sine function, however, would be no use at all for a logarithm.

For this reason, analog devices are normally composed of a number of independent parts each designed to perform a single, distinct part of a calculation. Because of their independence these parts can all act simultaneously in parallel with one another. Analog devices are, therefore, well suited to real-time applications in which the calculation must keep step with events in the external world. In contrast, digital systems typically reuse a single calculating unit sequentially for each step in a calculation, so that the speed is reduced as the complexity of the calculation increases.

The earliest calculating aids, the counting table and abacus, were digital, as they demanded very little in manufacturing skill yet combined a generous degree of precision with simple and effective use. Napier's invention of logarithms reduced multiplication to the simpler operation of addition and made possible the slide rule, a simple yet very effective analog device in which only a limited precision was required. Mechanical digital calculating devices first became widely available late in the nineteenth century when improved manufacturing techniques made the multitude of components required available at an economical price. Their limited speed of action effectively restricted these calculators to commercial calculations involving only simple addition operations.

Through the first half of the twentieth century, mechanical analog devices were developed extensively, particularly to handle the real-time calculations required in military applications. World War II brought the electronic technology that first made it possible for digital devices to operate at sufficient speed to perform higher mathematical functions than addition, at a speed competitive with even slow mechanical analog devices. The same technology also made possible improved analog devices that competed effectively with digital devices in many areas until well through the 1960s. It was the remarkable cost reductions of electronic digital devices in the 1970s that finally enabled them to supplant analog devices as the dominant technology for calculation.

Notes

1. In that integration is fundamentally a concept of the calculus, we must have some recourse to higher mathematics in the remainder of this chapter. Where possible, however, we have confined this to notes and figure captions. The other fundamental concept of the calculus is differentiation. This has very little application in mechanical devices—while an integrator tends to average out any small random errors in its input, a differentiator tends to accentuate them.

2. By setting the additional integrating wheels at angles of
   $$\pi/2 - 2\alpha \text{ and } 3\alpha,$$
   the moments
   $$y^2\, dx \text{ and } y^3\, dx$$
   can be found by using the trigonometric identities
   $$\sin^2\alpha = 1/2 - 1/2(\cos 2\alpha)$$
   $$\sin^3\alpha = 3/4 \sin\alpha - 1/4 \sin 3\alpha.$$

3. Thompson W. [Lord Kelvin], *Treatise on Natural Philosophy, Vol. 1* (Cambridge: Cambridge University Press, 1890), 498.

4. The method is based on De Moivre's theorem for complex numbers. If
$$z = r(\cos\theta + j\sin n\theta)$$
then
$$z^n = r^n(\cos n\theta + j\sin n\theta).$$
Given a polynomial
$$f(z) = a_n z^n + \ldots + a_1 z + a_0$$
we then have
$$f(z) = (a_n r^n \cos n\theta + \ldots + a_1 r \cos\theta + a_0 +$$
$$j\,(a_n r^n \sin n\theta + \ldots + a_1 r \sin\theta).$$

Both the real and imaginary parts are easily formed by a harmonic synthesizer for any given value of r. If both parts are plotted simultaneously in the complex plane, the result is a closed curve that circles the origin exactly as many times as there are roots of the polynomial with their modulus less than r. The roots can, therefore, be found by systematically varying r and replotting.

5. For example, if a circuit is available to form the square of a variable, then multiplication can be reduced to addition by taking advantage of the quarter-squares formula
$$ab = 1/4\,[(a + b)^2 - (a - b)^2].$$

Further Reading

Crank, J. *The Differential Analyzer*. Longmans, Green, 1947. The only textbook on this subject. It includes a detailed account of the practical aspects of using the Differential Analyzer.

Fifer, S. *Analogue Computations*. New York: McGraw-Hill, 1961. This is mainly devoted to electrical analog computers, but contains an excellent chapter on the Differential Analyzer.

Hartree, D. R. *Calculating Instruments and Machines*. Urbana: University of Illinois Press, 1953. Reprinted. Los Angeles and Cambridge, Mass.: Tomash Publishers and MIT Press, 1984. The first part of this book is devoted to differential analyzers and other analog instruments.

Horsburgh, E. M. *Handbook of the Napier Tercentenary Celebration or Modern Instruments and Methods of Calculation*. 1914. Reprinted for the *Charles Babbage Institute Reprint Series*. Los Angeles: Tomash Publishers, 1982. This volume contains an excellent description of mathematical instruments until 1914.

King, H. C. *Geared to the Stars*. Toronto: University of Toronto Press, 1978. A detailed history of the evolution of planetariums, orreries, and astronomical clocks.

Murray, F.J. *Mathematical Machines, Vol. II, Analog Devices*. New York: Columbia University Press, 1961. A well-known and very detailed account of scientific analog computing devices until 1960.

Svoboda, A. *Computing Mechanisms and Linkages*. New York: McGraw-Hill, 1948. The classic text on wartime work on the approximation of functions by simple mechanical linkages.

Chapter 6

Relay Calculators

Introduction

C harles Babbage had planned to power his Analytical Engine with a steam engine—steam being the only feasible prime mover available in the 1830s. In that same decade, however, others were making discoveries that led to the electric motor: a source of motive power more compact, cleaner, quieter, and most of all, much more flexible than steam. By the early twentieth century, calculators were just one of many machines that were powered by electricity.

But electricity could do more than replace the steam engine or human arm as a source of power; it could also represent the numbers themselves that a calculator handles. Electric circuits could replace the cams, pins, gears, and levers that actually do the computation. Hollerith's electric tabulators took advantage of this property, and we have already seen how the rival Powers system, developed after 1911 to compete with Hollerith, suffered in comparison because it used electricity only for motive power.

By the 1930s, a number of inventors recognized that the ability (as well as the power) offered by electric circuits allowed one to build a machine that could not only do arithmetic, but also direct a complex sequence of calculations automatically. That, of course, had been Babbage's dream, and by 1945 that dream had come true. It came true by combining traditional mechanical calculator architecture with

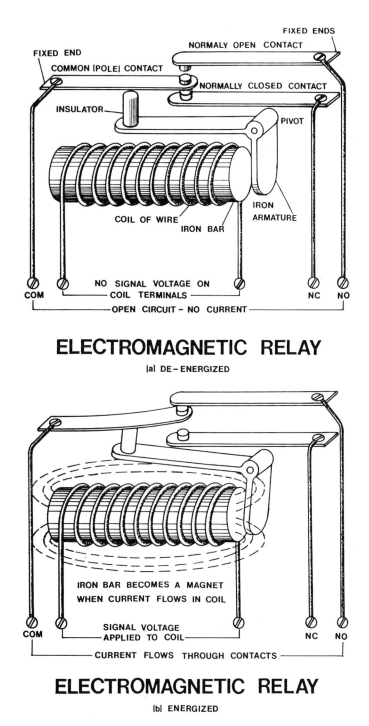

FIXED ENDS
NORMALY OPEN CONTACT
FIXED END
COMMON (POLE) CONTACT
NORMALLY CLOSED CONTACT
INSULATOR
PIVOT
IRON
ARMATURE
COIL OF WIRE
IRON BAR
NO SIGNAL VOLTAGE ON
COIL TERMINALS
COM
NC   NO
OPEN CIRCUIT - NO CURRENT

ELECTROMAGNETIC RELAY

(a) DE - ENERGIZED

IRON BAR BECOMES A MAGNET
WHEN CURRENT FLOWS IN COIL
COM
SIGNAL VOLTAGE
APPLIED TO COIL
NC   NO
CURRENT FLOWS THROUGH CONTACTS

ELECTROMAGNETIC RELAY

(b) ENERGIZED

Figure 6.1. (a) Typical relay used in telephone switching. The cylinder in front is the magnet; behind are the contacts. (b) Simple relay action. Drawings: Edwin Collen.

electric circuits and motors—a combination that allowed one to build a more complex and more powerful system that maintained the reliability and precision of simpler calculators.

Electromagnetic Relays as Computing Devices

Besides the electric motor which provided power, the key device of electromechanical calculators was the relay. A relay is a switch whose contacts are actuated by an electric current acting through an electromagnet. The device was originally developed to relay the dots and dashes of the Morse telegraph over long distances. (By having the original Morse signal activate a relay before it became too weak, one could transmit a message much farther—across the North American continent by the 1860s.)

Relays of this type usually have two switching states, with one activated by sending current through the magnet, the other activated by a return spring. It is basically a binary device (on or off), although one magnet can switch several contacts simultaneously. Typical relays may have up to ten sets of contacts switched by a magnet (Figure 6.1).

The telephone industry was also an early user of relays, but for a different purpose, namely switching. Telephone signals are not composed of discrete dots and dashes, like the telegraph, so they cannot be repeated by relay circuits for long distance transmission. But the telephone system can use a cascade of relays to allow an individual to select any other telephone without the need for an operator. The familiar rotary dial, first developed in America by Almon Strowger in 1890, transmits a string of discrete pulses (e.g., five pulses if the number 5 is dialed) that activates a series of relays connecting one caller's phone with another's. Unlike the simple two-position switches described above, the Strowger system uses ten-position relays—each pulse sent out by the dial advances a rotary contact by one position.

Devices of these types were in common use by the 1930s. Simple relays cost a few dollars each, and they were fairly rugged and reliable. But, for ordinary calculators, the relay offered few advantages over mechanical cams and gears. It was still cheaper and more reliable to store or add a decimal number on a train of ten-tooth gears than on a bank of multiple-contact relays. Mechanical calculators had a long heritage going back to Leibniz, during the intervening time the technology had reached a mature state of sophistication and a good deal of inertia had set in among designers. As long as one wanted only to do simple arithmetic, there was little incentive to abandon mechanical technology.

But, for something more than simple arithmetic, relays had a crucial advantage over mechanical systems, in that their circuits could be flexibly arranged (and rearranged) far more easily. One could arrange relays on a rack in rows and columns, and connect them with wires according to what one wanted the circuit to do. One could further reconfigure a relay system using a switchboard, with cables plugged into various sockets by a human operator. Going a step further, one could use a strip of perforated paper tape (originally developed to store telegraph messages for later transmission) to energize a separate set of relays that in turn reconfigured the system just as the plugboards did.

In this latter instance, the same devices—relays—perform the functions of both arithmetic and control. This seems to confer little advantage over mechanical calculators, as it appears that arithmetic and control are two different activities. But, in fact, the two are closely related, and for anything more than simple arithmetic both are required. A calculator designer who uses relays may exploit their ability to do both tasks—enabling the design of a machine with the general capabilities of Babbage's Analytical Engine, but with a much simpler overall design.

In the mid-1930s at least three individuals: Konrad Zuse in Berlin, George Stibitz in New York, and Howard Aiken in Cambridge, Massachusetts, conceived and developed calculating systems that exploited the relay's potential. In many ways their machines were different from one another, but each combined binary relays for control, other relays or electromechanical devices for number storage and arithmetic, and perforated tape for program input. And each was capable of carrying out an arbitrary sequence of elementary arithmetic operations, automatically storing and retrieving intermediate results as the need arose during a calculation. They were the fulfillment of Babbage's attempt to build an Analytical Engine, and it was relay technology that made it possible.

Konrad Zuse

Konrad Zuse, a mechanical engineering student in Berlin in the mid-1930s, was perhaps the first to make use of these properties of relays to build a working, general-purpose, program-controlled calculator. As a student, he faced problems in the analysis of load-bearing structures, like bridges or trussed roofs, whose analysis required the solution of large systems of linear equations. His textbooks taught a method (Gaussian elimination) for solving such systems, but in practice it required too much time and was too error-prone. Zuse knew little of the existing calculating machine industry, but in any case it was not a fancier calculator he wanted. Instead, he wanted a machine that could execute a sequence of simple calculations, and also store and retrieve intermediate results as needed during the solution of a problem. He recognized that, although the solution of typical problems might involve many arithmetic operations, a machine that would solve these problems would need only one calculating unit, provided it was linked to a storage unit that held and delivered initial, intermediate, and final values encountered in a solution. In addition to those two basic units, he also saw the need for a unit that stepped the other two through a sequence of operations depending on the overall plan of the problem's solution.

By 1935, while still a student at Berlin's Technical College, Zuse had sketched out a design for an automatic calculator and begun building it in a corner of his parents' apartment in Berlin. He had already decided to use the binary, not the decimal system of enumeration, with the machine itself performing the conversion between the two systems at the beginning and end of a calculating sequence, as needed. Binary arithmetic is so central to modern computer design that it is easy to overlook how radical a step this was in 1935. Nondecimal number systems were known and investigated by that time, but the established wisdom of the day among calculator manufacturers was that because human beings used decimal numbers, so should machines. Zuse, on the other hand, saw that a mechanical system could be much simpler and more reliable if its elements were designed to assume one of only two, instead of ten, values. It did not matter if the machine handled numbers in a form unfamiliar to humans; his machine would carry out a sequence of arithmetic operations, and during that sequence numbers stayed within the machine itself.

Zuse began building a machine that used mechanical computing

and memory elements, with electric motors supplying power. He was familiar with electromagnetic relays, but he felt a mechanical calculator would be less expensive and more compact. Within about a year, he succeeded in building a compact and reliable storage unit, but attempts to build a mechanical calculating unit met with less success. This unit was much more complex in that it had not only to store but also carry digits from one column to another during addition. He had further decided to represent numbers in floating-point form, a form most engineers took for granted, but which further complicated his design and construction.

So in 1938, after building a small prototype (later called the *Z1*), Zuse abandoned the purely mechanical approach to calculation. He was satisfied with mechanical techniques for memory, but for calculation and control he turned to telephone relays at the suggestion of Helmut Schreyer, a former schoolmate in electrical engineering. Schreyer had worked as a movie projectionist during his student days, and from that experience he further suggested punching holes in discarded movie film as an inexpensive way to enter the program into the machine. (The basic mechanism of a movie projector, which stops each frame of film briefly as it runs through, could be adapted to read the pattern of holes punched into the film.) Zuse adopted both these ideas, but he turned down Schreyer's suggestion to build an arithmetic unit using, not relays, but much faster vacuum tubes. Zuse was working on this project entirely in his spare time with his own personal funds, and felt that vacuum tube circuits would have been too expensive. Schreyer later pursued this approach on his own, as will be discussed in Chapter 7.

With a memory fashioned out of metal plates cut with a jigsaw, a calculating unit made from secondhand telephone relays, and a programming unit that recorded on discarded movie film, Zuse and a few of his friends built a prototype of a general-purpose calculator of this radical new design. This machine, later known as the *Z2*, did not work well but nonetheless demonstrated the soundness of the principles he had developed. It worked well enough to impress the German Aerodynamics Research Institute (DVL) to give him some money to build a more substantial machine, this time using telephone relays for all its units. In 1941, he completed the *Z3*—perhaps the world's first general-purpose, sequential calculator.

The Z3 used about 1,800 relays to store sixty-four 22-digit binary numbers, as well as about 600 additional relays for the calculating and control units. The operation sequence, memory storage and recall, binary-decimal conversion, and input and output all were directed by a control unit that took its instructions from perforated 35-mm movie film. A person entered numbers and operations on a calculator-style keyboard, and answers were displayed on small incandescent lamps. A drum rotating at 300 RPM synchronized all the units of the Z3; it took between three and five seconds to multiply two floating point numbers together. The total cost of the machine was around $6,500 (mostly materials, as many hours of labor were donated by Zuse and his co-workers).

Using the Z3 to solve a problem involved first of all writing out the sequence of commands to perform arithmetic operations and send to or retrieve data from storage. This sequence was then punched into a filmstrip, using an eight-hole pattern. Once this code was prepared, initial values were entered into the keyboard in floating-point, decimal form; the machine then converted the numbers into binary, carried out the sequence, and displayed the result on the lamps after reconverting it back to decimal notation.

Zuse wrote out calculating plans to solve small systems of linear equations, to find the determinants of matrices, and to locate the roots of quadratic equations. Because of its modest memory the Z3 could not attack the problem that at the time most concerned the Aerodynamics Research Institute, namely designing enough stiffnes into airplane wings so that they did not flutter like a flag at high speed—a problem in aerodynamics similar to the one that caused the Tacoma Narrows Bridge to collapse in 1940. But the Z3 was reliabl and flexible enough to persuade them to grant Zuse money for full-size machine, which eventually became the Z4, completed by t end of the war in 1945.

For the Z4, Zuse retained the overall design of the Z3 but returr to a mechanical memory instead of using relays. It was the only o of Zuse's machines to survive the war. Although in the immediat postwar years it was not functional, by 1950 it was running at the Swiss Federal Technical Institute (ETH) in Zurich with a mechanic memory of 512 binary numbers, giving it a power and versatility th matched other, more advanced electronic computers of the immediat postwar era (Figure 6.2).

Americans and Britons knew little of Zuse during or immediate after the war. The result was that his work had little influence on ti development of modern computing, and it remained for others i rediscover his fundamental concepts of binary, floating-point numbe representation and separation of memory, arithmetic, and contr

Figure 6.2. The Z4 at the Federal Technical Institute, Zurich (ca. 1950). Courtesy Konrad Zuse.

units. His Z4 influenced continental European computing in the early 1950s, but only modestly compared to several American projects, discussed below.

George Stibitz and Bell Laboratories

By the mid-1930s, Bell Telephone Laboratories was already one of America's foremost scientific research institutions, albeit with a mission closely wedded to the immediate needs of the American Telephone and Telegraph Company. Those needs centered around two technical problems concerned with establishing a nationwide telephone network. The first was the design and construction of long-distance circuits—Bell Labs was established in 1911 to investigate the use of the newly invented vacuum tube for this purpose. The second was in the design of automatic switching apparatus, which the Bell System introduced in the 1930s to replace human operators. Though long-distance circuits mainly used vacuum tubes to amplify the signal carrying the human voice, switching circuits used relays to route a call from one telephone to another. In modern terms, the first activity concerned analog circuits, the second digital.

The relay circuits that switched and routed calls also performed a modest amount of numerical processing. For example, some circuits converted the number dialed by a customer into another number more suitable for automatic switching. Other circuits might temporarily store a dialed number while the system searched for an open line from one central office to another. Still other relay circuits operated display panels revealing information about the internal workings of the network. In short, the telephone company's relay circuits performed all the functions of an automatic calculator, although they did not "calculate" in the ordinary sense of the word. With a few modifications, one could easily make an ordinary calculator out of relays.

In 1937, George R. Stibitz (b. 1904), a research mathematician at the Bell Labs, brought some relays home one evening and built a battery-operated device that added two binary digits together. His co-workers, however, were not impressed with his Model K. (Stibitz gave it this whimsical name because it was built on his kitchen table.) They reasoned that any practical relay computer, using binary arithmetic, would need perhaps hundreds of relays, thus making it both bulkier and more expensive than the commercial mechanical calculators then in use at the Labs.

But what Stibitz realized was that a relay calculator could perform not just one but a sequence of calculations, with relay circuits directing the order and storing interim results as needed. Specifically, it could perform the sequence of operations required to perform multiplication and division of complex numbers: two mathematical operations that researchers elsewhere at the Labs frequently performed in connection with filter and amplifier design for long-distance circuits.

Complex arithmetic manipulates numbers in pairs, one number

each for the "real" and "imaginary" parts. Electrical engineers modeled the performance of alternating current, amplifier, and filter circuits with complex numbers. For them both parts were equally "real": the first number represented a signal's amplitude or strength, the second its phase or relation to time. At Bell Labs in the 1930s, a roomful of human "computers" figured complex number quotients and products using commercial mechanical calculators. The calculations themselves are straightforward enough: a complex multiplication requires about six simple arithmetic operations, while complex division requires about a dozen operations, and each requires temporary storage of a few intermediate results.

Stibitz proposed building a machine out of relays that would perform these sequences automatically. Bell Labs approved. Work began in the early fall of 1939 and was completed that October. Initially the Complex Number Computer, as it was called, performed only complex multiplication and division, but later a simple modification enabled it to add and subtract as well. It used about 450 binary relays and ten multiposition, multipole relays called "crossbars" for temporary storage of numbers. The machine used the decimal system with the decimal point fixed at the beginning of each number. Internally, four binary relays coded each digit, using a code that represented a decimal digit n by the binary code for $n + 3$; this simplified the problem of digit carry and subtraction (excess-three binary coded decimal is still called "Stibitz-code" today). The machine handled ten-digit numbers in its registers, but displayed and printed eight-digit answers. It used "prefix" notation: that is, operators keyed in the arithmetic operations before they keyed in the operands. For example, to multiply $(3+5i)$ by $(4-2i)$, the operator would key in

$$M \ +.3 \ +i \ .5 \ +.4 \ -i \ .2 \ =$$

The "M" stands for multiply. Note the location of the decimal point before each of the four numbers. The machine would actually be calculating $(.3+.5i) \times (.4-.2i)$, and print the answer 0.22000000 $+i$ 0.14000000. The operator would have to scale the results accordingly. Complex multiplication took about forty-five seconds.

The Complex Number Computer was kept in an out-of-the-way room in the labs, where few ever saw it. Persons accessed it remotely using one of three modified teletype machines placed elsewhere. Only one keyboard could control the machine at any one time, but assuming a person would use it only briefly to do a calculation, no one would have to wait too long. As with the mechanical and human system it replaced, the engineers themselves did not usually operate the machine, but instead gave their problems to human operators who keyed in the numbers and recorded the answers.

Stibitz carried this idea of remote, multiple access one step further. In the fall of 1940 the American Mathematical Society met at Dartmouth College in Hanover, New Hampshire, a few hundred miles north of New York City. Stibitz arranged to have the Complex Number Computer connected by telephone lines to a teletype unit installed there. The Complex Number Computer worked well, and there is no doubt it impressed those who used it. The meeting was attended by many of America's most prominent mathematicians, as well as individuals who later led important computing projects (e.g., John von Neumann, John Mauchly, and Norbert Wiener). The Dartmouth demonstration foreshadowed the modern era of remote computing, but remote access of this type was not repeated for another ten years (until done by the National Bureau of Standards, in 1950).

The Complex Number Computer lacked an ability to carry out a sequence of operations other than those for complex arithmetic; however, Bell Labs used it for many years. Its success encouraged Stibitz to propose more ambitious designs that included an ability to modify the calculator's operations by perforated tape. At first the Labs turned down his proposals, but with the entry of the United States into the Second World War in December 1941, Bell Labs shifted its priorities toward military projects that involved more computation than its peacetime research. Most of their wartime accomplishments were in the design of analog computers, as described in the previous chapter. But they also built five digital relay computers for military purposes, and one more after the war's end for their own use, making a total of seven digital machines counting the Complex Number Computer.

The first of these calculators for military use was the Relay Interpolator, installed in Washington, D.C. in 1943 and later known as the Model II. It mainly solved problems related to directing antiaircraft fire, which it did by executing a sequence of arithmetic operations that interpolated function values supplied to the machine by paper tapes. Like the Complex Number Computer, it was a special-purpose machine; however, its arithmetic sequence was not permanently wired but rather supplied by a "formula tape" cemented into a loop. Different tapes therefore allowed one to employ different methods of interpolation. The Model II could not do much besides interpolation, but as interpolation is a process that lends itself to the solution of many problems in science and engineering the machine was kept busy by other government agencies long after the war ended. The machine was dismantled in 1961.

The next two machines, the Models III and IV, were identical machines, the first installed in 1944 at Fort Bliss, Texas, and the second in early 1945 in Washington. These machines also used paper tapes for data and formula input, with the arithmetic sequence supplied by a loop of paper tape. The Models III and IV, like the Model II, also solved problems relating to the aiming and tracking of antiaircraft guns. They were, however, more sophisticated machines, having the ability not only to perform interpolation but also to evaluate the ballistic equations describing the path of the target airplane and of the antiaircraft shell. An additional paper tape directed which of those functions the machine was to evaluate. Thus, the Models III and IV were the first of the Bell Labs digital calculators to have some degree of general programmability, although neither was a fully general-purpose calculator.

The largest computer in the series was the Model V, of which Bell Labs built two copies for the military in 1946 and 1947. Each contained over nine thousand relays and, like Zuse's Z3 and Z4, handled numbers expressed in scientific notation. The store could hold up to thirty numbers, and paper tape readers fed in both program steps and numerical data. A flexible and elaborate control unit allowed more than one tape loop to direct the machine while it was running, based on the results of a calculation just completed. This gave the Model V the ability to "branch" on a condition, modifying its own program instead of plodding down the same path each time.

This ability to branch to different sequences of instructions is a key to the power of the modern computer. Although branching had been recognized by Ada Augusta (and perhaps by Babbage as well), the practical difficulties of implementing it on a machine programmed by essentially linear paper tapes had prevented its use by earlier calculator designers. Relay calculators installed branching by means of multiple tape readers and loops of tape, which made for a rather baroque overall design.[1] A desire to circumvent the difficulties of providing conditional branching on machines like the

Model V was a major reason why computer designers adopted the principle of internal program storage that characterizes modern computer design.

A relay has a tendency to fail intermittently because of dust or dirt on its contacts. Therefore, all Bell Labs machines after the first employed a system whereby not four but seven relays encoded each decimal digit. The relays were grouped like the beads on a Chinese abacus, with one set of five relays having a unit's weight, the other two a weight of five—the so-called bi-quinary system, viz:

Table 6.1. The Bell Labs bi-quinary system of relays

Decimal digit	Bi-quinary code
0	01 00001
1	01 00010
2	01 00100
3	01 01000
4	01 10000
5	10 00001
6	10 00010
7	10 00100
8	10 01000
9	10 10000

As Table 6.1 shows, for each digit one and only one relay in each group is "on"; a separate set of relay contacts checked this condition and stopped the machine if it found otherwise. This arrangement was a forerunner of error-correcting codes now common in digital computing and communications.

The Model V was a powerful, general-purpose calculator that could and did solve problems in a variety of areas of physics, mathematics, and engineering—many of these problems related to classified wartime work. But at the same time it represented the end of the line for relay technology applied to computing, as its computing power was in many ways offset by increased complexity, cost, bulk, and power requirements. Bell's engineers frankly admitted that their Models III and IV, which had less programming power, represented a better balance between the users' needs and the relay's inherent abilities. The last machine of the series, the Model VI built for Bell's own use in 1949, abandoned the dual-processor and master control programming facilities of the Model V, its designers believing the increased complexity was not worth the trouble or expense. By 1949, it was clear that computing's future lay in the direction of vacuum tube circuits and program input from an internal store instead of a paper tape. Bell Labs did not design or produce electronic computers at that time, but its relay machines were nonetheless an important bridge from the mechanical calculator to the electronic computer.[2]

Howard Aiken and the Harvard Computation Laboratory

The same year that Stibitz was experimenting with relay circuits on his kitchen table, a Harvard graduate student named Howard Aiken began looking for ways to adapt existing calculating machines to help him with calculations for his dissertation research in physics. Aiken began by taking a thorough look at existing calculator technology and its history; he also studied the capabilities of commercial punched-card and calculating machines. He saw that they had sophisticated powers, but primarily for business and accounting applications. For the scientific applications he had in mind (specifically for his thesis on space charges, which required the numerical solution of differential equations) their capabilities were inappropriate. For example, business equipment handled positive values rarely greater than a million, and rarely with more than two places to the right of the decimal point. But scientific problems involved positive and negative numbers of a much wider range and decimal precision; they also used functions like sine, cosine, and logarithm, which business machines did not supply.

Most important, scientific calculations often required iterative solutions, in which the results of a previous calculation are recycled as input data for a subsequent stage in the approximation of a solution. But typical punched-card installations did not permit this kind of approach. With punched-card machines, if one were to evaluate, say, a payroll formula for employees, one would first multiply the number of hours worked by the hourly rate for each employee, producing a new deck of cards as output. This deck would then be submitted to another machine (or to the first machine after making some wiring changes) to compute the deductions for each employee, and so on. Only at the very last step in this process would one have a complete evaluation of the entire formula—and at this step one would have it for every employee (cf. Chapter 4, section 2). Aiken wanted a machine that could compute the whole formula for each value of n, before going on to the next iteration. That implied that the machine would have to alter the arithmetic operations it performed on each input value automatically. And as he intended to use it for problems in which the value of the independent variable was incremented by a constant amount each time, he also wanted the machine to automatically increment the variable and step through the process without human intervention. Implicit in that requirement is the further ability to stop processing upon reaching the desired number of iterations.

Aiken sketched out these ideas in a memorandum entitled "Proposed Automatic Calculating Machine," written in 1937. He discussed these issues, stating above all that the proposed machine had to automatically carry out sequences of different operations. The picture that emerged from this 1937 proposal is one of a set of commercial punched-card machines linked to one another by cables, with separate units for input of initial data, storage and retrieval of interim results, and control of the sequence of operations by the rest of the machine. His proposal also stressed the machine's ability to print the results of its work without the need for manual typesetting or proofreading—this of course would eliminate one of the main sources of errors in printed tables, as Babbage had astutely noted a century earlier.

Aiken tried to interest calculating machine firms in his proposed calculator, but had little success at first. The Harvard astronomer Harlow Shapley then suggested that he approach IBM by way of T. H. Brown, a professor at the Harvard Business School who was on good terms with IBM's chairman, Thomas J. Watson. Watson had already initiated the use of IBM machines in scientific work at Wallace Eckert's lab in New York (cf. Chapter 4); he believed that collaboration with Aiken would lead to a similar involvement at Harvard. Watson assigned the experienced and respected IBM engineer James W. Bryce to implement Aiken's proposal; Bryce in turn assigned three engineers and the facilities of IBM's Endicott, New York plant. Aiken spent the summers of 1941 and 1942 in Endicott, where he sketched out what he wanted his machine to do, but it was the IBM personnel who actually designed and built the machine, using existing IBM punched-card technology. IBM also paid most of the estimated half a million dollars the machine cost.

The Automatic Sequence Controlled Calculator (ASCC)—so named to call attention to its method of evaluating formulas—was completed in Endicott early in 1943 and moved to Harvard the next year. It was covered with an attractive stainless-steel and glass enclosure, and on August 7, 1944 was publicly unveiled at an elaborate ceremony attended by Watson, Aiken, President Conant of Harvard, and a number of other VIP's. The ASCC thus became the first large-scale automatic digital calculator made known to the public. News of its dedication was overshadowed by the war, but nonetheless many newspapers and popular scientific journals reported the event. Some reports found their way to Germany, where Konrad Zuse heard them as he was building his own Z4.

The ASCC was long and slender: 51 feet long, 8 feet tall, and only 2 feet deep. By 1944 standards it was awfully large for a "calculator," but today it would be dwarfed by typical mainframe installations with their rows of tape and disk drives. It had that shape because all its individual calculating units were powered (and synchronized) by a constantly turning drive shaft that ran along its base—not unlike a nineteenth-century New England textile mill. Numbers were transferred by relay circuits, which activated clutches that coupled the drive shaft to one of seventy-two sets of wheels called "accumulators." By activating the clutch connected to an accumulator for, say, five units of time, the number 5 was added to whatever contents were already in that unit. A typical addition took about one-third of a second.

The seventy-two accumulators were adapted from similar devices found in IBM punched-card machines, and comprised both the ASCC's store and mill—that is, they both stored numbers and performed nearly all of the arithmetic operations needed to solve a typical problem. Like punched-card machines, the accumulators used fixed decimal arithmetic, although they could store and add numbers having many more digits—twenty-three digits plus sign, with the decimal point fixed after the twelfth digit. (Commercial punched-card machines handled numbers from eight to twelve digits in length.) Numbers were inputed by paper tape or cards, or by setting a bank of manual switches (Figure 6.3); the calculating sequence was entered by a 24-column, punched-paper tape (Figure 6.4).

Additional equipment included a separate device for multiplication (and division) and a device for interpolating function values supplied on paper tapes. A device similar to the interpolator supplied logarithmic and trigonometric functions. Two "electromatic" typewriters provided output.

The key piece of the ASCC was its sequence control unit. This device read 24-column paper tapes containing the operation sequences needed to solve a problem. The columns were grouped into three fields: out-, in-, and miscellaneous-field. The first specified from which accumulator or other unit a number was to be taken. The second specified where it was to go (the terminology is the reverse of today's). The third, or miscellaneous field could specify a number

Figure 6.3. A bank of manual switches on the Automatic Sequence Controlled Calculator, used for input of constant numerical values. Courtesy Cruft Laboratory, Harvard University.

of operations, but it was not strictly speaking used as an operation field. A number routed to a given accumulator would automatically be added to whatever was already in it; hence, there was no need to give the command "add," but only a command (punched into the third field) to continue with the next operation. Typical operation sequences for the ASCC consisted of a long series of transfers from one accumulator (or input device) to another, with the command to "continue" punched in the miscellaneous field. Even multiplication was handled in this way: the multiplier unit was given an address, which was punched into the in-field when one wanted to use it.

Aiken assembled a small staff of mathematicians and technicians to service and program the ASCC. Support for the machine's daily operations came from the Navy; hence most of this staff were either fresh recruits or recently commissioned Naval officers. One of the latter was Grace Hopper, who had taken leave as an instructor in

Figure 6.4. Twenty-four-column punched-paper tape for input of calculating sequence on the Automatic Sequence Controlled Calculator. Courtesy Cruft Laboratory, Harvard Univeristy.

mathematics at Vassar College to attend the Navy's Midshipmen's School. In 1943, the Navy ordered her to go to Harvard and join Aiken's staff. Very quickly she assumed the task of preparing codes for the ASCC to solve a variety of problems, and so began a long and productive career as one of America's pioneers in what is now known as computer "software."

Recall that from the telegraph and telephone industries came not just the electromagnetic relay but also the techniques of paper tape and plugboards, which calculator designers adopted for the control functions of their machines. Reflecting its hybrid ancestry, the ASCC used both: paper tape for input of its operation sequence, and plugboards for operations like the routing of results to the several output devices, or the formatting of typed output intended for publication.

Even before its public unveiling, the calculator was kept busy doing classified work for the United States Navy. At least one of the problems it worked on involved a calculation of the blast effects of the first atomic bomb. After the war, the machine settled into a more prosaic role of calculating and printing tables of Bessel and other related functions, the tables reproduced by photolithography directly from the machine's typewriters. Thus, Babbage's dream of computing and printing mathematical tables finally came true, even as the ASCC ushered in an age of computers that would transform the whole process of compiling and using tables, in some cases making tables themselves obsolete.

The ASCC was finally retired in 1959; a part of it may still be found in the foyer of the Harvard Computation Laboratory. Aiken went on to supervise the design of three more large-scale calculators; as these were completed they took on the names Mark II, III, and IV, and the ASCC became known as the Harvard Mark I. The Mark II (completed in 1947) was a calculator more in the spirit of the Bell Labs Model V, computing entirely with relays, not mechanical driveshafts or clutches. It was a big machine by any standards: it contained 13,000 relays and occupied a large room at the Navy's proving ground at Dahlgren, Virginia. Like the Mark I, it was controlled by a combination of sequence tapes and plugboards; like the Bell Labs Model V, it could be operated as two independent machines and work on two problems simultaneously.

By the time the Mark II was installed at Dahlgren, many were beginning to feel that vacuum tubes offered a number of advantages over relays for automatic calculator circuits. Aiken was leery of the what he perceived as the inherent unreliability of tubes, but for the Marks III and IV he did employ some tubes to gain higher speeds. In many respects these calculators were anachronisms, but the Mark III did pioneer the use of a high-speed magnetic drum for the storage of numbers and instructions. The drum became the most popular storage device for electronic computers of the "first generation," even though the architecture of those computers was far different from what Aiken developed. His influence on postwar computing was strong, not so much as a designer of machines, but as the director of the Harvard Computation Laboratory, which was one of the few places where what we now know as "computer science" was taught. Aiken's students were among the first to receive a thorough training in the fundamentals of computing, and after leaving Harvard many of them helped steer the direction of academic, commercial, and military computing for the next three decades. Aiken also frequently travelled to continental Europe, where he inspired and influenced many computer projects otherwise out of the Anglo-American mainstream.

Conclusion

R elay technology seemed to hold the potential for building powerful computing machines that were cheap and reliable, yet it never really fulfilled that promise. Relays were indeed mechanically rugged and relatively cheap, but calculator circuit design imposed severe constraints not found in telephone circuits. Most critical was the fact that relays were prone to intermittent failures, usually caused by a piece of dirt or dust between the contacts.[3] In a telephone circuit this was of little consequence, as the telephone system can still function acceptably with some degradation of service. Indeed, the highest priority in a telephone system is to maintain service—any service—despite the failure of many of the system's components (this is especially important during a storm or flood). But the philosophy of calculator design is diametrically opposite: if there is any chance that the machine might deliver a wrong answer, say a misplaced sign or decimal point, it is better to shut the whole system down and fix the problem before continuing.

The result was that relay calculators needed elaborate checking circuits or redundancy, which made them costly and overly complex. Where there were no self-checking circuits, as on the Mark I, its operators had to periodically run portions of a problem through the machine twice, using different registers to ensure that everything was all right. By contrast, when a vacuum tube fails, it usually does so catastrophically, i.e., it burns out. That renders the whole circuit inoperative, so it is less likely to spew out wrong answers before the problem is noticed. So although it was true that tubes were less reliable than relays, they actually allowed one to build a total system that in the long run was more reliable when measured in terms of the average number of arithmetic operations between failures. These characteristics of tubes, coupled with their higher speeds, spelled the end of relay calculator development. The invention of the transistor by Bell Labs scientists in 1947 eventually allowed the construction of computing machines that combined the ruggedness of relays with the speed of tubes, and rendered the question moot.

During the immediate postwar years, a few relay machines were built to take advantage of lower initial costs and development time. Relay technology was especially appealing in Europe, where capital was hard to raise in the late 1940s. In West Germany, Zuse founded a commercial company, Zuse K. G., of Neukirchen, that produced several compact and reliable relay calculators in the 1950s. One of them, the Z11, sold well and continued to be used into the 1980s. But in 1955 he changed over to electronics—first with vacuum tube and later with transistorized computers. (In the mid-1960s his company was absorbed by the German electronics firm Siemens.) Some European groups adopted the relay design philosophy advocated by Aiken, who made several trips across the Atlantic at that time. Two such machines were the BARK and the ARRA, which introduced automatic computing to Sweden and the Netherlands in 1950 and 1952. At King's College in London, A. D. Booth built the ARC—a machine whose architecture reflected the latest ideas on internally stored programming from John von Neumann and other Americans, but which used relays to save costs.

In the United States, Engineering Research Associates designed a high-speed magnetic drum for the storage unit of an electronic computer, but before assembling the computer they built a relay processor to test the drum's powers. This combination (called the *Abel*) turned out to be so useful that the United States Office of Naval Research installed it in Washington, D.C. and continued to use it for many years for a wide range of problems, mainly logistics calculations. Modest relay devices were also built in Japan in the early 1950s.

These examples illustrate the place of the relay calculator in the history of computing: almost from the start they were eclipsed by the faster vacuum tube computers, but at the same time they played a vital role as the machines that introduced to the world the concept of automatic, sequential calculation. It was with relay technology that the first functional automatic calculators finally came into existence, after years of hope and promise.

Notes

1. Neither the Z4 nor the ASCC, described later in this chapter, had conditional branching at first, but the capability was retrofitted to both machines after the end of the war.

2. One reason AT&T did not then produce computers was that it was a regulated monopoly, whose main line of business was domestic telephone service; and it was prohibited by law from entering into a business such as computing, which was outside their main line of business.

3. In one famous instance, Grace Hopper found that a moth trapped between two relay contacts was causing the Mark II to malfunction; she removed the moth and taped it in the logbook, noting that she had found the "bug" that was causing the problem!

Further Reading

Aiken, Howard. "Proposed Automatic Calculating Machine." Reprinted in *The Origins of Digital Computers: Selected Papers*, 3d ed. Edited by Brian Randell. New York: Springer-Verlag, 1982. A description of the general needs for an automatic calculator for scientific problems, and how one might construct such a machine.

Berkeley, Edmund. *Giant Brains, or Machines that Think.* New York: Wiley, 1949. A good survey of the automatic electromechanical and electronic calculating machines available in the years following the end of World War II.

Ceruzzi, Paul E. *Reckoners: The Prehistory of the Digital Computer.* Westport, Conn.: Greenwood Press, 1983. Case studies of the calculating machines built by Zuse, Stibitz, Aiken, and Eckert and Mauchley. Especially detailed description of Zuse's work.

Dunsheath, Percy. *A History of Electrical Power Engineering.* Cambridge, Mass.: MIT Press, 1962. A general history of the principles and history of electrical engineering technologies that were the basis for the electromechanical calculators.

Harvard University, Computation Laboratory. *A Manual of Operation for the Automatic Sequence Controlled Calculator.* Harvard University Press, 1947. Reprinted by MIT Press, 1985. A detailed description of the ASSC (Harvard Mark I), written mainly by Grace Hopper under Howard Aiken's direction. The 1985 reprint edition contains a new foreword and introduction, which both provide valuable historical information about Aiken's work.

Stibitz, George. "Computer." In *The Origins of the Digital Computer.* Edited by Brian Randell, 247-52. An informal and easy-to-understand description by the inventor of the Bell Labs Model I calculator.

Chapter 7

Electronic Calculators

Introduction

It was not until the mid-1930s that anyone began to think seriously of using high-speed electronic circuits in digital calculating machinery. The vacuum tube itself, a device that could switch current many times faster than electromagnetic relays, was known and heavily used for other applications for at least the previous two decades. Suggestions for why it was not applied to computing earlier and what finally triggered the change are discussed as this chapter traces the introduction of vacuum tubes into calculating machinery.

In 1883, Thomas Edison, as part of his work in developing commercial electric lighting, first noted that an evacuated tube could pass an electric current. Edison did not follow up that discovery and failed to notice the tube's ability to regulate and control currents. Not long after that discovery, J. J. Thompson explained this "Edison effect" as a boiling off of negatively charged particles (named "electrons" in 1894; hence the term "electronic") from the tube's filament, from which they would travel across the vacuum to a metal plate. In 1904, J. A. Fleming used such a "diode"—so-called because it had two working elements: a filament and a plate—to detect weak radio signals. Two years later, Lee DeForest added a third element to the diode, thereby transforming it into a device that could not only detect, but also amplify signals.

DeForest's triode touched off the first of what has become a steady stream of applications of electronics technology, which have affected the character of twentieth-century life. It transformed the radio industry by making it possible to transmit more powerful signals at higher frequencies than before, and at the receiving end it allowed extremely faint signals to be amplified and thus made intelligible. It transformed the telephone industry by permitting voice signals to be amplified and thus sent across long distances—something that hitherto had been possible only with the dot-dash signals of the telegraph. Each of these advances led in turn to further developments in communication and control.

But the calculator and accounting machines industries were not among those so rapidly transformed. One reason was that engineers who worked with the vacuum tube did not perceive it as a switch that could route electrical pulses through a circuit. Indeed, they designed circuits to minimize the tube's tendency to act as a digital switch, while maximizing its ability to produce an amplified, but smooth, continuous copy of its input.[1] The telephone engineer's goal was to get the circuit to reproduce as accurately as possible the nuances of the original signal and to minimize any tendency the tube had to latch on to either extreme of letting all or none of the available current through. Applications requiring all-or-nothing switching, as in routing telephone calls, or transmitting the discrete dots and dashes of Morse telegraph signals, were well served by electromechanical relays. Given these two apparently separate arenas of tube and relay applications, there was a general perception that tubes were ill-suited for calculators, which handled discrete digits and not continuous signals.

In the 1930s, relays and mechanical devices still served the calculating machines industry well. These devices permitted rapid calculation compared to manual methods, which satisfied most users (except for men like Wallace Eckert, L. J. Comrie, and Howard Aiken who wanted to use these machine to solve highly complex scientific problems). Furthermore, electromechanical calculating speeds were in balance with the speeds of the other activities like recording and reading data, and directing the sequence of calculations: activities still done by hand. The limits of the relay's speed to a few arithmetic operations a second did not form a bottleneck that machine designers were concerned with breaking.

First Digital Applications of Tubes

As early as 1919, Eccles and Jordan published a description of a vacuum tube "trigger" circuit that could hold one of two states indefinitely, like an ordinary relay only capable of operating much faster. Their circuit got little attention at first, but eventually it found an application in solving a problem whose nature precluded the use of slower relays. Advances in atomic physics had led researchers to an interest in recording and counting cosmic rays and related phenomena. The Geiger-Mueller counter, itself an ingenious application of a vacuum tube, allowed one to record this radiation; but to count the actual flux of particles required speeds far in excess of what relay circuits could deliver. At the Cavendish Laboratory in Cambridge, England, in 1930, C. E. Wynn-Williams built a device capable of resolving events occurring less than a millisecond apart. His circuit did not use evacuated tubes, but rather gas-filled "thyratrons," which were able to hold a state of either conducting or not-conducting, like Eccles' and Jordan's "flip-flop." The circuits were chained to one another in such a way that for every two firings of the first one, its neighbor would fire once, and so on down the chain. Thus, if there were n such circuits, the firing of the nth would indicate that the first had receive 2^{n-1} events. By making the chain long enough, the speed at which the last tube fired could be scaled down to a point at which it could be recorded by a mechanical counter.[2] Such a circuit was an electronic counterpart of a mechanical register consisting of toothed wheels with a carry occurring after one full revolution of a given wheel.

By the late 1930s such "ring-counters" were well known in the physics community. Variations of Wynn-Williams's design, many using the Eccles-Jordan vacuum tube design instead of thyratrons, appeared in the literature, especially in the journal *Review of Scientific Instruments*.

With additional circuits, these ring counters could be made to calculate as well as count. As early as 1936, William Phillips, an actuary for the British office of the Manufacturers Life Insurance Company, described a machine that computed in the binary scale, which in theory was capable of very high speeds. Although the public description of it did not explicitly mention vacuum tube circuits, Wynn-Williams was thinking of using ring counters to achieve multiplication speeds of between five and ten a second.

Whatever the merits of his design, there was one basic flaw in using such ring counters for numerical calculation. Arithmetic devices, especially those used for banking, insurance, or accounting, must be exact. Ring counters, as built and used by physicists, were not. Cosmic-ray counters were perfectly acceptable if they missed a few events over a long span of time.[3] It would not do to simply build a calculator by substituting ring counter circuits for relays or gears. Nonetheless, it was from these basic concepts that some of the first electronic calculating circuits emerged.

One other development in electronics during the 1930s contributed to the perception of the vacuum tube as a digital as well as an analog device. This was the development of radar, which used pulses of radio-frequency energy to locate objects. Radar devices are fundamentally analog—they typically display the location of the object by an analogous displacement of a spot on a cathode-ray-tube. But a successful radar device requires circuits that can generate very short pulses of current, on the order of a few microseconds in duration. Such pulses had to be of a high intensity and had to be switched on and off cleanly. The intense effort devoted to radar development as World War II approached helped dispel the notion of tubes as strictly analog amplifiers, while generating a wealth of experience in circuit design that calculator designers later drew heavily from. By the late 1930s, these advances in electronic engineering combined with the ever-increasing demands for routine calculation to make the idea of electronic digital calculation at least within the realm of the practical.

Atanasoff

Not surprisingly, a serious attempt to apply electronic devices to calculation occurred independently in America, England, and Germany between 1935 and 1943. But each of these applications was in a sense precocious, in that their arithmetic speeds outstripped their ability to handle input, output, and programming functions. The ENIAC, completed in 1945, shared this problem; but it struck at least a workable balance, and so may be regarded as the first working system to solve practical numeric problems at electronic speeds. Before looking at the ENIAC, we shall examine its immediate predecessors.

In the mid-1930s, John V. Atanasoff, a professor of physics at Iowa State College in Ames, began exploring the feasibility of using electronic computing circuits to help solve systems of linear equations. Such systems occur in nearly every branch of physics; furthermore, many problems described by differential or other equations can be recast and solved as linear systems. Basically, the technique for solving linear systems is straightforward and the same regardless of the number of equations or unknowns, and involves a sequence of ordinary arithmetic operations. But the number of operations grows so large that systems greater than about ten equations in ten unknowns are impractical to solve by hand. Atanasoff, like some other physicists, saw the need to mechanize this process. He first considered analog devices, then configurations of punched-card equipment, but eventually realized that the order-of-magnitude increase in speed that electronics offered was the only way to attack the explosive growth of calculations required to solve large systems of linear equations.

Atanasoff has often recounted the story of how he invented his electronic calculator. One night in the winter of 1937, he got in his car and went for a drive to clear his mind. As he later described the evening, he must have been quite agitated, for he did not stop until he arrived at a roadside tavern across the Mississippi River in Illinois, almost two hundred miles from Ames along two-lane roads. He went in, ordered a drink (something one could not legally do in Iowa in the 1930s), and collected his thoughts.

Atanasoff claims that that night he settled on the overall design of his calculator. It would be an electronic, digital machine; and it would use the binary system. Because the calculating speed had to be matched by equally high speeds for the storage and retrieval of temporary results of previous calculations, he decided on storing the numbers electronically as well. To store the digits he decided to use banks of capacitors (called "condensers" at that time), which in turn would be periodically refreshed to prevent their contents from leaking away.

Finally, he made a preliminary decision as to the arithmetic circuits themselves, although he would not actually build such circuits until 1939. His design differed from Wynn-Williams's ring counters mainly in that the holding of digits before and during an arithmetic operations would take place in banks of capacitors, not in rings of triodes. Vacuum tube circuits, consisting of only fourteen triodes enclosed in seven glass envelopes, would handle the addition of 30-bit binary numbers, while the other three arithmetic operations would be derived from addition.

The machine he envisioned would be hard-wired to carry out the arithmetic sequences to solve linear systems.[4] It did so by the method of successive elimination: first, the coefficients of one equation were multiplied by a constant, so that at least one coefficient was equal to a coefficient of the equivalent term of another equation; then the two equations were subtracted from each other. Because at least one term of each was equal to its counterpart in the other equation, the subtraction eliminated that term, and yielded a new equation having one fewer term. This process was repeated, until it yielded the value for one of the unknowns. That value could then be substituted in each of the equations, yielding a new system of equations with one fewer variables. The method could be repeated until the values of all the variables were determined.

By the end of 1939, Atanasoff and a graduate assistant, Clifford Berry, completed a prototype that could add and subtract binary numbers equivalent to about eight decimal digits of precision. The next summer, Atanasoff submitted a proposal to Iowa State College to fund the construction of a full-scale machine that would solve linear systems automatically. With a modest contribution from the college and a grant of about five thousand dollars from a private foundation, Atanasoff and Berry built a machine that functioned in every respect except for its input-output device, a novel method of punching cards at high-speed that made just enough errors to prevent an accurate solution of large systems of equations.

The most striking feature of their machine was its two drums mounted along a common shaft, each drum containing banks of capacitors that stored thirty numbers of up to fifty bits in length. (Figure 7.1) The capacitors were mounted radially, with a common contact at the center of the drum and wipers that made contact with a row of thirty on the drum's surface. One row of capacitors held the nth bit of each of thirty numbers; the machine therefore handled the digits of each number one at a time, or serially, but in parallel regarding all thirty coefficients of an equation. The drums rotated at about one revolution per second. The system was designed to read the charge of each capacitor (binary 1 was +40 volts, binary 0 -50 volts), and immediately refresh that charge with another set of brushes following those that read its value. Without such refreshing, the charges would leak away, but the circuits ensured that there was a more than adequate margin of safety given the speeds at which it

Figure 7.1. The Atanasoff calculator. Courtesy Iowa State University
Archives.

operated. Atanasoff called this process "jogging"; it was the forerunner of the concept of dynamic memory so common to modern computer design.

Each drum held the coefficients of one equation of the linear system; and by a process of repeated subtraction the values on one drum were subtracted from those on the other, until one coefficient was reduced to zero. If one coefficient was not an exact multiple of the other, the machine would subtract one extra time (giving a negative coefficient value), then shift the circuits one binary place and add this new value (which would be one-half the old value of the subtrahend) to the remainder. This process would be repeated until it produced zero. In this manner, the machine was able to reduce the coefficients of the system of equations by successive elimination, using only the operations of subtraction, addition, and shifting. Although this method is similar to many modern machine implementations of binary division, Atanasoff's machine did not actually produce the quotient of the two numbers, as it kept no record of the number of times it performed the repeated subtraction.

As each pair of equations was reduced, its new coefficients were punched onto cards by a novel method of depositing a conductive spot on a card by an intense electric spark. This interim storage on cards was an integral part of the process of solving a system of equations, and it had to proceed at high speeds to remain in balance with the electronic circuits that performed the arithmetic. Ordinary card readers and punches might suffice for the initial input of a problem or the output of the final answer, but they were too slow for this intermediate storage function. It was the occasional malfunctioning of this device which prevented the computing machine from ever being put into routine use solving large systems of equations.

The machine remained at this stage of refinement until 1942, when both men left Iowa: Atanasoff for the Naval Ordnance Laboratory near Washington, D.C., and Berry for Consolidated Engineering in California. The machine was never made fully reliable and never put to use. For many years its existence was forgotten. During its construction it never even had a name, although in some later descriptions it was called the ABC for Atanasoff-Berry-Computer. Thirty years after work on the machine was abandoned, when the invention of the electronic digital computer became the subject of a lawsuit, attorneys representing one of the parties rediscovered the work. By that time, the ABC itself, save for a memory drum, had long since vanished.

Helmut Schreyer

The idea of computing with vacuum tube circuits occurred to Helmut Schreyer in Germany at the same time. Schreyer was a schoolmate of Zuse at the Berlin Technical College, where Schreyer was studying electrical engineering. He had helped Zuse with the construction of the Z1 and had suggested to Zuse the possibility of using modified film projection as a way of programming the machine. But whereas Zuse had early on favored mechanical or electromechanical computing elements, Schreyer saw that one could construct an electronic circuit that worked just like the binary relays Zuse was using, only at much higher speeds. He based his circuits on a combination of triodes coupled to gas-filled lamps (somewhat like neon light bulbs), which had well-defined voltage levels that would hold a state of either conducting or not conducting. Such circuits were slower than Eccles-Jordan flip-flops, but still much faster than ordinary relays. He designed a number of switching circuits using his so-called tube relay, and in 1941 he received a doctorate from the Berlin Technical College for a thesis on the subject.

Schreyer's thesis did not discuss the application of these relays to computing, but he did mention to Zuse the possibility of building a computer based on the Z3's design, using tubes instead of relays (recall that the Z3 was completed and working by 1941). Schreyer proposed to the German Army Command that he build a full-scale programmable electronic computer having about fifteen hundred tubes and about as many lamps. But he was turned down. The German Army Command felt the two years time Schreyer needed to complete his machine was too long: given their perception of the course of the war at that time, they chose to concentrate on projects that could be completed sooner.

Schreyer did not give up. The German army was not interested, but the Aviation Research Office (DVL) was; and they supplied him with funds to begin a more modest project: an electronic device that converted three-digit decimal numbers to and from binary. In the meantime, the Telefunken Company had developed a special tube well suited for Schreyer's designs.[5] Schreyer combined this tube with three fast-acting lamps and nine resistors to give a reliable and fast (up to 10 kHz) circuit that accepted up to three inputs and produced their logical addition (or), multiplication (and), or negation (not). The lamps were bathed in ultraviolet light to increase the reliability of their operation at high speed (Figure 7.2).

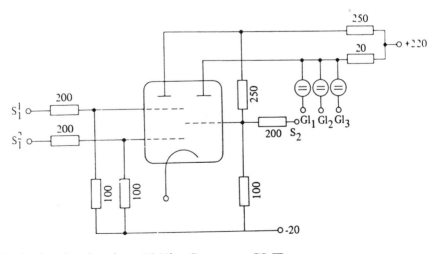

Figure 7.2. Schreyer's logic circuits (ca. 1942). Courtesy GMD, Bertin.

Work on the binary-to-decimal converter began in 1941 but proceeded slowly as Schreyer was called to do other work, including work on radar and on an accelerometer for the V-2 ballistic missile. In November 1943, the converter was damaged during a bombing raid on Berlin, and further work on electronic computing came to a halt. After the war, Schreyer left Germany and never again returned to computing. Thus, the priorities of the war diverted both Schreyer and Atanasoff from further progress in electronic computing, although government support for Atanasoff's computer work was somewhat greater than for Schreyer's.

The Colossus

If the war hindered progress for Atanasoff and Schreyer, it had the opposite effect on the first British steps toward electronic calculation. During the War, the British Foreign Office's Department of Communications designed a machine called the Colossus, which used high-speed electronic circuits to assist the British in decoding intercepted German radio messages that had been encrypted on a machine called the *Geheimschreiber* (Secret Writer). The first Colossus was operational late in 1943, and by the end of the war at least ten were built along the same design. The first one contained fifteen hundred vacuum tubes and operated at a frequency of five thousand pulses per second.

Unlike the two electronic calculators just described, the Colossus's logic circuits performed not ordinary arithmetic, but rather Boolean comparisons of one string of pulses with another. These operations are logically equivalent to binary arithmetic, but strictly speaking the Colossus was not a calculator. The Colossus *was* capable of high-speed internal generation and storage of data; and its sequence of operations could be modified by setting switches, while certain characteristics of the message to be decoded were entered into the machine by plugging cables. These features gave the machine a sophistication lacking in contemporary electronic and relay calculators.

The interception and decoding of German messages was a significant factor in the Allied victory, a fact kept secret until recently. The work was carried out in great secrecy at Bletchley Park, a Victorian estate about fifty miles north of London. No single person was the Colossus's inventor, but of the many who worked at Bletchley, Alan M. Turing, M. H. A. Newman, and Thomas H. Flowers were the key individuals responsible for the machine's design, construction, and method of operation. Many others played important roles, including C. E. Wynn-Williams mentioned above.

The immediate ancestor of the Colossus was a partially electronic machine called the "Heath Robinson," after a well-known British cartoon character (Americans might have called it a "Rube Goldberg"). This machine compared two streams of data entered on two paper tape readers and counted the Boolean sums or products of the holes punched on each tape with those on the other. One tape contained the encrypted German message, the other a coded representation of what the British believed the German's enciphering device did to a message (this information was itself arrived at by a combination of guesswork and mathematical theory, and by taking advantage of occasional German lapses in encrypting every message thoroughly). By performing this comparison of the two tapes over and over, each time moving one letter sequence a single place relative to the other, a clue might emerge as to the exact code the Germans had used on the particular message.[6] This clue in turn would lead to another tape with which to repeat the process, and so on until the original scrambling of letters was exactly reversed.

Because of the great number of runs needed, and because of the more general fact that the value of reading enemy messages rapidly diminishes with time, it was of utmost importance that the machine process messages quickly. The Heath Robinson's tapes fed data at the rate of up to two thousand characters per second—at this speed ordinary electromechanical tape readers were useless, and a special photoelectric reader was specially developed for this function. This reader, developed by the Post Office Research Establishment at Dollis Hill, was vital to the success of both the Heath Robinson and later the Colossi, where an even higher speed of up to five thousand characters per second was obtained.

The Heath Robinsons, however, suffered from difficulties in reading the two tapes in synchrony at high speeds. Even a slight misalignment would render the whole process worthless. Flowers, who had explored the substitution of electronics for relays in telephone circuits before he was transferred to Bletchley Park in 1942, suggested that one of the tapes be completely replaced with an internally stored table for the trial "key" tape, which could be delivered in the proper phase and sequence to the rest of the machine at high speeds. Stepping this pattern relative to the tape of the German's code could likewise be done electronically. This at once solved the problem of synchronizing the tapes and greatly reduced the Heath Robinson's "Rube Goldberg" complexity.

But as Flowers said: "My suggestion, made in February 1943, was met with considerable skepticism. The first reaction was that a machine with the number of tubes that was obviously going to be needed would be too unreliable to be useful. Fortunately, this criticism was defeated by the experience of the Post Office using thousands of tubes in its communication network. These tubes were not subject to movement or handling, and the power was never switched off. Under these conditions tube failures were very rare."[7]

The main group at Bletchley continued work on the two-tape Heath Robinsons, while engineers at Dollis Hill began almost immediately building an electronic device. After eleven months of intense effort, they completed their first model. The machine contained about fifteen hundred vacuum tubes and generated the "key-tape" data from parameters stored internally in ring counters. In early December 1943, it was put into service at Bletchley, where it acquired the name "Colossus" because of the number of tubes it contained. It soon proved to be a fast and reliable machine, producing far more useful output than the Heath Robinsons, while breaking down less often than many had feared. Its tape reader operated at a speed of five thousand characters per second, with the tape moving through it at over thirty miles an hour. The tape reader's photoelectric scanner had an ingenious double-crescent mask that produced a square-shaped pulse of current from the photocell reading the passage of light through a round hole in the tape. Special timing holes on the tape triggered an internal electronic clock, whose pulses synchronized reading the tape with comparing the internal key data, thus avoiding problems of synchronizing the two streams of data at such high speeds.

The success of the Dollis Hill engineers did not go unnoticed—in February 1944 they were told to produce twelve more machines by the summer! Flower's reaction was "flatly that it was impossible." Increasingly, the Allied ability to keep up with the German encryption depended on the Colossus's powers. Although the Germans had not caught on to the fact their messages were being read, they were slowly introducing new operating practices and a new, slightly more advanced coding machine. The code-breakers at Bletchley were always at least a half-step behind the Germans at any time, and they were facing the prospect of falling so far behind they would never catch up—just as the Allies were preparing the cross-Channel invasion.

Flowers promised to have at least one new Colossus working by the first of June, and once again the Dollis Hill group did the "impossible." They met the deadline (the first of the new machines was not working the evening of May 31, but was set right by an engineer overnight). What was more, the new Colossus incorporated a number of improvements over the first, not the least of which was its ability to process not one, but five streams of data from the tape in parallel, thus increasing its speed fivefold. And unlike the original Colossus, the new model contained circuits that could automatically alter its own program sequence. If it sensed a potentially meaningful pattern, a circuit permitted it to redirect its stepping through the internal table in such a way that would more quickly find a path to a solution. Within a decade, this ability became a defining feature of digital computers.

By V-E Day in May 1945, a total of ten Colossi were in use at Bletchley. Design changes continued to be made, but after the first one, each of the following contained about twenty-four hundred tubes, twelve rotary switches, and about eight hundred relays. Input of tabular data was made by plugging cables into pairs of sockets, which in turn directed the firing of ring counters. The pattern stored in these rings was compared with the pattern read from a tape, according to various Boolean operations. Usually the bit streams were added modulo-2, but a number of other functions were possible if so desired by the cryptanalysts.

After each pass the comparison was repeated, only with one pattern offset by one position relative to the other, as set by a rotary switch. The results of the comparison, as well as the positions of the rotary switches, were printed out on a typewriter for further processing by the human cryptanalysts at Bletchley. The Colossus did not produce a decoded message, but rather an intermediate text that required further work, not always leading to success.

The Colossus's place in the history of the invention of the computer is hard to fix. Compared to other machines of the day, it was both more and less than what we now recognize as a digital computer. It performed all logical functions electronically at very high speeds, stored data internally in high-speed, fixed, and alterable stores, and stepped through a sequence of operations also at electronic speeds. In a rudimentary way, it could also alter that sequence.

But it was a machine capable of attacking one and only one problem: the analysis of German messages, which themselves were encrypted in a specific way. The Colossus did not perform ordinary arithmetic, nor could it solve other logical problems not cast in the same mold as those for which it was designed. Its greatest legacy—besides the enormous contribution it made to the Allied war effort—was that those who worked on it gained an experience with computing circuits that allowed them after the war to design and build a number of general-purpose electronic computers. These computers, built at Manchester, Cambridge, and London, were among the first to be placed in operation anywhere. In the context of the postwar evolution of digital computer architecture, the Colossus had less influence. The computers built after the war were general-purpose devices that could perform numerical or logical work, but they were immediate descendants of machines that had been built for numerical work, not from logic machines like the Colossus. The architecture of the modern stored-program computer hardly resembles that of the ENIAC, but it evolved from the ENIAC—a special-purpose electronic computer optimized for certain numerical problems.

The ENIAC

Of the machines described above, only the Colossus was able to take advantage of high processing speed, by balancing it with a fast photoelectric tape reader and plugboard programming. The first machine that could solve complex numerical problems electronically, and whose programming was flexible enough to allow it to solve a variety of such problems, was the ENIAC, completed in late 1945 at the Moore School of Electrical Engineering at the University of Pennsylvania. The ENIAC is the most famous of the early computers, but not always for the right reasons. It deserves its fame not for its electronic circuits, which several other machines already had, nor for its architecture, which although ingenious and full of promise was rejected by subsequent designers. One should rather remember the ENIAC as the first electronic machine to consistently and reliably solve numerical problems beyond the capability of human and in many cases relay computers as well.

The ENIAC owed its existence, like the Colossus, to the pressures of the Second World War. It grew out of the need by the United States

Army to compute firing tables for ordnance then being employed in the field. The rapid deployment of various new types of artillery to widely dispersed battle fronts strained the capabilities of the Army's Ballistic Research Laboratory (BRL) at Aberdeen, Maryland, to supply field officers with firing tables, without which the guns were useless. After 1935, the BRL began to employ a variety of methods for preparing these tables, including one method that used differential analyzers of the type described in Chapter 5. At the Moore School in Philadelphia, there was one such analyzer; teams of human computers (many of them recent graduates of women's colleges in and around Philadelphia) also prepared tables using mechanical calculators. Although each of these methods worked, none was able to produce firing tables fast enough for the Army's needs after the United States's entry into the war in 1941.

Against that background at the Moore School, John Mauchly conceived of an electronic calculator that he felt would be able to compute tables much faster than any other method. Like the teams of human computers, his would be a digital machine, solving the differential equations of ballistics by numerical methods. But like the Differential Analyzer in which the integrators were connected via servomechanisms and cables, this machine would have a flexible arrangement for interconnecting its individual units, thereby allowing it to be used to solve a wide variety of problems.

John W. Mauchly (1907-1980) received a Ph.D. in Physics from Johns Hopkins in 1932 and from 1933 to 1940 taught physics at Ursinus College outside Philadelphia. While at Ursinus, he pursued an interest in meteorology and began investigating mechanical aids to assist with a problem he had a long interest in, namely correlation between weather and sunspots or other periodic solar activity. He built a small electrical analog computer to assist with the analysis of weather data, and began searching the literature for information on other mechanical aids to calculation.

Mauchly also explored the use of punched-card equipment, and for a while considered building a special-purpose harmonic analyzer like Kelvin's tide predictor. Sometime around 1940, he began considering the use of vacuum or gas-filled tubes for counters and storage of numbers. He was familiar with cosmic-ray counters then in common use by physicists, and at that time he also built one or two vacuum tube circuits to explore these concepts.

In December 1940, Mauchly attended a meeting of the American Association for the Advancement of Science, where he presented a paper on the weather analysis he did using his analog computer. Atanasoff was among those who heard the talk, and afterward he introduced himself and told Mauchly of the electronic machine then being built in Iowa. The two men corresponded frequently on the subject of computing, and in June 1941, Mauchly drove out to Iowa to visit Atanasoff for five days. While there as Atanasoff's guest, Mauchly examined the partially completed machine, and the two had long discussions about its details, as well as about the general philosophy of calculator design.

When he returned, Mauchly enrolled in a special summer course in electronics at the Moore School designed to acquaint professionals with the recent developments in electronics that were expected to play a role in the war. Mauchly completed the course and stayed on at the Moore School as an instructor. His correspondence with Atanasoff and others at that time reveals a growing conviction that a calculating machine using vacuum tubes and digital circuits was indeed both feasible and potentially useful—not only for meteorology but also for a range of problems the military might be interested in, including the preparation of firing tables. Correspondence continued through 1941 and into the next year, but tapered off after that, and the two men went their separate ways.

In December 1941, the United States entered the war, and the Ballistic Research Lab pressed on with even greater urgency in computing firing tables. At the Moore School, Mauchly met J. Presper Eckert, who at the time was studying for a master's degree in electrical engineering and who had already done significant work on several advanced electronics projects, including the Moore School's Differential Analyzer.

By the time he met Eckert, Mauchly had conceived of an electronic calculating machine that would eventually become the ENIAC. His visit with Atanasoff and their exchange of letters suggest that Atanasoff's work was a spark that ignited Mauchly's growing interest in digital electronic devices. The fact that in Iowa Mauchly saw another physicist building such a complex machine might have helped convince him that his own, independent ideas were not all that farfetched (it might easily have seemed so at Ursinus, where Mauchly had few colleagues with whom he could discuss such grand schemes).

Many years later, the issue of who deserved credit for the invention of the computer became the subject of a court case, *Honeywell vs. Sperry Rand*. Briefly, the court case arose because Sperry Rand held a basic patent on the computer (# 3,120,606).

Honeywell challenged its validity and thus Sperry's right to collect royalty payments from other computer manufacturers. The patent itself was for the ENIAC, and was applied for in 1947 by Mauchly and several other members of the ENIAC team. Sperry Rand acquired the rights to this patent after its merger in 1955 with Remington Rand, which had in 1950 acquired the Eckert-Mauchly Computer Corporation. The patent was finally granted in 1964, although Sperry Rand had been collecting royalties prior to that time. In 1973 Judge Earl Larson of the U.S. District Court for Minnesota ruled the patent invalid, primarily due to Atanasoff's prior work and his influence on Mauchly.

Mauchly strongly denied the influence of Atanasoff. The ENIAC had a very different structure from Atanasoff's machine. Most of all, the ENIAC was designed to solve different problems, and it could be reconfigured to solve a range of such problems—something that Atanasoff's machine could not do. If Atanasoff is the inventor of the electronic digital computer, as the courts judged in 1973, then it is in the restricted sense outlined here. At the same time, evidence uncovered at the trial reveals that prior to his visit to Iowa, Mauchly had only vague and ill-defined ideas about how to use vacuum tubes to build circuits that could perform digital calculation. Atanasoff, by contrast, was skilled at circuit design and had a thorough understanding of the difference between electronic circuits used for analog as opposed to digital applications.[7] However, the ENIAC's circuits were not derived from Atanasoff's. Atanasoff deserves credit as one of the persons who made the electronic digital computer a reality, but he is not the "inventor" of the digital computer.

In August 1942, Mauchly wrote a brief memorandum on "The Use of High Speed Vacuum Tube Devices for Calculating," in which he outlined his thoughts on the feasibility of such machines. That memo received little immediate response, but by the following spring, as the problem of computing firing tables mounted, the Army was more willing to entertain Mauchly's notion. In April 1943 he and Eckert submitted a formal proposal to the Army for the Construction of an "Electronic Diff. Analyzer," with "diff." standing for "difference" but intentionally abbreviated to suggest a kinship with the analog Differential Analyzer already familiar to the Army. The proposal was accepted, funds were made available, and design and construction begun. A year later, the basic design was complete—and the name was changed to ENIAC, for Electronic Numerical Integrator and Computer.

The heart of the ENIAC, and the first part its creators began designing, was a set of accumulators in which numbers were both stored and added.[8] Eckert and Mauchly were familiar with thyratron scaling circuits used by physicists, but rejected that design because it could not guarantee enough accuracy. They settled instead on a ring counter having ten positions for each of the decimal digits, but which stored each digit in an Eccles-Jordan flip-flop. The result was an electronic counterpart to a mechanical calculator's decimal wheel, with one flip-flop corresponding to each tooth of the wheel. In the ring counter, the state of one (and only one) flip-flop would be different from all the others. When the ring received a pulse or train of pulses, the flip-flop having the different state would cycle around the ring accordingly, sending out a carry pulse to the next ring counter if it passed through the nines position (Figure 7.3).

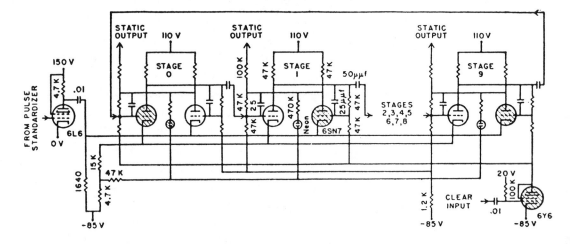

Figure 7.3. ENIAC's ring counter. Courtesy IEEE.

A unit of ten ring counters stored a ten-digit decimal number. Because a carry mechanism was built in, the unit could also perform addition and subtraction. One set of counters, together with circuits that gated pulses into and out of it, made up one accumulator. Each accumulator required 550 tubes; it was the need for reliability that dictated this rather large number of tubes to handle a single ten-digit number. The whole ENIAC, with twenty accumulators, a multiply-divide unit, and other units for control and input-output, contained about 18,000 tubes and consumed 150 kilowatts of power.

Besides the twenty accumulators, the ENIAC contained a separate unit that performed multiplication and division, a bank of ten-position switches that stored up to one hundred numbers for use during a calculation, and standard IBM punched-card readers and printers for input and output. A separate cycling unit delivered electronic pulses at 100 kHz to all other units to keep them synchronous. The basic machine cycle, or addition time, was 200 microseconds; a multiplication took 14 cycles or 2.8 milliseconds.

If the ENIAC's number registers were akin to those found in mechanical calculators, its method of programming was a direct descendant of the Differential Analyzer's. Cables, plugged into large plugboards distributed throughout the machine, directed the sequence of operations, while a cycling unit orchestrated the overall flow of instructions. This method, though cumbersome and time-consuming when it came to configure the ENIAC to solve a new problem, was nevertheless the only feasible way to exploit its high arithmetic speeds. The ENIAC's accumulators were capable of adding five thousand numbers a second; no electromechanical input device (save possibly the Colossus's paper tape reader) could have supplied instructions to it at that rate. It took up to two days to make all the necessary connections that set up the ENIAC to solve a new problem; once set up, it might solve that problem in minutes.[9]

In programming the ENIAC by plugging cables, its users were literally rewiring the machine each time, transforming it into a special-purpose computer that solved a particular problem. In a sense this is what happens whenever one programs a modern computer; only with the ENIAC, as with the Differential Analyzer from which the concept was derived, the changes were made by a person rather than automatically by the computer itself.

The important point is that however time-consuming the setup period was, it allowed the ENIAC to solve a wide range of mathematical problems, including many that its designers never anticipated. It was not fully a "general-purpose computer"—for example, it could not solve large systems of linear equations as Atanasoff's machine was designed to do. But its ability to be reconfigured to perform an almost limitless sequence of steps, including iterative loops of operations, sets the ENIAC apart from the other electronic calculators described thus far, and places it astride the categories of "calculator" and "computer."

The ENIAC was completed late in 1945 (well after the end of the war) and publicly dedicated in February 1946. The dire predictions that a machine with so many tubes could never be reliable did not come true: Eckert had carefully designed all the circuits so that the tubes drew far less current than they were rated for. And once completed, the ENIAC's operators left the tube heaters on all the time, preventing the extreme temperature changes that cause filaments to burn out. After an initial run-in period, the ENIAC routinely ran up to twenty hours between tube failures—not as good as some relay calculators, but during those twenty hours the ENIAC could do more work than a relay machine could do in months. Like the Colossus, ENIAC's speed allowed it to tackle problems that in practice were insoluble by any other method. From the very start, the ENIAC solved a steady stream of problems in a variety of fields; its first job was a still-classified problem relating to a design of the hydrogen bomb. In fact, the ENIAC was kept so busy at first that its installation at the BRL's Aberdeen Proving Ground was delayed a year. It was finally moved, in 1946-47, to Aberdeen, Maryland where it computed firing tables reliably until it was shut down in 1959. Also while at Aberdeen it solved a number of other problems, ranging from number theory to meteorology, that demonstrated its versatility and power.

There is no question that the machine was successful in doing the kind of work it was designed to do, but the ENIAC's shortcomings of limited memory size and tedious programming were apparent from the start. These two deficiencies were remedied to a limited extent by two modifications to the machine's original design.

At Aberdeen, the ENIAC was modified in 1948 so that the pulses that directed its program sequence came not from cables laboriously plugged into plugboards, but rather from one of the banks of switches originally intended to be used as a function table. It was done by exploiting a symmetry of the ENIAC's design, namely that cables carrying numbers from one unit to another contained eleven channels (for the ten decimal digits plus the sign), the same as the number of program channels the cycling unit delivered to each unit. In that a program pulse in the ENIAC was electronically identical to a number pulse, it was easy enough to route the pulses delivered by a function table onto the 11-wire program trunk. Eckert has stated that he purposely designed this symmetry into the ENIAC from the start, but in any case it was not exploited until after 1948. Its effect was to shorten the setup time greatly, while slowing down the execution time somewhat (because steps could no longer be executed simultaneously in different parts of the machine).

In 1953, a mass storage device was fitted, which increased the ENIAC's memory capacity from 20 to 120 numbers. This device used small magnetic cores, whose direction of magnetization represented a binary value analogous to the flip-flops of a ring counter. This modification, together with the internal storage of the machines's instructions in numerical (albeit nonalterable) form, foreshadowed two salient features of nearly every computing machine built thereafter.

To summarize, the ENIAC was a transitional device that incorporated many of the features of what we now define as computers: high processing speed, flexible (and from 1948, internally stored) programming, and the ability to solve a wide range of problems in practice insoluble by any other means. But at the same time, it exhibited many of the features—and the inherent limitations—of calculators: a tedious method of setup, internal use of decimal instead of binary numbers, and the use of accumulators that performed the dual functions of storage and arithmetic.

But the most important thing was that it worked, and worked well. Its existence was well publicized from 1946, and news of the ENIAC helped dispel the skepticism about the feasibility of electronic calculation. Its place as a milestone in computer history has become controversial, especially since the 1973 legal judgement declaring Eckert and Mauchly's patent on the ENIAC invalid.

Other Electronic Calculators

It was from the ENIAC team that the concept of the modern stored-program computer emerged. As its designers recognized the ENIAC's deficiencies, they wisely chose not to abandon the project (cf. Babbage) but rather deferred their ideas for a new design to the future. That design produced the EDVAC, and later a host of other computers that embodied the stored-program principle. But for almost ten years, even well after the advantages of the EDVAC-type design were recognized, other electronic calculators continued to be built. A few of these deserve a brief mention here.

The IBM SSEC

IBM equipment was used with little modification for the ENIAC's input-output devices. Although the head of IBM, Thomas Watson, Sr., hardly foresaw the future trend toward electronic computers, he did embark on an ambitious project to build an electronic computer for IBM. This machine was finished quickly, by 1948, and was called the SSEC, for Selective Sequence Electronic Calculator. Its design was a hybrid of traditional IBM punched-card technology, Howard Aiken's ideas, and some of what IBM gleaned from the ENIAC and the Moore School staff. Wallace Eckert directed the overall project, while Frank Hamilton, one of the builders of the Harvard Mark I, was the chief engineer at IBM's Endicott, New York plant. Hamilton was reluctant to build a fully electronic machine, and the result was an awkward architecture of a high-speed electronic store holding only eight, 20-digit decimal numbers, together with a much slower relay store that held 150 numbers. A third store, consisting of an array of paper-tape devices, held an additional twenty thousand numbers. Like the ENIAC, the SSEC was huge, occupying a prominent windowed showroom at IBM's New York offices on 57th St. The machine did incorporate a number of innovative features, including the ability to store and even modify instructions in the 8-number electronic store, but the awkward compromises of its design gave it few of the advantages, while retaining most of the disadvantages of both relay and vacuum tube technology. It did solve a number of problems at a time when few other machines of its size were operating reliably (and of these few, most were under strict control of United States military organizations).

Wallace Eckert used the SSEC for astronomical work; his computation of tables of the Moon's position helped to guide the Apollo astronauts twenty years later. The SSEC was dismantled in 1952, after a modestly productive but short life.

The Aviation Industry Calculators

By 1950, a general consensus was beginning to emerge as to the best way to build an automatic calculating machine. It was agreed that the machine should have a large-capacity read-write memory in which both program instructions and data are stored. It should use the binary system, and its circuits should be electronic.

But there were serious difficulties in getting such machines completed and working. In particular, the question of how to construct a memory of adequate capacity and sufficient speed was unresolved (and remained so until the perfection of the magnetic core in the mid-1950s). Meanwhile, the need to solve large systems of linear equations, and linear and nonlinear differential equations was growing, especially within the booming aviation industry. In the United States this industry was centered in Southern California, where its engineers took the initiative in designing several electronic calculators that had unique and interesting designs and performed a lot of computation for them for many years.

In 1951, engineers at Northrop Aircraft developed a machine in many ways reminiscent of Atanasoff's machine, in that it used a rotating drum on which successive approximations of the solution to a problem were computed and stored. They called their machine "MADDIDA" for Magnetic Drum Digital Differential Analyzer.[10] The original model was built under an Air Force contract for the Snark guided missile project, but after the completion of a prototype in 1949, Northrop built a production model, of which at least ten were installed by the early 1950s. The production model contained about one hundred tubes; its drum stored about ten thousand 29-bit binary numbers. The MADDIDA's processor consisted of twenty-two circuits that performed numerical integration iteratively on pieces of data, at an addition speed of ten microseconds.

Despite its limitations, the MADDIDA was a successful machine and was highly regarded by those who used it. For Northrop engineers the important point was that with it they were getting solutions to their problems (while the BINAC, a stored program computer they contracted from Eckert and Mauchly for the Snark project, never worked at all for them.) The MADDIDA's ability to deliver solutions to problems was clearly more important to Northrop. Besides their MADDIDA, three or four other companies made and sold similar devices through the early 1950s. After about 1955, manufacturers of stored-program computers learned to produce simple, compact, and reliable machines, thereby taking away the MADDIDA's *raison d' etre*. Meanwhile, its designers went on to found a host of computer companies on the West Coast, including Computer Research Corporation, ElectroData, and Teleregister. These companies formed the basis for much of the dynamic computer industry in California during the next decade.

Another machine developed at Northrop and used heavily by the aviation industry was an adaptation of IBM accounting equipment. Northrop engineers coupled an IBM Type 604 calculator to a Type 402 accounting machine, which they controlled through a plugboard device of their own design. The combination worked well, and later IBM extended the concept by adding a type 521 summary punch and a type 941 memory unit, which gave the system an ability to store up to fifty 10-digit decimal numbers. IBM marketed this system as the Card Programmed Calculator, or CPC; nearly seven hundred were installed and used until the late 1950s. Its type 604 calculating unit used vacuum tubes operating at 50 kHz, performing eighty multiplications a second. Programming was carried out by a combination of plugboards and punched cards, with conditional branching and loops of up to ten lines of instructions possible. For companies like Northrop, the CPC filled the need for computing power at a time when good commercial stored-program computers were unavailable.

Conclusion

The high speeds of electronic circuits offered dramatic increases in the power of mechanized arithmetic, but also brought forth serious design challenges. The variety of calculator designs described in this chapter reveals that there was little agreement on how best to use vacuum tubes. One serious problem was the perceived unreliability of tubes compared to relays; as it turned out, engineers like Presper Eckert found ways to design tube circuits that were even more reliable than relay circuits. More serious was the integration of high arithmetic speeds with the speeds of input, output, and programming. Each of the machines just described addressed this issue in a different way, with varying degrees of success. None of them achieved a good balance among the various functions. Only with the adoption of the stored-program concept was this problem adequately met, allowing the technology of electronic calculating circuits to realize its potential.

Notes

1. In British Commonwealth countries the vacuum tube is called a "valve," a name which might further suggest its function as a regulator of the flow of current, as well as an all-or-nothing switch.

2. By connecting the chains of thyratrons in rings, one could count in any number base besides binary, with the base determined by the number of tubes in each ring.

3. This is generally true of counters: consider an automobile odometer, which counts the total miles a car has traveled. It is usually off by a few percent due to numerous factors, but for its use in an automobile the error is tolerable.

4. The sequence was fixed for this process and did not need to be altered.

5. This tube enclosed a tetrode, having two grids, and a triode in the same glass envelope.

6. The exact nature of this clue and how it was observed is still kept secret, but it is derived from the statistical properties of a sequence of letters that in some way represents a meaningful message.

7. Indeed, Atanasoff was the first to use the word "analogue" to describe that type of computer ; "digital" was first used by George Stibitz in 1942.

8. The 1943 proposal called for the ENIAC to have ten accumulators; later this was doubled to twenty.

9. Because the input of data was through punched cards and not cables, it was easy to have the ENIAC solve a set of problems in which the basic operation sequence remained unchanged. This was the kind of operation the designers had intended, although with the end of the war the ENIAC assumed a much different role that required the frequent changing of its programs.

10. Unlike Atanasoff's computer, MADDIDA stored digits on the drum magnetically and was dedicated to solving differential equations.

Further Reading

Atanasoff, John V. "The Advent of Electronic Digital Computing." *Annals of the History of Computing* 6(1984):229-82. A well-written and carefully documented account of the invention of his calculator.

Burks, Arthur. "The ENIAC: The First General-Purpose Electronic Computer." *Annals of the History of Computing* 3(1981):310-99. A detailed historical and technical description of the ENIAC, by one of the members of the Moore School team that built it.

Eccles, W. H., and F. W. Jordan. "A 'Trigger' Relay Utilizing Three-electrode Thermionic Vacuum Tubes." Reprinted in *Computer Design Development: Principal Papers.* Edited by Earl Swartzlander. Rochelle Park, N.J.: Hayden Books, 1976. Generally acknowledged as the first published description of an electronic circuit that could perform digital switching.

Flowers, Thomas H. "The Design of the Colossus." *Annals of the History of Computing* 5(1983):239-52. The most detailed account available about the Colossus and related British code-breaking computers, by one of the persons who worked on them.

Randell, Brian. *The Origins of Digital Computers: Selected Papers.* 3d ed. New York: Springer-Verlag, 1982. A comprehensive collection of seminal papers on computing, from Babbage's day to the completion of the EDSAC in 1949. In addition to the papers reprinted, the book contains valuable commentaries by Randell, as well as an excellent annotated bibliography.

Steele, F. G. and D. E. Eckdahl. "MADDIDA." *Electrical Engineering* 69(1950):722-23. A description of the digital computer built by Northrop Aircraft.

Stern, Nancy. *From ENIAC to UNIVAC: An Appraisal of the Eckert-Mauchly Computers*. Bedford, Mass.: Digital Press, 1981. The history of Eckert and Mauchly's role in the establishment of a commercial computing machines industry.

Wynn-Williams, C. E. "A Thyratron Scale-of-two Counter." *Proceedings of the Royal Society of London* 136(1932):312-24. A description of one of the earliest attempts to utilize the high speeds of electronic tubes to count or otherwise handle numeric information.

Epilog

Today we see computers almost everywhere we turn: in our banks, our schools, our factories, our offices, our homes. How this happened, and what it has to do with those technologies we have discussed in this book, are described in the following few pages. In doing so, we will argue that the computer has evolved from the long line of calculating technologies we have traced from antiquity, and that it may not be the revolutionary technology some people suppose it to be.

All computers, from the giant brains of the 1950s to the sleek microcomputers of the 1980s, have the same fundamental design. The computer is not a single device, but rather an integrated system of hardware. A control unit directs the operations of the constituent units, coordinating them to carry out the thousands or millions of small steps in the information-processing task the computer has been programmed to do. Input-output units transfer data and instructions from the user to the computer system. Memory units store data and instructions until they are needed for processing. And an arithmetic-logic unit performs the basic arithmetic operations and logical comparisons that comprise an information-processing task.

Computers are *general purpose* in the sense that they can carry out any information-processing task a programmer can break into suitable basic operations and feed to the computer in an appropriate code. Computers are *automatic* in the sense that once the instructions and data have been appropriately coded and sent to the computer through the input equipment, no human intervention is required throughout the course of the computation; the computer is able automatically to transfer information and data between various units of the system as needed, carry out the sequence of arithmetical and logical operations in the appropriate order, and even modify data and instructions in the course of a computation as the circumstances warrant. Computers are *digital* devices in the sense we discussed in Chapter 5.

There are two general features of computers that set them apart from earlier calculating technologies and help to explain why the computer has become so prevalent in contemporary western society. The widespread use of electronics makes the computer thousands of times faster than any mechanical or electromechanical calculating device. This speed advantage opens up many new computing opportunities, e.g., real-time applications, like air traffic control, in which the calculator must provide an answer as rapidly as the activity progresses, and supercomputing problems in which billions of arithmetic and logical operations may be required to achieve a single result. The use of stored programming (i.e., instructing the machine through the use of programs which the machine stores internally and modifies and executes automatically) makes practical the computer's general-purpose capability. A stored-program computer can process in rapid succession, or even simultaneously, a wide range of problems. This is accomplished, without the lengthy and tedious rewiring or replugging of the machine between problems, by simply using the input equipment to enter a string of symbols representing a new program.

For all of the design similarities among computers, the changes over the past forty years are perhaps more significant to the technology's incorporation in society. In comparison with those of even thirty years ago, today's computers are smaller and more reliable, require less maintenance, consume less power, cost considerably less, and have much better absolute performance and price-performance characteristics. The microcomputers used by today's hobbyist outperform in almost every respect the computers of the 1950s, which were affordable only to the largest organizations. These changes are explained by the rapid stream of inventions and innovations in the hardware that implement the various functions of the computer, and in the software that instructs this hardware how to operate. These innovations include the transistor, the microprocessor, virtual memory, parallel processing, operating systems, and high-level programming languages.

The implementation of these innovations widened the market for the computer. In the 1950s, only large organizations (e.g., the Census Bureau, military agencies, and aerospace and oil companies) with large computing or data processing needs could afford computers. In the 1960s, computers came within reach of many medium-sized businesses, universities, and smaller scientific organizations. In the 1970s, price-performance continued to improve so that individual research laboratories and business offices could afford their own computers. By the 1980s, the cost had declined to the point where computers appeared in the home and on the desks of individuals in the office place. These changes, which could not have occurred without continuous dramatic decreases in price, were also dependent on many other technical innovations that made the machines smaller, more powerful, more reliable, and easier to use. This whole, interrelated set of changes have enabled the computer to attain its position in what some now call the "Information Age." But it is beyond the scope of this work to trace these changes and their impacts in the detail they deserve.

Contrary to the popular perception of the computer as an entirely novel invention, it adapted to its own needs features from many different earlier calculating technologies. Many of the early American and British computer designers built directly upon their experiences building large electronic calculators, like Colossus and ENIAC. The idea of a program-controlled calculating machine was developed by Charles Babbage in the mid-nineteenth century. Inspired by Babbage, Howard Aiken built his Harvard Mark I, which would execute an arbitrary sequence of operations specified by a program. The concept of program control was carried much further forward by the invention of stored programming.

Many of the first digital computer projects had their origins in punched-card equipment or analog calculators. International Business Machines, the world leader in computer manufacturing, achieved the transition from punched-card equipment manufacture to computer manufacture partly through an intermediate technology, the Card Programmed Calculator (CPC). Built in 1948, the CPC wired together into a system an IBM 603 electronic punched card multiplier and an IBM 405 accounting machine. The University of Pennsylvania's ENIAC project, out of which grew the first plans for the modern computer, had its own origins in MIT's Rockefeller Differential Analyzer; in fact ENIAC was known originally as an electronic difference analyzer. MIT's Whirlwind computer evolved from an Air Force project to construct an analog calculating device to control an aircraft simulator.

Peripheral equipment used in prewar calculating systems was adapted to the computer. The prime example is punched-card equipment. Contrary to the prediction of MIT mathematician Norbert Wiener that computers would make punched cards obsolete, their use expanded exponentially in the 1950s and remained popular until time-sharing became commonplace in the 1970s. Paper tape, used earlier in the Harvard Mark I, Colossus, and several of the Bell Labs relay calculators, was a principal input medium of the early computers. The Flexowriter, a "smart" typewriter used in direct mailing and other applications before the Second World War, was employed as the principal output device on the Harvard Mark I and several computers of the 1950s.

Early computer designers also appropriated electronic technology from other fields. The vacuum tube flip-flop, the fundamental switching component of computers in the 1950s, was first tested and refined in cosmic ray counters of the 1930s. Mercury delay lines, used during the Second World War to store radar signals, were modified to store information in the EDVAC and several other early computers. Cathode ray tubes, developed for television and radar, served as the basis for the popular Williams tube memory of the 1950s and also as an input-output device on the Whirlwind. Magnetic tape and wire, introduced by the German broadcast industry, was pioneered as a storage medium on the first National Bureau of Standards computer, the SEAC.

This continuity in technology is mirrored in the organizations that manufactured it. The computer industry of the 1950s emerged largely from the business equipment manufacturing industry that had supplied card punches, sorters, tabulators, and desk calculators between the two world wars. National Cash Register acquired Computer Research Corporation in 1953 to update their line of retail equipment. Burroughs acquired ElectroData in 1956 in order to computerize their traditional line of banking equipment. IBM's 650 and 1401 computers of the 1950s replaced the punched-card equipment IBM had supplied for decades to insurance companies and other large businesses.

This same pattern of continuity is apparent among users. Industries that used calculating technology extensively in the 1930s became a ready market for the computer in the 1950s. For example, the aircraft manufacturers, which employed thousands of Friden and Marchant calculators and many punched-card systems in test data reduction in the 1930s and 1940s, replaced these with computers as soon as they became available. In some instances companies were not satisfied with the computing power available from commercial sources and participated in the development of the new products themselves. For example, IBM worked with Northrop Aviation to develop the Card Programmed Calculator and with United Aircraft on the first high-level programming language, Fortran.

The story is similar for government users. In the 1930s and 1940s the heaviest government users of calculating equipment were the Census Bureau and the military organizations. The first commercial computer delivered in the United States went to the Census Bureau in 1951. The Navy supported the start-up of a new firm, Engineering Research Associates, in 1946 in order to ensure that state-of-the-art computing equipment would be available for cryptanalysis. Those who founded Engineering Research Associates were some of the same engineers who built or operated cryptanalytic calculating equipment as military personnel during the war.

Scientists were among the most innovative and demanding users of calculating technology in the 1930s and the war years. Astronomers, psychologists, and agricultural statisticians found new ways of using business calculating equipment in the 1930s. Physicists from Los Alamos used desk calculators, punched-card tabulators, relay calculators, and differential analyzers on the Manhattan Project during the war. But they switched to computers as soon as they became available in the 1950s. The NORC, the MANIAC, the Institute for Advanced Study computer, and others were used heavily for research in nuclear physics, molecular biology, fluid dynamics, and many other scientific areas in the first decade of modern computing.

These remarks only suggest the rich connections between the technology we have set out in this book and the electronic, stored-program computer. Our incomplete understanding of these connections, of events that have occurred so recently that we may still speak to the participants, may seem odd to some readers. But it requires time to gain perspective, especially in a field in which most participants are too busy looking to the future to devote time to the past. Many of the advances in computing have been made in the context of government-classified or company-proprietary projects, in which information has not been shared yet with the historian. But as we learn more our appreciation for a single, continuous history of computing grows deeper. And within the next few years we should be able to present the events of the first half-century of the computer era as we have been able here to account for the development of those earlier calculating technologies.

Index